LOUISVILLE
& SOUTHERN INDIANA

D1714271

Five-Star Trails: Louisville & Southern Indiana
40 Spectacular Hikes in the Derby City Region
1st edition 2013
2nd edition 2023
Copyright © 2013 and 2023 by Valerie Askren

Cover design: Scott McGrew
Text design: Annie Long
Front cover photo: Tioga Falls. *(See Hike 17, page 105.)* © Valerie Askren
Interior photos: Valerie Askren
Cartography and elevation profiles: Valerie Askren and Steve Jones
Project editor: Holly Cross
Copy editor: Kerry Smith
Proofreader: Emily Beaumont
Indexer: Rich Carlson

Cataloging-in-Publication Data is available from the Library of Congress.
ISBN 978-1-63404-356-4 (pbk.); ISBN 978-1-63404-357-1 (ebook)

 MENASHA RIDGE PRESS
An imprint of AdventureKEEN
2204 First Ave. S., Ste. 102
Birmingham, AL 35233
menasharidge.com
800-678-7006; fax 877-374-9016

Visit menasharidge.com for a complete listing of our books and for ordering information. Contact us at our website, at facebook.com/menasharidge, or at twitter.com/menasharidge with questions or comments. To find out more about who we are and what we're doing, visit blog.menasharidge.com.

SAFETY NOTICE Though the author and publisher have made every effort to ensure that the information in this book is accurate at press time, they are not responsible for any loss, damage, injury, or inconvenience that may occur while using this book—you are responsible for your own safety and health on the trail. The fact that a hike is described in this book does not mean that it will be safe for you. Always check local conditions (which can change from day to day), know your own limitations, and consult a map.

For information about trail and other closures, check the "Contacts" listings in the hike profiles.

LOUISVILLE
& SOUTHERN INDIANA

40 SPECTACULAR HIKES
in the Derby City Region

VALERIE ASKREN

MENASHA RIDGE
PRESS

Five-Star Trails: Louisville & Southern Indiana

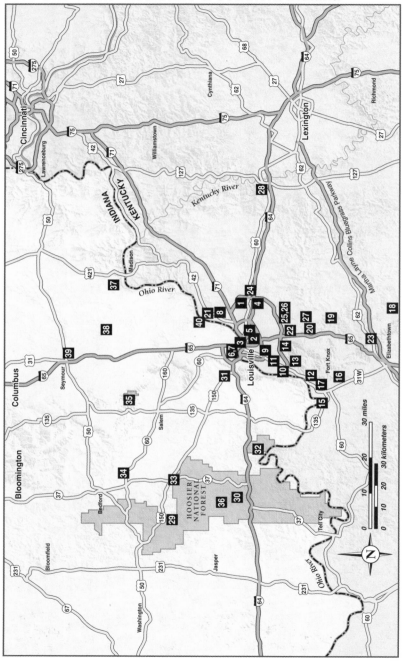

Contents

Indiana: North of Louisville and West of I-65 167

Indiana: North of Louisville and East of I-65 213

Appendixes and Index 236

Dedication

To my parents, who shared their love of the outdoors with me;
to my husband, who understands my need to be immersed in nature;
and to my children, who have inherited the joy of frolicking with
Mother Earth.

 # Acknowledgments

HIKING AND WALKING OPPORTUNITIES ABOUND in the Greater Louisville area, thanks in part to those 19th-century visionaries who believed that communing with nature was essential in order for urban dwellers to thrive. With the establishment of the city's first park, Baxter Square Park, in 1880 and the purchase of a 313-acre tract of land called Burnt Knob (which later became Iroquois Park) authorized by Mayor Charles Jacob in 1888, Louisville laid the foundation for a metropolitan area laced with urban forests, walking trails, picnic areas, and other forms of outdoor recreation.

Louisville established the Board of Parks Commissioners in 1890 with the intent of developing a park in each section of the city: east, west, and south, with the north bounded by the Ohio River. A year later the city hired Frederick Law Olmsted, the father of American landscape architecture, to design seven parks plus several interconnecting parkways. Olmsted was already well known for designing such notable spaces as Central Park in New York; the Niagara Reservation, adjoining Niagara Falls; George Vanderbilt's Biltmore Estate in North Carolina; Chicago's "Emerald Necklace" of parks and boulevards; and the grounds surrounding the US Capitol. Clearly, the city of Louisville was aiming high in its desire to build a world-class park system.

Throughout the 20th century, Louisville continued investing in that system by acquiring land to establish the Jefferson Memorial Forest—now the nation's largest urban forest—in 1946 and the "Rainbow Chain of County Parks" in the 1950s, as well as creating a unified city–county Metropolitan Park and Recreation Board in 1968.

And Louisville hasn't even begun to slow down. The 21st century has brought a host of new land acquisitions, including the Louisville Extreme Park and the nearly 4,000-acre Parklands of Floyds Fork, as well as several historic properties. To preserve and expand the city's park system in perpetuity, Louisville works with several nonprofit organizations such as 21st Century Parks, the Olmsted Park Conservancy, the Future Fund Land Trust, the Trust for Public Land, and the Louisville and Jefferson County Environmental Trust.

Many other nongovernmental entities work diligently to protect our natural areas while providing additional opportunities for outdoor recreation. Private endowments (such as the Bernheim Arboretum and Research Forest, the Creasey Mahan Nature Preserve, and the Waterfront Botanical Gardens); nonprofit organizations (including the Nature Conservancy); state agencies (both Kentucky's and Indiana's state parks and nature preserves); and national forests and wildlife refuges all provide an endless array of hiking opportunities.

It is these partners and others whom we should acknowledge and thank for their vision and perseverance.

—*Valerie Askren*

THE PAVED ANCHORAGE TRAIL IS PERFECT WHEN WOODLAND PATHS ARE MUDDY.
(*See Hike 1, page 20.*)

Preface

DESPITE THE MYRIAD HIKING POSSIBILITIES in the Greater Louisville area, many people are familiar with only a few of the better-known outdoor locales. While these might be terrific choices, the most popular places tend to be packed to the gills on beautiful weekends and holidays. Further, hiking the same places again and again can become a bit tedious.

Wouldn't you love to find some new places to explore?

Hiking is enjoying an explosion in popularity, as more people are turning to walking for its health and relaxation benefits. And now that Boomers are beginning to retire, more people are looking for recreational opportunities. Simultaneously, Gen Xers and millennials are increasingly strapped with children and demanding careers that compete for their free time, yet they're not ready to give up their outdoor pursuits.

But how many of us have the time to hike the Appalachian Trail in its entirety? And who wants to spend more time driving to a day hike than actually being out on the trail?

Happily, Louisville and the surrounding countryside brim with hiking opportunities off the beaten path. Nearly everyone will discover a trail in this book that's just right for them—from a half-mile stroll on a level trail to a 12.5-mile hike across rugged terrain. Family visiting from out of town? Try a paved path on the riverfront. Kids out of school for the day? Check out one of the many hiking areas with a nature center. Looking for a romantic but cheap date? Seek out one of the region's many waterfalls. History buff? Geology nerd? There are trails for you too!

Situated along the Ohio River, the Louisville area is chock-full of stunning wildflower displays, towering forests, fascinating caves, quiet trails, and friendly naturalists. Stroll a paved riverfront trail during lunch to clear your head or burn off some steam. After work, you're just minutes away from a heart-pumping power walk through a forest or a slice of solitude overlooking a peaceful stream. On half- or full-day trips, you can explore a multitude of small, narrow gorges; steep ravines; tumbling creeks; and dazzling overlooks.

Five-Star Trails: Louisville & Southern Indiana lets you experience all this and more.

Recommended Hikes

Best for Waterfalls

Best for Waterfowl

Best for Wildflowers

CATCH TIOGA FALLS ANY TIME OF YEAR, BUT IT'S BEST AFTER A GOOD RAIN.
(See Hike 17, page 105.)

FRENCH LICK HAS MORE TO OFFER THAN POSH SPAS AND ROULETTE TABLES.
(See Hike 29, page 168.)

Introduction

About This Book

Five-Star Trails: Louisville & Southern Indiana covers 40 hikes in the city and surrounding area. Given that Louisville is situated on the Ohio River, about two-thirds of the hikes are south of the river, in central Kentucky, and about one-third are north of the river, in southern Indiana.

Geologically speaking, Louisville sits on the far western fringe of the Outer Bluegrass, characterized by rolling hills and narrow ridgetops. Deciduous-hardwood forests dominated by oak, maple, beech, and hickory cover most of this area, except for the occasional meadow, a leftover remnant of land that was cleared for farming. Just south of Louisville lies the Knobs, a region distinguished by distinctive steep-sloping, often cone-shaped hills capped with limestone and sandstone, rendering their peaks more erosion-resistant compared with the rock beneath. Southwest of Louisville lie the Mississippian Plateau and the far-eastern edge of the Muldraugh Hills. Unlike the isolated hills of the Knobs, the Muldraughs are an escarpment, or ring of continuous hills, that divides the Plateau from the Bluegrass.

North of Louisville, in southern Indiana, the terrain is also quite hilly and in geological terms is referred to as the Southern Hills and Lowlands. This part of the Hoosier State was largely untouched by encroaching glaciers, preserving a rich ecosystem of plants and animals that thrive on the steeper topography found closer to the river.

The hikes in this book are divided into five geographic regions:

LOUISVILLE: INSIDE I-265 This section comprises hikes close to the heart of the city, bounded by Interstate 265 to the south (in Kentucky, where it's known as the Gene Snyder Freeway) and to the north (in Indiana). Most of these hikes are lightly wooded trails traversing a gently rolling landscape in urban parks, or they consist of level paved walkways adjacent to the Ohio River. (The exception is the trail at Iroquois Park, which ascends a 260-foot knob.) Several of the hikes begin at nature centers, making them perfect for cold or rainy days.

KENTUCKY: SOUTH OF LOUISVILLE AND WEST OF I-65 The trails southwest of Louisville generally travel through moderately hilly woods, including the Jefferson

Memorial Forest. Four hikes lie just south of the Ohio River and several others include lake, creek, and waterfall views.

KENTUCKY: SOUTH OF LOUISVILLE AND EAST OF I-65 Most of the terrain in this region encompasses gently rolling hills, with the exception of the Knobs area due south of Louisville. Adding to the diversity of trails in this region are Fairmount Falls Park, Pine Creek Barrens, and Salato Wildlife Education Center.

INDIANA: NORTH OF LOUISVILLE AND WEST OF I-65 Hiking areas in the northwest quadrant can vary from rolling hills to steep ravines and cliffs, the latter being representative of the karst geology of southern Indiana. The Hoosier National Forest dominates much of this region. Also found here are the remnants of an old-growth forest.

INDIANA: NORTH OF LOUISVILLE AND EAST OF I-65 The terrain in this section varies tremendously, from small, intimate gorges (which escaped the leveling glacial flows that transformed other parts of Indiana) to the shallow lakes and waterfowl-breeding grounds of the Muscatatuck Plateau.

How to Use This Guidebook

The following section walks you through this guidebook's organization, making it easy and convenient to plan great hikes.

Overview Map, Regional Maps, and Map Legend

The overview map on page iv shows the primary trailheads for all 40 of the hikes described in this book. The numbers on the overview map pair with the table of contents on the facing page. Each hike's number remains with that hike throughout the book. Thus, if you spot an appealing hiking area on the overview map, you can flip through the book and find those hikes easily by their numbers at the top of the first page for each profile. This book is divided into regions, and prefacing each regional chapter is a regional map. These maps provide more detail than the overview map, bringing you closer to the hikes. A legend explaining the map symbols used throughout the book appears at right.

Trail Maps

In addition to the overview map, a detailed map of each hike's route appears with its profile. On each of these maps, symbols indicate the trailhead, the complete route, significant features, facilities, and topographic landmarks such as creeks, overlooks, and peaks.

Featured trail	Alternate trail Directional arrows	Off-map pointer

Interstate	Major road	Minor road

Unpaved road	Boardwalk	Stairs

Power line	Railroad	Borderline

Park/forest	Water body	River/creek/ intermittent stream

Amphitheater	Church	Playground
Barn	Dump station	Phone access
Baseball field	Fishing	Restroom
Beach access	Gate	Scenic view
Bench	General point of interest	Shelter
Bicycle trail	Golf course	Spring
Boat launch	Park office	Tennis court
Bridge	Parking	Tower
Camping	Picnic area	Trailhead
Cemetery	Picnic shelter	Waterfall

To produce the highly accurate maps in this book, I used a handheld GPS unit to gather data while hiking each route, then sent that data to the expert cartographers at Menasha Ridge Press. Be aware, though, that your GPS device is no substitute for sound, sensible navigation that takes into account the conditions that you observe while hiking.

Further, despite the high quality of the maps in this guidebook, the publisher and I strongly recommend that you always carry an additional map, such as the ones noted in each profile opener's "Maps" listing.

Elevation Profile (Diagram)

For trails with significant changes in elevation, the hike descriptions include this graphical element. Entries for fairly flat routes, such as a lake loop, do *not* display an elevation profile. Also, each entry's key information lists the elevation at the start of that specific route to its highest and/or lowest point.

For hike descriptions that include an elevation profile, this diagram represents the rises and falls of the trail as viewed from the side, over the complete distance (in miles) of that trail. On the diagram's vertical axis, or height scale, the number of feet indicated between each tick mark lets you visualize the climb. To avoid making flat hikes look steep and steep hikes appear flat, varying height scales provide an accurate image of each hike's climbing challenge.

The Hike Profile

Each profile opens with the hike's star ratings, GPS trailhead coordinates, and other key information—from the trail's distance and configuration to contacts for local information. Each profile also includes a map (see "Trail Maps," page 2). The main text for each profile includes four sections: Overview, Route Details, Nearby Attractions, and Directions (for driving to the trailhead area). Below is an explanation of each of those elements.

STAR RATINGS

The hikes in *Five-Star Trails: Louisville & Southern Indiana* were carefully chosen to provide an overall five-star experience and represent the diversity of trails found in the region. Each hike was assigned a one- to five-star rating in each of the following categories: scenery, trail condition, suitability for children, level of difficulty, and degree of solitude. It's rare that any trail receives five stars in all five categories; nevertheless, each trail offers excellence in at least one category.

Here's how the star ratings for each of the five categories break down:

FOR SCENERY:

★ ★ ★ ★ ★	Unique, picturesque panoramas
★ ★ ★ ★	Diverse vistas
★ ★ ★	Pleasant views
★ ★	Unchanging landscape
★	Not selected for scenery

FOR TRAIL CONDITION:

★ ★ ★ ★ ★   Consistently well maintained

★ ★ ★ ★   Stable, with no surprises

★ ★ ★   Average terrain to negotiate

★ ★   Inconsistent, with good and poor areas

★   Rocky, overgrown, or often muddy

FOR CHILDREN:

★ ★ ★ ★ ★   Babes in strollers are welcome

★ ★ ★ ★   Fun for any kid past the toddler stage

★ ★ ★   Good for young hikers with proven stamina

★ ★   Not enjoyable for children

★   Not advisable for children

FOR DIFFICULTY:

★ ★ ★ ★ ★   Grueling

★ ★ ★ ★   Strenuous

★ ★ ★   Moderate—won't beat you up, but you'll know you've been hiking

★ ★   Easy, with patches of moderate

★   Good for a relaxing stroll

FOR SOLITUDE:

★ ★ ★ ★ ★   Positively tranquil

★ ★ ★ ★   Spurts of isolation

★ ★ ★   Moderately secluded

★ ★   Crowded on weekends and holidays

★   Steady stream of individuals and/or groups

GPS TRAILHEAD COORDINATES

As noted in "Trail Maps," on page 2, I used a handheld GPS unit to obtain geographic data and sent the information to the cartographers at Menasha Ridge Press. In the opener for each hike profile, the coordinates—the intersection of latitude (north) and longitude (west)—will orient you from the trailhead. In some cases, you can drive within viewing distance of a trailhead. Other hiking routes require a short walk to the trailhead from a parking area.

This guidebook uses the degree–decimal minute format for expressing GPS coordinates. The latitude–longitude grid system is likely quite familiar to you, but here's a refresher, pertinent to visualizing the coordinates.

Imaginary lines of latitude—called *parallels* and approximately 69 miles apart from each other—run horizontally around the globe. The equator is established to be 0°, and each parallel is indicated by degrees from the equator: up to 90°N at the North Pole and down to 90°S at the South Pole.

Imaginary lines of longitude—called *meridians*—run perpendicular to lines of latitude and are likewise indicated by degrees. Starting from 0° at the Prime Meridian in Greenwich, England, they continue to the east and west until they meet 180° later at the International Date Line in the Pacific Ocean. At the equator, longitude lines also are approximately 69 miles apart, but that distance narrows as the meridians converge toward the North and South Poles.

To convert GPS coordinates given in degrees, minutes, and seconds to degree–decimal minute format, divide the seconds by 60. For more on GPS technology, visit usgs.gov.

DISTANCE & CONFIGURATION

Distance indicates the length of the hike from start to finish, either round-trip or one-way depending on the trail configuration. If the hike description includes options to shorten or extend the hike, those distances will also be factored here. **Configuration** defines the type of route—for example, an out-and-back (which takes you in and out the same way), a point-to-point (or one-way route), a loop, a figure-eight, or a balloon.

HIKING TIME

A general rule of thumb for hiking the trails in this book is 2–3 miles per hour, depending on the terrain and whether you have children with you. That pace typically allows time for taking photos, for dawdling and admiring views, and for alternating stretches of hills and descents. When deciding whether or not to follow a particular trail in this guidebook, consider your own pace, the weather, your general physical condition, and your energy level on a given day.

HIGHLIGHTS

This section lists features that draw hikers to the trail: waterfalls, historic sites, and the like.

ELEVATION

Each hike's key information lists the elevation (in feet) at the trailhead and another figure for the peak height or low point you will reach on the trail. For routes that involve significant ascents and descents, the hike profile also includes an elevation diagram (see page 4).

ACCESS

Fees or permits required to hike the trail are detailed here—and noted if there are none. Trail-access hours are also listed here.

MAPS

Resources for maps, in addition to those in this guidebook, are listed here. As noted earlier, we recommend that you carry more than one map—and that you consult those maps before heading out on the trail.

FACILITIES

For planning your hike, it's helpful to know what to expect at the trailhead or nearby in terms of restrooms, phones, water, picnic tables, and other niceties.

WHEELCHAIR ACCESS

Paved sections or other areas where wheelchairs can safely be used are noted here.

COMMENTS

Here you'll find assorted nuggets of information, such as whether or not dogs are allowed on the trails.

CONTACTS

Listed here are phone numbers and websites for checking trail conditions and gleaning other day-to-day information.

Overview, Route Details, Nearby Attractions, and Directions

These four elements compose the heart of the hike. **Overview** gives you a quick summary of what to expect on that trail; **Route Details** guides you on the hike, from start to finish; and **Nearby Attractions** suggests appealing adjacent sites, such as restaurants, museums, and other trails (note that not every hike profile has these). **Directions** will get you to the trailhead from a well-known road or highway.

Weather

As a river city, Louisville can get quite hot and humid during the summer. For that reason alone, hiking during June, July, and August can be less than ideal. During this time of year, you may want to consider a shorter trail or one with a reprieve from the heat, such as a nature center. Fall and spring are by far the most popular times of the year for hiking. Colorful leaf and wildflower displays always draw crowds. During busy months, try to avoid hiking the more popular spots on holidays and beautiful weekends. If possible, hike during the week, after work when the days get longer, or on a less well-known trail.

For many hikers, wintertime presents an excellent opportunity to get out on the trails. Crowds (and bugs) disappear, cliffs and rocky outcrops are easier to see, and the contours of the earth become more apparent. Plus, if we get a good snow, animal tracks marking the trails, birds at their feeders, and ice formations on the waterways make for wonderful sights along the way.

The following chart provides a month-by-month snapshot of the weather in the Louisville area. For each month, "Hi Temp" shows the average daytime high, "Lo Temp" gives the average nighttime low, and "Rain or Snow" lists the average precipitation.

MONTH	HI TEMP	LO TEMP	RAIN OR SNOW
January	43°F	27°F	3.24"
February	48°F	30°F	3.18"
March	58°F	38°F	4.17"
April	69°F	47°F	4.01"
May	77°F	57°F	5.27"
June	85°F	66°F	3.79"
July	89°F	70°F	4.23"
August	88°F	69°F	3.33"
September	82°F	60°F	3.05"
October	70°F	49°F	3.22"
November	58°F	40°F	3.59"
December	46°F	30°F	3.83"

Source: usclimatedata.com

Water

How much is enough? One simple physiological fact should convince you to err on the side of excess when deciding how much water to pack: you can sweat nearly 2 quarts of fluid each hour you walk in the heat, more if you hike uphill in direct sunlight and during the hottest time of the day. A good rule of thumb is to hydrate prior to your hike, carry (and drink) 16 ounces of water for every mile you plan to hike, and hydrate again after the hike. For most people, the pleasures of hiking make carrying water a relatively minor price to pay to remain safe and healthy. So pack more water than you anticipate needing, even for short hikes.

If you find yourself tempted to drink "found water," proceed with extreme caution. Many ponds and lakes you'll encounter are fairly stagnant, and the water tastes terrible. Drinking such water presents inherent risks for thirsty trekkers. *Giardia* parasites contaminate many water sources and cause the dreaded intestinal ailment giardiasis, which can last for weeks after onset. For more information, visit the Centers for Disease Control and Prevention website: cdc.gov/parasites/giardia.

In any case, effective treatment is essential before you drink from any water source along the trail. Boiling water for 2–3 minutes is usually a safe measure for camping, but day hikers can consider iodine tablets, approved chemical mixes, filtration units rated for giardia, and ultraviolet purification. Some of these methods (for example, filtration with an added carbon filter) remove bad tastes typical in stagnant water, while others add their own taste. As a precaution, carry a means of water purification in case you've underestimated your consumption needs.

Clothing

Weather, unexpected trail conditions, fatigue, extended hiking duration, and wrong turns can individually or collectively turn a great outing into a very uncomfortable one at best—or a life-threatening one at worst. Proper attire plays a key role in staying comfortable and, sometimes, staying alive. Here are some helpful guidelines:

★ *Choose quick-dry, wool, or synthetics* for maximum comfort in all of your hiking attire—from hats to socks and in between. Cotton is fine if the weather remains dry and stable, but you won't be happy if that material gets wet.

★ *Wear a hat,* or at least tuck one into your day pack or hitch it to your belt. Hats offer all-weather sun and wind protection as well as warmth if it turns cold.

★ *Be ready to layer up or down* as the day progresses and the mercury rises or falls. Today's outdoor wear makes layering easy, with such designs as jackets that convert to vests and pants with zip-off or button-up legs.

★ *Mosquitoes, ticks, poison ivy, and thorny bushes* found along many trails can generate short-term discomfort and long-term agony. A lightweight pair of pants and a long-sleeved shirt can go a long way toward protecting you from these pests.

★ *Wear hiking boots, trail shoes, or sturdy hiking sandals* with toe protection. Flip-flopping along a paved urban greenway is one thing, but you should never hike a trail in open sandals or casual sneakers. Your bones and arches need support, and your skin needs protection.

★ *Pair that footwear with good socks.* Again, wool is the preferred choice and comes in a variety of weights for all-year use. If you prefer not to sheathe your feet when wearing hiking sandals, tuck the socks into your day pack—you may need them if temperatures plummet or if you hit rocky turf and pebbles begin to irritate your feet. And if it's cold and you've lost your gloves, you can use the socks as mittens.

★ *Don't leave rainwear behind,* even if the day dawns clear and sunny. Tuck into your day pack, or tie around your waist, a jacket that's breathable and either water-resistant or waterproof. Investigate different choices at your local outdoor retailer. If you are a frequent hiker, ideally you'll have more than one rainwear weight, material, and style in your closet to protect you in all seasons in your regional climate and hiking microclimates.

Essential Gear

You can neatly stow all of these items in your day pack or backpack, ready-to-go for your next adventure. The following list showcases never-hike-without-them items—in alphabetical order, as all are important:

★ *Extra clothes:* raingear, a change of socks, and, depending on the season, a warm hat and gloves

★ *Extra food:* trail mix, granola bars, or other high-energy snacks

★ *Flashlight or headlamp* with extra bulb and batteries

★ *Insect repellent.* For some areas and seasons, this is vital.

★ *Maps and a high-quality compass.* Even if you know the terrain from previous hikes, don't leave home without these tools. And, as previously noted, bring maps in addition to those in this guidebook, and consult your maps prior to the hike. If you're GPS-savvy, bring that device, too, but don't rely on it as your sole navigational tool—battery life is limited, after all—and be sure to check its accuracy against that of your maps and compass.

★ *Pocketknife and/or multitool*

★ *Sun protection:* sunglasses with UV tinting, a sunhat with a wide brim, and sunscreen. (Tip: Check the expiration date on the tube or bottle.)

★ *Water.* Bring more than you think you'll drink. Depending on your destination, you may want to bring a means of purifying water in case you run out.

★ *Whistle.* It could become your best friend in an emergency.

★ *Windproof matches and/or a lighter,* as well as a fire starter, for real emergencies. Please don't start a forest fire.

★ *Finally, don't forget your sense of adventure!*

First Aid Kit

In addition to the preceding items, those that follow may seem daunting to carry along for a day hike. But any paramedic will tell you that the products listed here—again, in alphabetical order, because all are important—are just the basics. The reality of hiking is that you can be out for a week of backpacking and acquire only a mosquito bite. Or you can hike for an hour, slip, and suffer a bleeding abrasion or broken bone. Fortunately, the items listed pack into a very small space. You may also purchase convenient prepackaged kits at your local outdoor retailer or pharmacy, or online.

★ Adhesive bandages (such as Band-Aids)

★ Antibiotic ointment (such as Neosporin)

★ Aspirin, acetaminophen (Tylenol), or ibuprofen (Advil)

★ Athletic tape

★ Blister kit (moleskin or an adhesive variety such as Spenco 2nd Skin)

★ Butterfly-closure bandages

★ Diphenhydramine (Benadryl), in case of mild allergic reactions

★ Elastic bandages (such as Ace) or joint wraps (such as Spenco)

★ Epinephrine in a prefilled syringe (EpiPen), typically by prescription only, for people known to have severe allergic reactions

★ Gauze (one roll and a half dozen 4-by-4-inch pads)

★ Hydrogen peroxide or iodine

Note: Consider your intended terrain and the number of hikers in your party before you exclude any article listed above. A botanical-garden stroll may not inspire you to carry a complete kit, but anything beyond that warrants precaution. When hiking alone, you should always be prepared for a medical need. And if you're a twosome or with a group, one or more people in your party should be equipped with first aid supplies.

General Safety

Here are a few tips to make your hike safer and easier:

★ *Always let someone know where you'll be hiking and how long you expect to be gone.* It's a good idea to give that person a copy of your route, particularly if you're headed into any isolated area. Let them know when you return.

★ *Always sign in and out of any trail registers provided.* Don't hesitate to comment on the trail condition if space is provided; that's your opportunity to alert others to any problems you encounter.

★ *Don't count on a smartphone for your safety.* Reception may be spotty or nonexistent on the trail, even on an urban walk—especially one embraced by towering trees or buildings.

★ *Always carry food and water,* even for a short hike. And bring more water than you think you'll need.

★ *Ask questions.* Public-land employees are on hand to help. It's a lot easier to solicit advice before a problem occurs, and it will help you avoid a mishap away from civilization when it's too late to amend an error.

★ *Stay on designated trails.* Even on the most clearly marked trails, you usually reach a point where you have to stop and consider in which direction to head. If you become disoriented, don't panic. As soon as you think you may be off-track, stop, assess your current direction, and then retrace your steps to the point where you went astray. Using a map, a compass, a GPS device or smartphone, and this book, and keeping in mind what you've passed thus far, reorient yourself, and trust your judgment on which way to continue. If you become absolutely unsure of how to continue, return to your vehicle the way you came in. Should you become completely lost and have no idea how to find the trailhead, remaining in place along the trail and waiting for help is most often the best option for adults and always the best option for children.

★ *Always carry a whistle.* It may become a lifesaver if you get lost or hurt.

★ *Be especially careful when crossing streams.* Whether you're fording the stream or crossing on a log, make every step count. If you have any doubt about maintaining your balance on a log, ford the stream instead: use a trekking pole or stout stick for balance and *face upstream as you cross.* If a stream seems too deep to ford, turn back. Whatever is on the other side isn't worth the risk.

★ *Be careful at overlooks.* While these areas may provide spectacular views, they are potentially hazardous. Stay back from the edge of outcrops, and make absolutely sure of your footing—a misstep can mean a nasty and possibly fatal fall.

★ *Standing dead trees and storm-damaged living trees pose a significant hazard to hikers.* These trees may have loose or broken limbs that could fall at any time. While walking beneath trees, and when choosing a spot to rest or enjoy your snack, look up!

★ *Know the symptoms of subnormal body temperature, or hypothermia.* Shivering and forgetfulness are the two most common indicators of this stealthy killer. Hypothermia can occur at any elevation, even in the summer, especially if you're wearing lightweight cotton clothing. If symptoms develop, get to shelter, hot liquids, and dry clothes as soon as possible.

★ *Likewise, know the symptoms of heat exhaustion, or hyperthermia.* Here's how to recognize and handle three types of heat emergencies: Heat cramps are painful cramps in the legs and abdomen, accompanied by heavy sweating and feeling faint. Caused by excessive salt loss, heat cramps must be handled by getting to a cool place and sipping water or an electrolyte solution (such as Gatorade). Dizziness, headache, irregular pulse, disorientation, and nausea are all symptoms of heat exhaustion, which occurs as blood vessels dilate and attempt to move heat from the inner body to the skin. Find a cool place, drink cool water, and get someone to fan you, which can help cool you off more quickly. Heatstroke is a life-threatening condition that can cause convulsions, unconsciousness, or even death. Symptoms include dilated pupils; dry, hot, flushed skin; a rapid pulse; high fever; and abnormal breathing. If you should be sweating and you're not, that's the signature warning sign. If you or a hiking partner is experiencing heatstroke, do whatever you can to cool down and find help.

★ *Most important, take along your brain.* A cool, calculating mind is the single most important asset on the trail. Think before you act. Watch your step. Plan ahead. Avoiding accidents before they happen is the best way to ensure a rewarding and relaxing hike.

Watchwords for Flora and Fauna

Hikers should remain aware of the following concerns regarding plant life and wildlife, described in alphabetical order.

MOSQUITOES Ward off these pests with insect repellent and/or repellent-impregnated clothing. Long pants and a long-sleeved shirt may offer your best protection. In general, mosquitoes are at their worst during spring and early summer. In warm weather, mosquitoes typically hatch four to six days after significant rainfall. However, recent mild winters in the Louisville area have extended the mosquito season to whenever nighttime temperatures don't dip below freezing for a prolonged period of time. When examining your hiking options, consider the presence of low-lying areas (including wetlands) and bodies of water such as lakes and ponds, which may provide a breeding ground for those little minions of evil. In some areas, mosquitoes are known to carry the West Nile virus, so take extra care to avoid their bites. Several cases of West Nile are reported in Jefferson and surrounding counties each year.

POISON IVY Recognizing and avoiding poison ivy are the most effective ways to prevent the painful, itchy rashes associated with this plant. Poison ivy occurs as a vine or ground cover, three leaflets to a leaf. Urushiol, the oil in the sap of this plant, is responsible for the rash. Within 14 hours of exposure, raised lines and/or blisters will appear on your skin, accompanied by a terrible itch. Try to refrain from scratching, though, because bacteria under your fingernails can cause an infection.

POISON IVY *Tom Watson*

Wash and dry the affected area thoroughly, applying a topical ointment to help dry out the rash. If the itching or blistering is severe, seek medical attention. To keep from spreading the misery to someone else, wash not only any exposed parts of your body but also any oil-contaminated clothes, hiking gear, and pets. Again, long pants and a long-sleeved shirt may offer the best protection.

SNAKES Rattlesnakes, cottonmouths, copperheads, and corals are among the most common venomous snakes in the United States, and their hibernation season is typically October–April. But despite their fearsome reputation, rattlesnakes like to bask in the sun and typically won't strike unless threatened.

COPPERHEAD
Creeping Things/Shutterstock

Although unlikely, you may encounter a copperhead while hiking in the Louisville area. The snakes you'll most likely see, however, are nonvenomous species and subspecies, particularly Eastern garter and rough green snakes. The best rule is to leave all snakes alone, give them a wide berth as you trek past, and make sure your hiking companions (including dogs) do the same.

When hiking, stick to well-used trails, and wear over-the-ankle boots and loose-fitting long pants. Don't step or put your hands beyond your range of detailed visibility, and avoid wandering around in the dark. Step *onto* logs and rocks, never *over* them, and be especially careful when climbing rocks. Always avoid walking through dense brush or willow thickets.

TICKS These arachnids are often found on brush and tall grass, where they seem to be waiting to hitch a ride on warm-blooded passersby. Adult ticks are most active April–May and again October–November, but Louisville's relatively mild winters have greatly extended the tick season to year-round. In addition, seed ticks (the larval stage of a tick) are particularly problematic since they are so prolific and their small size makes them difficult to spot. The black-legged (deer) tick is the primary carrier of Lyme disease. Although reported incidents of Lyme disease in Kentucky remain relatively rare, all hikers should be able to recognize the symptoms of this potentially debilitating disease. If you hike with a canine companion, be sure your pet is protected as well, since dogs can also get Lyme disease. *A few precautions:* Wear light-colored clothing, which will make it easier for you to spot ticks before they migrate to your skin. After hiking, inspect your hair, the back of your neck, your armpits, and your socks. During your posthike shower, take a moment to do a more complete body check. To remove a tick that is already embedded, use tweezers made just for this purpose. Treat the bite with disinfectant solution.

DEER TICK
Jim Gathany/Centers for Disease Control and Prevention (public domain)

Hunting

A number of rules, regulations, and licenses govern the various hunting types and their related seasons. In Kentucky and Indiana, hunting seasons vary each year by animal, county, location, and type of weapon. Though no problems generally arise, hikers may wish to forgo their trips during these times, when the woods suddenly seem filled with orange and camouflage. For more information, visit the websites of the Kentucky Department of Fish & Wildlife Resources (fw.ky.gov) and the Indiana Department of Natural Resources (in.gov/dnr).

Trail Etiquette

Always treat the trail, wildlife, and your fellow hikers with respect. Here are some reminders.

★ *Plan ahead in order to be self-sufficient at all times.* For example, carry necessary supplies for changes in weather or other conditions. A well-planned trip brings satisfaction to you and to others.

★ *Hike on open trails only.*

★ *Respect trail and road closures.* Avoid trespassing on private land (ask if you're not sure), and obtain all permits and authorizations as required. Also, leave gates as you found them or as marked.

★ *Be courteous to other hikers, bikers, equestrians, and others* you encounter on the trails.

★ *Never spook wild animals or pets.* An unannounced approach, a sudden movement, or a loud noise startles most critters, and a surprised animal can be dangerous to you, to others, and to itself. Give animals plenty of space.

★ *Observe any yield signs you encounter.* Typically they advise hikers to yield to horses, and bikers to yield to both horses and hikers. Observing common courtesy on hills, hikers and bikers yield to any uphill traffic. When encountering mounted riders or horsepackers, hikers can courteously step off the trail, on the downhill side if possible. Calmly greet riders before they reach you, and do not dart behind trees. Also, don't pet a horse unless you are invited to do so.

★ *Leave only footprints.* Be sensitive to the ground beneath you. This also means staying on existing trails and not blazing any new trails.

★ *Pack out what you pack in.* No one likes to see the trash someone else has left behind. The Leave No Trace Center for Outdoor Ethics is an excellent resource (visit lnt.org for more information).

Tips for Enjoying Hiking in Greater Louisville

THINK INSIDE THE CIRCLE. Hiking opportunities abound inside both I-265 and I-264 (also known as the Gene Snyder Freeway and the Watterson Expressway, respectively). For quick lunchtime power walks, consider the Olmsted Parks, such as Cherokee and Iroquois, as well as the paved multiuse trails along the riverfront. The other urban trails listed in this book are within easy reach of most Louisville residents, so they're good for parents while the kids are in school or for family outings after school and on weekends.

THINK OUTSIDE THE CIRCLE. Just outside I-265 are a handful of trails perfect for after work, particularly when the days are a bit longer. Creasey Mahan Nature Preserve, Blackacre State Nature Preserve, Fairmount Falls, and all of the Jefferson Memorial Forest are just minutes outside the beltway. Even Mount St. Francis, in southern Indiana, is just 20 minutes from downtown Louisville.

THINK SOCIAL. Friends in town for the weekend? Family coming to visit? Not everyone wants to sit on the living-room couch all afternoon. Looking for an inventive (and cheap) date idea? A first-run movie and popcorn may set you back more than you care to spend. So head out to an urban trail or catch a cascading waterfall. Enjoy the natural beauty around you, pack a picnic or maybe a kite, and you've got instant fun.

THINK INDOORS. Weather too cold or wet to hit the trail? Are the kids driving you absolutely crazy? Check out one of the many free nature centers around Louisville. Blackacre State Nature Preserve and Creasey Mahan Nature Preserve are free to enter, although donations are always appreciated. Salato Wildlife Education Center, Spring Mill State Park, Bernheim Arboretum, and Falls of the Ohio State Park charge only nominal admission fees.

If you're feeling brave, bring boots and a raincoat and let the rug rats stomp every puddle from one end of the trail to the other. Tuck in a change of shoes and maybe some clothes for the ride home, and everyone will sleep well tonight.

THINK WINTER. During the cold months, bugs and crowds vanish and non-stop views take their place. Cliffs and waterfalls become a winter wonderland as icicles sparkle like stalactites in the sun. Even a light snowfall can turn a simple walk in the woods into a gorgeous adventure.

THINK INTELLECTUAL. If asked "Hey! Wanna trudge 3 miles, swat mosquitoes, and get blistered feet?," how many people would say "Heck yeah!"? Only the hardcore among us exercise purely for fun. But each trail on this hike can offer an exploration into history, geology, biology, photography, art, and more. Once you're mentally engaged, the miles can fly by.

THINK ADVENTURE. To keep your hikes fresh, try new trails, new hiking partners, new seasons for discovering the natural world around you. Bring your maps, your raingear, even the entire contents of your favorite local outdoors store. But don't forget to bring your sense of adventure and your smile. You'll be sure to come back for more.

BERNHEIM FOREST IS A GREAT PLACE TO PUT YOUR FEET UP AND RELAX IN THE SHADE. (*See Hike 20, page 122.*)

Louisville: Inside I-265

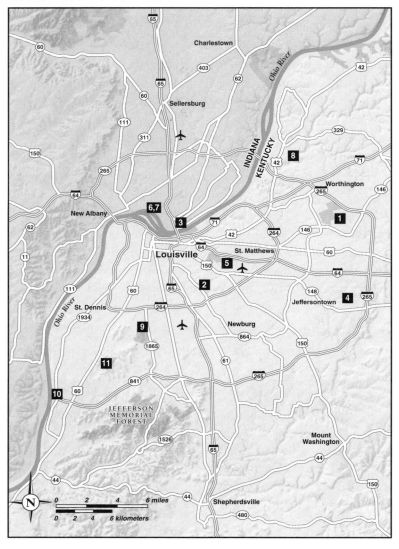

Louisville: Inside I-265

WAVERLY PARK IS ONE OF URBAN LOUISVILLE'S MANY WOODLAND RETREATS.
(See Hike 11, page 71.)

1

Anchorage Trail

SCENERY: ★ ★ ★
TRAIL CONDITION: ★ ★ ★ ★ ★
CHILDREN: ★ ★ ★ ★ ★
DIFFICULTY: ★
SOLITUDE: ★ ★

AUTUMN IS A LOVELY TIME TO HIKE THE ANCHORAGE TRAIL.

GPS TRAILHEAD COORDINATES: N38° 15.987' W85° 32.426'

DISTANCE & CONFIGURATION: 2.0-mile balloon

HIKING TIME: 1 hour

HIGHLIGHTS: Herringbone brick and paved path, Willow Lake

ELEVATION: No appreciable change in elevation

ACCESS: Daily, sunrise–sunset; free admission

MAPS: tinyurl.com/AnchorMap

FACILITIES: None

WHEELCHAIR ACCESS: None

COMMENTS: Pets must be leashed.

CONTACTS: Evergreen Real Estate; anchorageky.info or tinyurl.com/AnchorTrail

Overview

The Anchorage Trail starts in quaint downtown Anchorage and wanders for 2 miles through a parklike setting, along open farm fields, and past Willow Lake before ducking under a lightly forested canopy once again. The 10-foot-wide trail begins with a herringbone brick walk, which turns to pavement just before it crosses the second of two bridges. Mowed and dirt paths lightly crisscross the property, which is bordered by hidden homes and country estates.

Route Details

What? Who can afford to lay brick, let alone in a herringbone pattern, on a public-access trail? The town of Anchorage, a suburb of eastern Louisville, is undoubtedly affluent, and many of the homes and businesses are on the National Register of Historic Places. But this kind of paved trail is expensive, so before we start walking, let's learn a little bit of the background story.

In 1773 Isaac Hite, one of the original surveyors of what later became Jefferson County and an officer in the Virginia militia, was gifted a land grant in exchange for his military service during the French and Indian War. A portion of his land grant included the property where the E. P. Tom Sawyer State Park and the Central State Hospital are now located. Another part of Hite's estate later became the town of Anchorage, which was named in honor of James W. Goslee, a riverboat captain, when the town was incorporated in 1878.

From there on, Anchorage has been home to many of the wealthy elite, including Virginia Pearson, the silent movie star, and Isaac Wolfe Bernheim, whose legacy has long been associated with bourbon and philanthropy. It was Bernheim who commissioned the Olmsted Brothers, sons of the "Father of Landscape Architecture," Frederick Law Olmsted, in 1914 to develop a plan for the future growth of the town of Anchorage, replete with stone bridges, triangular intersections, and tree-lined streets.

Since that time other notables have called Anchorage their home, such as singer-songwriter Joan Osborne; the CEO of Yum! Brands, David Novak; and John Schnatter, of Papa John's fame and fortune. After moving to Anchorage, Schnatter restored many of the historic buildings in the city center and in 2008 built the Anchorage Trail to be used freely by the public. The paved trail runs across private property and is managed by Evergreen Real Estate LLC, which is owned by Schnatter.

Anchorage Trail

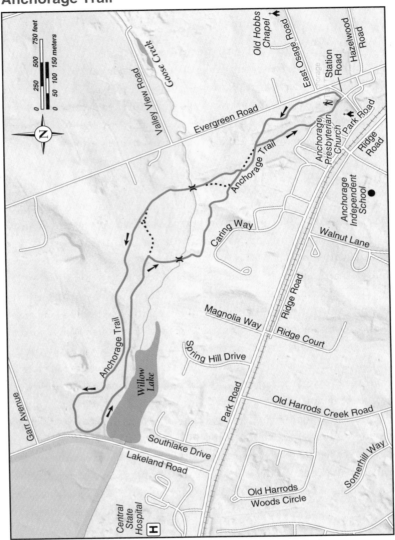

Now that you've read a little history of both Anchorage and the trail, it will give you something to mull over as you walk the 2.0-mile loop. Starting from the corner of Evergreen and Station Roads, the brickwork is beautiful, including the large compass that forms the starting point of the path, which immediately passes over a small stone bridge. For the first 0.2 mile, the Anchorage Trail gently parallels Evergreen Road, until the brick sidewalk ends and the trail turns to pavement, where it crosses another bridge over Goose Creek.

To walk the trail counterclockwise, bear right (north) at the first inter-section. A horse trail crosses the paved trail, and occasionally you'll see a few other dirt and mowed paths taking off here and there. As the Anchorage Trail continues, the scenery becomes a mixture of lightly wooded areas and open fields surrounded by a four-plank fence. Supposedly, 150 different species of birds, as well as the local deer population, also have free access to the trail and its environs, and they seem to make good use of it.

At 1 mile into your walk, the trail curves back southeast at the halfway point. Willow Lake will become visible on your right, ringed with yellow iris (a beautiful yet invasive species) on the trail side of the modest lake and lucky homeowners on the far shore. There are several small wood decks, allowing walkers a better view of the water, including a longer walkway that traverses the wetlands where Little Goose Creek drains into the lake. Unfortunately, other invasive species, in particular bush honeysuckle and Bradford pear trees, have run amuck here, both of which are extremely difficult to contain.

Anchor Trail soon doubles back on itself, and you can simply return the way you came or bear right to finish the trail behind the Anchorage Presbyterian Church. As a means of thanks to the vision and generosity of those who came before us, some of you may wish to celebrate with a toast of good bourbon and a slice of brick-fire-oven pizza.

Nearby Attractions

The town of **Anchorage** is quite walkable, including the lovely neighborhoods and the small downtown area. Several local establishments have well-earned reputations for excellent food and spirits. **Mouthwatering MozzaPi** (mozzapi .com) has long been a local favorite, but we'll discuss two other equally fine choices. Both restaurants have a strong fan base, especially on weekends, so you may want to consider reservations.

The **Village Anchor** is composed of the Village Anchor Restaurant and the Anchor Bar on the main floor and the Sea Hag Patio (which is enclosed during inclement weather) on the lower level. While the restaurant is a bit more upscale, the Sea Hag leans a little more on the casual side. See villageanchor.com for hours and menus. They are located at 11507 Park Road, just a stone's throw from the trailhead.

Selena's at Willow Lake Tavern describes its food as a fusion of Creole and Sicilian, with an emphasis on fresh seafood. Customers are welcome to dine inside by the fire or outdoors in the courtyard next to the small, artificial water-fall. Selena's is located at 10609 Lagrange Road, 0.7 mile from the trailhead. See selenasrestaurant.com for more information.

Only 20 minutes from Anchorage is the fabulous **Yew Dell Botanical Gardens.** Plan on spending the better part of the day here, as there is so much to see, from the Kitchen and Sunken Rock Gardens, to the Holly Allee and the Greenhouse Terrace, to the Klein castle. And on Sundays, except for during the winter season, the gardens offers hounds on the grounds! Go to yewdellgardens .org for hours, admission prices, special events, class offerings, and an extensive online plant market. Yew Dell is located at 6220 Old Lagrange Road in Crest-wood, Kentucky.

Directions

From the intersection of I-264 and US 60 (near the Mall at St. Matthews), head northeast on New La Grange Road/KY 146E for 4.7 miles. Once you pass Selena's at Willow Lake Tavern, this becomes Park Road. Bear left (northeast) on Station Road. The US Post Office will be on your left and the Village Anchor Restaurant on your right. The city of Anchorage has provided a map of downtown public parking at tinyurl.com/AnchorParkMap.

DEER FREQUENTLY GRAZE IN THE OPEN FIELDS ADJACENT TO THE ANCHORAGE TRAIL.

2

Beargrass Creek
State Nature Preserve:
White Oak Nature Trail

SCENERY: ★ ★ ★
TRAIL CONDITION: ★ ★ ★ ★
CHILDREN: ★ ★ ★ ★
DIFFICULTY: ★
SOLITUDE: ★ ★

THE WATER FEATURE AND NATIVE PLANTINGS AT THE EDUCATION CENTER OFFER VISITORS AN INVITING RECEPTION.

GPS TRAILHEAD COORDINATES: N38° 12.594' W85° 42.669'

DISTANCE & CONFIGURATION: 1.5-mile loop

HIKING TIME: 1 hour, as measured by a kid's pace

HIGHLIGHTS: Nature playground, sensory garden, and bird blind

ELEVATION: 533' at trailhead, descending to 453' at low point

ACCESS: Trails are open daily, sunrise–sunset. The nature center is open Monday–Saturday, 9 a.m.–4 p.m.; closed Sundays and holidays. Free admission; donations welcome.

MAPS: Available on-site and at the first website below

FACILITIES: Nature center, restrooms, and picnic tables

WHEELCHAIR ACCESS: Only at the nature center

COMMENTS: Pets are not permitted.

CONTACTS: Louisville Nature Center, 502-458-1328; louisvillenaturecenter.org/beargrass-creek or tinyurl.com/BGCSNP

Beargrass Creek State Nature Preserve: White Oak Nature Trail

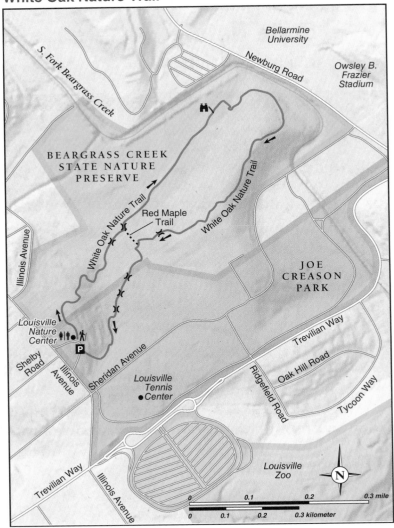

Overview

Beargrass Creek State Nature Preserve lies near the heart of Louisville and within easy reach of every child in Jefferson County. Take your kids (or someone else's) to explore every nook and cranny of this 41-acre woodland wonder. Beargrass Creek is the only urban forest owned by the Kentucky State Nature Preserve Commission. Comanaged with the Louisville Nature Center, the preserve provides four seasons of opportunity to tire those little rascals out and get them to bed early.

Route Details

If this is your first visit, you should begin at the Louisville Nature Center. As you approach, you'll notice small signs identifying many of the trees and native plantings that dot the landscape. A sensory garden is located in front of a small pond, with a raised "table" for planting flowers and vegetables. Rain chains dangle as downspouts on both sides of the front entrance to the center, designed to catch both your eye and the surplus water that runs off the gutters. Operated as a nonprofit, the nature center gratefully accepts donations for the upkeep of its facilities and sells rain barrels as one of its fundraisers.

Inside the center you'll find several hands-on exhibits for the kids to investigate and a room that serves as both a library and a gift shop. Be sure to say hello to Amie the stuffed armadillo, who's visiting from Texas.

The nature center also has an informative display on the Beargrass Creek watershed, which drains 61 square miles of Jefferson County. Every drop of metro-Louisville runoff ends up in this watershed—encompassing Muddy, Middle, and South Forks—on its way to the Ohio River. Think about that impact while you try to keep your lawn and garden chemical-free.

The Louisville Nature Center takes its educational outreach programs seriously, offering a preschool program for the little tykes, hosting school groups throughout the year, and operating youth camps in the summer. Scout troops frequently roam the area dressed in those easily identifiable blue and brown outfits, complete with neckerchiefs. The facility is also available for rent (think birthday parties), and the Jefferson County Master Gardener Association uses it for luncheons and meeting space.

A large bird blind lies just out the back door of the nature center, overlooking several feeders. Frequent avian visitors include dark-eyed (or slate-colored) juncos, cardinals, white-breasted nuthatches, tufted titmice, and downy woodpeckers. Walk about the blind slowly and quietly—although the exterior wall has tinted one-way glass, the birds are very aware of shadows and noise as you move about the room.

A good hike for anyone is the White Oak Nature Trail, which starts just to the left of the bird blind and offers 20 information markers posted along the way. To follow the guided trail sequentially, start your hike here, looping clockwise to return to the parking lot on the front side of the nature center. Highlights include several small wooden bridges and walkways, the sycamore "hugging tree," and some of the largest poison ivy vines you've ever seen. Known in scientific circles as *Toxicodendron radicans*, poison ivy produces an irritating oil called urushiol. Curiously, wildlife is immune to this irritant: a variety of birds, deer, rabbits, and other small mammals eat the grayish-white berries throughout the fall and winter. Adhere to the old adage "leaves of three, let it be," and maybe you won't wake up itching. (For more on the subject, see page 13.)

If you want to limit your hike to less than 0.5 mile, take the shortcut across Red Maple Trail to the other side of White Oak Nature Trail. But if one of your objectives is to wear out the kids, don't even mention that as an option.

Shortly after you pass the Red Maple Trail, about 0.3 mile into the hike, you'll notice an increasing number of old bricks embedded within the dirt path. This section of the White Oak Nature Trail was an old paved roadbed that led to Basil Prather's homestead. Prather, a Revolutionary War captain, bought this property in 1789.

At the far northeastern end of the trail, about 0.7 mile from the trailhead, the path traverses a wooden walkway before ascending gently and eventually returning to the nature center. Along the second half of the trail, you may see two or three paths veering left (southeast); these lead to Joe Creason Park, just south and east of the preserve.

To keep kids interested as they walk along the trail, try a photo scavenger hunt. Provide an inexpensive digital camera or phone and a list of sights to find and record photographically. Hunt items could include a left- or right-hand mitten hidden in one of the many old sassafras trees that line the trail; white blooms or red berries on an invasive honeysuckle; sightings of snakeroot, witch hazel, or poplar (Kentucky's state tree); a photo op with the creek. . . . You get the idea.

And don't forget about Beargrass Creek on inclement-weather days. Load up with raincoats and boots or a warm winter coat with hat and mittens, and look for animal tracks. It's always surprising how many mammals frequent our urban backyard. And on cold days, the bird blind will be chattering with activity.

Nearby Attractions

Both **Joe Creason Park** and the **Louisville Zoo** are just south of the preserve. All three parks share adjacent borders, with Creason in the middle and Beargrass and the zoo serving as bookends. A 1.5-mile multiuse trail encircles Joe Creason

Park; the 3.1- and 6.2-mile loops are popular with cross-country runners. Ambitious hikers can use one of the connector paths between Beargrass Creek and Creason Park to hike both trail systems. Joe Creason Park also has nine clay tennis courts, soccer fields, and two pedestrian bridges that cross Beargrass Creek. In winter, the large hill in front of the Metro Parks Administrative Office is great for snow sledding.

Directions

From I-264 (Watterson Expressway), take Exit 14 (Poplar Level Road/KY 864), head north on Poplar Level Road, and drive 0.7 mile. Turn right (east) at Trevilian Way, and in 0.1 mile turn left (north) on Illinois Avenue. The Louisville Nature Center is 0.2 mile ahead, on your right. Park in this lot for access to the nature preserve.

I WONDER WHAT'S AROUND THAT NEXT BEND IN THE TRAIL?

Big Four Bridge and Waterfront Park

SCENERY: ★ ★ ★ ★ ★
TRAIL CONDITION: ★ ★ ★ ★ ★
CHILDREN: ★ ★ ★ ★ ★
DIFFICULTY: ★
SOLITUDE: ★

WALK THE BIG FOUR BRIDGE IN ALL SEASONS, DAY OR NIGHT, FOR FABULOUS VIEWS.

GPS TRAILHEAD COORDINATES: N38° 16.258' W85° 44.491'

DISTANCE & CONFIGURATION: 4.2-mile balloon loop

HIKING TIME: 2 hours

HIGHLIGHTS: Panoramic views of the Ohio River and downtown Louisville and Jeffersonville, water features, sculptures

ELEVATION: 448' at trailhead, with no significant elevation change

ACCESS: Daily, 6 a.m.–11 p.m.; free admission

MAPS: Available at the website below

FACILITIES: Restrooms, picnic tables, drinking fountains (in season), playgrounds, splash park

WHEELCHAIR ACCESS: Yes

COMMENTS: Parking is free and plentiful. Pets are permitted on leash on the paved trails but NOT on the Big Four Bridge.

CONTACTS: Waterfront Park, 502-574-3768; ourwaterfront.org

Overview

Bring the family. Bring a date. Bring your walking shoes and head to the river-fronts of both downtown Jeffersonville and Louisville. The Big Four Bridge links these two urban venues and provides access to the River City's Waterfront Park, an 85-acre linear green space on the Kentucky side of the Ohio River. The paved path offers stunning views of the river and both cities as it passes multiple sculptures and water features, urban gardens, the Lincoln Memorial, and more.

Route Details

The Big Four Bridge and Waterfront Park is such a prominent feature that it's hard to imagine what downtown Louisville was like before. Groundbreaking for Phase I of the park started in 1994, and the conceptual master plan for Phase IV is complete. The city continues to dream big with its efforts to transform this former industrial riverfront into an integral spoke of the social hub of downtown Louisville. And on the Indiana side of the river, the Big Four Bridge leads you to Jeffersonville, which is undergoing an exciting urban renewal of its own.

The Falls of the Ohio, just downstream of the park, is the only natural obstruction along the nearly 1,000-mile Ohio River as it flows from Pennsylvania before joining the Mississippi River in Cairo, Illinois. For thousands of years, migrating buffalo crossed the Ohio here to reach the salt licks and cane that grew along the riverbanks. Various indigenous tribes followed these migrations, and the crossing soon became a point of commerce. As development occurred on both sides of the river, Louisville quickly grew as a point of warehousing and support for the shipping industries. Eventually, the Louisville and Portland Canal was built to move boat traffic through the locks and avoid the portaging that was necessary to bypass the falls.

The construction of the six-span, railroad-truss "Big Four Bridge" (named for the Cleveland, Cincinnati, Chicago, and St. Louis Railway), began in 1888 and ultimately claimed the lives of 37 workers. Twelve men drowned after the collapse of a caisson that was supposed to hold the water back when they were building the pier foundation, and another four men died when a wooden beam broke while they were working on another caisson. The worst disaster occurred in December 1893, when heavy winds knocked over a crane, which in turn caused a truss to fall into the river, bringing with it 41 men and killing 21 of them.

In 1928–29, the bridge was rebuilt using much of the original structure. But in the 1960s, the bridge again fell into disuse and was abandoned in 1969.

Big Four Bridge and Waterfront Park

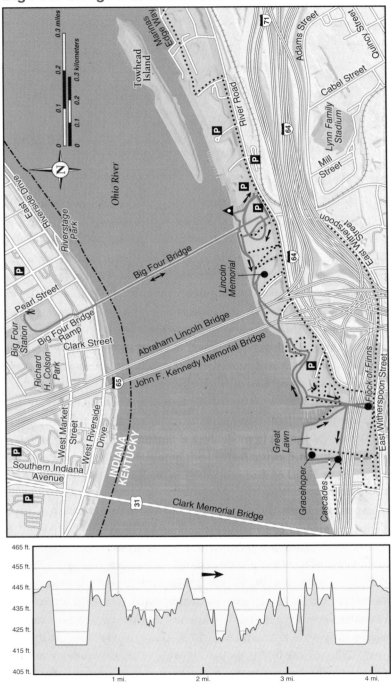

The original rail approaches on both ends of the bridge were removed in 1974–75 and sold for scrap, resulting in the epithet "the Bridge That Goes Nowhere." During this same time period, the continued transformation of the transportation industry led to a significant decline in commercial boat traffic along the Ohio. Louisville's waterfront fell into deep neglect until a revitalization project was launched in the late 1980s.

Whereas Louisville's waterfront had become an eyesore, it is now eye candy for those wanting to enjoy the amenities a park can bring: paved walkways, water features, gardens, benches, and artwork—all in an outdoor urban environment. Likewise, the city of Jeffersonville has conducted its own waterfront redevelopment initiative with paved walking paths, restaurants, and historic homes. Carrying more than 1.5 million pedestrians and cyclists a year, the mile-long Big Four Bridge allows casual walkers and commuters to cross these political boundaries with ease, while providing seamless access to miles and miles of paved trails on both sides of the river.

There is ample and free parking at the base of the Big Four Bridge on both sides of the river, and walkers can hike either way over the bridge, but let's start in Jeffersonville. After parking (see detailed directions on page 34), head up the entrance ramp on the Indiana side of the bridge. The views quickly become prodigious, from renovated cottages to historic homes, the flood wall along the levee, and the dazzling skyline of Louisville more than a mile away. Downstream (west) of the bridge, are the Abraham Lincoln, John F. Kennedy, and George Rogers Clark memorial bridges.

At the Kentucky side of the Big Four Bridge, descend the spiraling ramp until you reach ground level and the parking lots on either side. The 2.7-mile Waterfront Park loop trail begins at the far side of the west parking lot adjacent to the ramp of the Big Four Bridge, near the river. Our route runs along the riverfront and circles back around, before completing the loop back along the river.

From the parking lot, walk north toward the riverfront. Turn left (west) and head downstream along the promenade toward the I-65 bridge over the Ohio. The first thing you'll pass on your left is the Swing Garden, a wide, grassy knoll scattered with bench-style swings facing the water. The Lincoln Memorial is just past the swings. The paved path continues along the waterfront, past the Fred Wiche Grove (named after the beloved local gardening expert who had his own radio show) and then past the Upland Meadows. Feel free to wander off the path at any point to explore the inner workings of this linear park.

Past the meadows, the trail takes a left turn away from the river as it bears south along the Harbor (aka the Great Lawn Docks). Continue straight to see *Flock of Finns,* a group of sculptures created by the late folk artist Marvin Finn, which sits at the corner of Witherspoon Street and River Road. Loop back north again toward the river and the Great Lawn, the Cascades, and *Gracehoper,* a black painted-steel abstract sculpture designed by the late Tony Smith.

From the base of the Big Four Bridge in Jeffersonville where you started, you are now a little more than 2 miles into your walk. Bear east and work your way back along the waterfront to the base of the Big Four Bridge on the Kentucky side. Ascend the spiral entrance ramp to the Big Four and head back across the river to Jeffersonville.

Nearby Attractions

If all this water has you waxing nostalgic, make time for the **Howard Steamboat Museum.** Located just 1.1 miles from Big Four Station in Jeffersonville, the museum is housed in a beautiful Victorian mansion built by the Howard family in 1894. The Howards were among the major steamboat builders of their time, and the master craftsmen who worked for the shipyard helped construct the house. The museum is located at 1101 East Market Street in Jeffersonville, Indiana; hours are Tuesday–Saturday, 10 a.m.–3 p.m., and Sunday, 1–3 p.m. Discounted ticket prices are offered for children and seniors. For more information, call 812-283-3728 or visit howardsteamboatmuseum.org.

Jeffersonville is filled with a tantalizing array of restaurants, ice-cream shops, and tap houses, including more than a dozen located just a few minutes' walk from Big Four Station. For those trying to strike a balance between calories in and calories out, you'll find several worthy competitors for your wallet just within striking distance. Signature events for the city of Jeff range from the Chili & Brew Bonanza to the Holiday Open House and the Chocolate Stroll, all located in the historic downtown area. See jeffmainstreet.org for more information.

Directions

For access to the Big Four Bridge in Jeffersonville, Indiana: From Louisville, head north on I-65, then take Exit 0. Turn right (east) on West Court Avenue. Drive 0.2 miles. Turn right (south) on Pearl Street and drive another 0.2 miles.

Big Four Station and the entrance ramps to the bridge will be on your right. Free street parking and public lots are typically available, unless special events are going on, including activities at the KFC Yum! Center.

Waterfront Park is located between River Road and the Ohio River, just north of the spaghetti junction where I-64, I-65, and I-71 intersect in downtown Louisville; see ourwaterfront.org for detailed directions and the location of multiple (and free) parking lots.

THE BIG FOUR BRIDGE WAS NAMED FOR THE CLEVELAND, CINCINNATI, CHICAGO, AND ST. LOUIS RAILWAY.

Blackacre State Nature Preserve

THE SPRINGHOUSE HERE CAPTURED WATER FOR ONE OF THE FIRST LICENSED DISTILLERIES IN KENTUCKY.

GPS TRAILHEAD COORDINATES: N38° 11.727' W85° 32.015'

DISTANCE & CONFIGURATION: 3.2-mile loop with less mileage readily available

HIKING TIME: 1.5 hours

HIGHLIGHTS: Historic home, working farm

ELEVATION: 721' at trailhead, descending to 648' at low point

ACCESS: Open daily sunrise–sunset. The Presley Tyler House is open on a seasonal basis on the second and fourth Sunday of each month, 1–4 p.m. Free admission; donations welcome (some special events incur a small fee).

MAPS: Blackacre State Nature Preserve, USGS *Jeffersontown*

FACILITIES: Nature center, house and farm tours, picnic tables, restrooms

WHEELCHAIR ACCESS: None on trails; first floor of house during tour is accessible.

COMMENTS: No dogs or smoking permitted on the grounds

CONTACTS: Blackacre State Nature Preserve and Historic Homestead, 502-266-9802; visitblackacre.org

Overview

Are your little ones restless? Or perhaps the grandparents are in town and you're looking for a way to entertain them for a few hours? Then consider Black-acre State Nature Preserve and Historic Homestead. Listed on the National Register of Historic Places, Blackacre offers a fine example of farm life in the 1800s among the landed gentry. Docent tours and several miles of trails provide an interesting and relaxing visit for all. The loop trail described here is an easy walk along the Waterfall Trail, out old Mann's Lick Road to the cattail pond, then back to the springhouse and double-crib barn.

Route Details

Comprising almost 300 acres of historic buildings, open pasture, and wooded trails, Blackacre Nature Preserve was created in 1979 by Judge Macauley Smith and his wife, Emilie Strong Smith, who sought to preserve the working farm and homestead. Phoebe and Moses Tyler first settled the land in 1789 and built a one-room stone cottage mortared with limestone and horsehair. With 10 children, the Tylers had plenty of mouths to feed and a built-in labor force to work the fields. Moses later built an addition to the cottage to accommodate—no . . . not his growing family, but one of the first licensed distilleries in the state. At the time, a distiller's license was difficult to obtain and allowed the licensee to keep a portion of the customer's corn in exchange for the distillation of the grain.

Years later, the Tylers' son, Presley, and his wife, Jane, built their home here in 1844. Designed in the Federal style, the house is open seasonally for docent-led tours. Historic Mann's Lick Road traverses the property and at one time led to other farms owned by the Tylers. But be forewarned—with all the roughness of a working farm, Blackacre Preserve is not My Old Kentucky Home.

This hike was awarded five stars for the diversity of views and experiences found at the preserve, in particular the historic home, barn, and other outbuildings. Six trails are available for hiking anytime the preserve is open. If you're looking for an open-meadow hike, consider the Sunrise Meadow Trail or the Lower or Upper Sunset Trail. For a more wooded experience, Tyler's Trace Trail and Mann's Lick Road are good choices. But if water attracts you like a divining rod, consider the Waterfall Trail, which follows a creekside, meanders through lightly wooded areas before reaching Jackson's Pond, and returns to the homestead via historic Mann's Lick Road. In order to add a bit more mileage, let's include the spur to the cattail pond as well. To reach the trailhead,

Blackacre State Nature Preserve

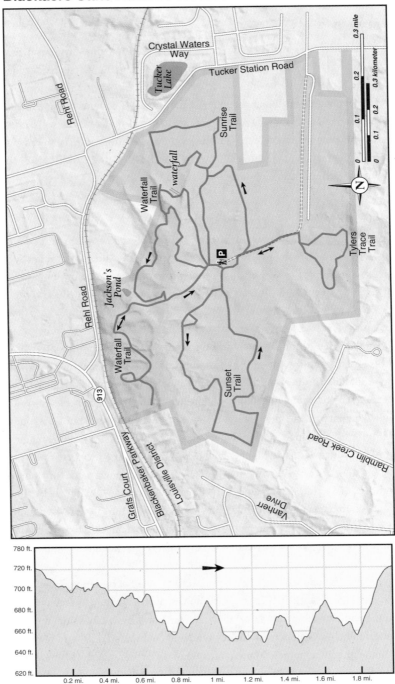

begin at the large kiosk at the far northeastern edge of the primary parking lot. Head north toward the Tyler House, then bear right (east) to get to the Schick Nature Center.

Before you start your hike, it's worth spending a little time at Schick. To the left of the nature center's front door hangs an unusual map of the homestead, fashioned from metal and stamped with Braille lettering. To the right of the front door hangs an old farm gate painted with a picture of the homestead in *American Gothic* style.

Feel free to go inside and explore the nature center. Despite several preserve signs admonishing NO STICKS, RUNNING, OR SHOUTING. QUIET VOICES ONLY, the nature center is all about kids. The exterior of the quaint yet rustic wooden building has a 1970s contemporary look, yet the inside is set up like an old one-room schoolhouse. From the plastic snake dangling below the deer antlers to the extensive collection of children's nature books, the atmosphere will make kids feel immediately at home.

The nature center hosts many programs throughout the year, with topics ranging from owls and tree frogs, to planets and stars, to heirloom tomatoes and canning. Special summer programs include Pioneer Day and camps for the kids. More information, including farm-animal feeding schedules, is available on the center's website. Out the back door of the Schick Nature Center stands a separate building housing the bathrooms, fully outfitted with Clivus Multrum composting toilets long before such facilities were fashionable. The preserve notes that the compost is indeed used on the farm to fertilize the crops. It's nice to know that what we give will keep on giving.

Behind the nature center and next to the bathrooms you'll see the sign for the Waterfall Trail. Several small waterfalls form where various drainages tumble down the hillsides. About 0.3 mile from the trailhead, a small footbridge takes hikers from one side of the creek to the other. Cedar, redbud, and dogwood trees provide plenty of seasonal interest along the way.

Approximately 0.5 mile from the trailhead, the path splits into a Y. The left branch heads southwest toward Mann's Lick Road, while the right branch heads northwest toward Jackson's Pond. Take a right here and walk about 0.4 mile to reach the pond. An old beaver lodge is embedded within the earthen berm containing the pond, close to the outtake pipe. Other evidence of beaver activity includes nibbled tree branches and stumps lining the pond.

The trail loops left (south) before rejoining Mann's Lick Road. Just don't expect a paved thoroughfare with yellow painted lines and rumble strips. This road was built long before Henry Ford was knee-high to a grasshopper, and it's easy to see why wagon wheels broke down so often.

Turn right (north) on Mann's Lick and cross a small bridge, just below Jackson's Pond. Mann's Lick Road ascends a small hill until you reach one of the oldest trees in the preserve, a white oak measuring 17 feet in circumference, just to the right or east of the trail. If you look to your left, west of the road, a spur trail heads to a small pond. Honestly, the pond is not much to look out, but this spur goes through some of the loveliest parts of the preserve. Invasives, including honeysuckle and privet, are a serious problem at Blackacre, but this stretch of woods remains considerably more pristine.

After hiking the spur, return to Mann's Lick, turn right, and follow the old road south to the back side of the circa-1795 springhouse. A small spring in front of the stone building flows under the structure and enters a small pond. Food was kept cool in the springhouse during warm summer days, and the pond provided swimmers a welcome relief from the heat.

The trail continues behind the springhouse, between the smokehouse and the weaving shed. Bear right (west) down the gravel road 20 yards or so until you reach the Appalachian-style barn, also built in 1795. The barn is a rare double-crib style, with an enclosed dogtrot down the middle. Here the rough-hewn walls are hung with old farm equipment, including harnesses, yokes, pitchforks, scythes, cross draw saws, plows, barrel hoops, reaping hooks, hay crooks, corn knives, and the like. A corn sheller and cider press sit opposite the wall, where several old horseshoes hang open-side up to catch all the luck before it falls out. Note the magnet used by veterinarians to remove wire from cows' stomachs. Stored on the other side of the barn are several old horse-drawn vehicles, including buggies, farm wagons, and an old sleigh. If heaven has a fragrance, it must include the smell of fresh hay in an open-air barn.

Just outside the barn, several fields house the resident horses, sheep, goats, and donkeys. The goats and donkeys will love your attention, while the horses happily reach for your open palm, sniffing for treats. The parking lot and your horseless carriage will be sitting just north of the pasture.

Nearby Attractions

Blackacre also offers community garden plots, starting at $15 for the season. For more information, including a complete calendar of events, see the website.

If you enjoy old homes, public gardens, and early-American history, historic **Locust Grove** is another great place to spend the day. The restored Georgian house was home to Revolutionary War hero General George Rogers Clark during his later years. Locust Grove sits on 55 acres of woods and meadows, sprinkled with period-style gardens featuring rare and historic plants. Admission fees apply. For more information, call 502-897-9845 or go to locustgrove.org.

Directions

From I-265 (KY 841/Gene Snyder Freeway), head west off Exit 23 (Taylorsville Road) and drive 0.8 mile. Turn right (north) on Tucker Station Road, drive 0.3 mile, and turn left (west) at the sign for Blackacre State Nature Preserve. Pass through the old green metal farm gate, and follow the gravel road around to the Tyler House. Park in the large lot to your left. Parking for the disabled is available near the house.

TOURS OF THE PRESLEY TYLER HOUSE ARE FREE WITH YOUR CULTURAL PASS, AVAILABLE FROM ANY OF THE LOUISVILLE PUBLIC LIBRARIES.

Cherokee Park Scenic Loop

SCENERY: ★ ★ ★ ★
TRAIL CONDITION: ★ ★ ★ ★ ★
CHILDREN: ★ ★ ★ ★ ★
DIFFICULTY: ★ ★
SOLITUDE: ★ ★

THE MIDDLE FORK OF BEARGRASS CREEK RUNS THROUGH MUCH OF CHEROKEE PARK.

GPS TRAILHEAD COORDINATES: N38° 14.363' W85° 41.786'

DISTANCE & CONFIGURATION: 2.3-mile paved loop

HIKING TIME: 1.5 hours

HIGHLIGHTS: Hogan's Fountain, Christensen Memorial Fountain, Baringer Hill

ELEVATION: 540' at trailhead, descending to 437' at low point

ACCESS: Daily, sunrise–sunset; free admission

MAPS: Louisville Metro Parks, tinyurl.com/CherokeeParkMap, USGS *Louisville*

FACILITIES: Picnic tables and shelters, restrooms, playground

WHEELCHAIR ACCESS: The entire trail is paved but includes several moderate hills.

COMMENTS: Pets must be leashed.

CONTACTS: Louisville Metro Parks, 502-456-8100; tinyurl.com/CherPark or olmstedparks.org

Overview

Cherokee Park—part of one of only four city-park systems in the United States created by Frederick Law Olmsted—has long served as a gift to all urbanites. Designed by Olmsted and his firm in 1891, it's among Louisville's 18 parks and six interconnecting parkways attributed to the father of American landscape architecture. Cherokee Park is undergoing a lengthy revitalization process to reclaim its former glory as a sanctuary for outdoor recreation. The paved Cherokee Park Scenic Loop takes hikers through much of the heart of this 389-acre park.

Route Details

Frederick Law Olmsted, who also designed Central Park in New York City; the Biltmore Estate outside of Asheville, North Carolina; and the grounds of the US Capitol, believed that city parks were an essential element of healthy urban communities. His design philosophy encompassed three elements: recreative use (such as walking or relaxing), gregarious use (picnicking and other social activities), and exertive use (including ball fields and courts).

Originally Cherokee Park was surrounded by beautiful homes to the north and south, and Seneca Park (another Olmsted park) to the west. Today the Louisville Presbyterian Theological Seminary lies to the east, I-64 crosses the northern tip of Cherokee Park, and a golf course lies to the west. Consequently, Cherokee Park has suffered from the growing pains of overuse due to increased urban density. In addition, a 1974 tornado destroyed many of the large, mature trees that dominated the landscape. The loss of canopy has resulted in less-desirable and more-invasive plant species taking root in the park. Nevertheless, the "bones" of Cherokee Park remain sound, and Louisvillians continue to be drawn to its natural beauty. The last several years have seen a tremendous push to revitalize all the Olmsted parks. Several nonprofits and foundations are working together with the city to bring the Louisville park system back to its glory days.

The main artery for travel in Cherokee Park is the 2.4-mile Scenic Loop, a one-way paved road divided evenly between vehicular and pedestrian use. On almost any day of the week, and on most evenings as well, the pedestrian lane is filled with walkers, joggers, cyclists, and parents pushing strollers. The Scenic Loop combines historic features within a pastoral backdrop of natural forests and tumbling creeks. Multiple stone bridges and two large fountains provide the hardscape that completes the look. Notably, Cherokee Park contains an

Cherokee Park Scenic Loop

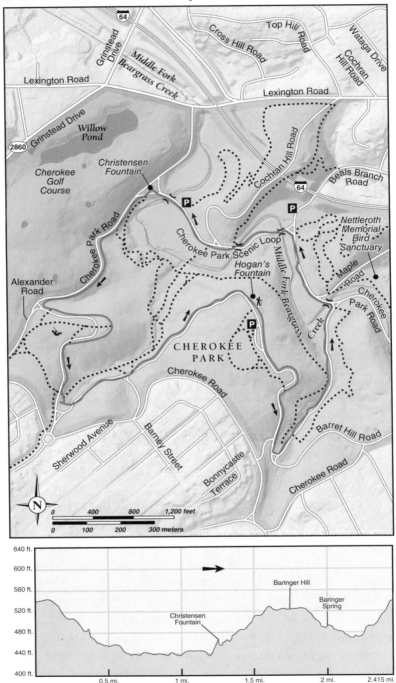

incredible maze of trails, including paved, multiuse, mixed-use, and just-plain-rogue paths that can confuse the first-time or casual hiker. The trail described here, in contrast, prepares you for repeat visits by sharpening your sense of bearing and navigational skills.

The Scenic Loop can be accessed at a multitude of locations, but let's start at Hogan's Fountain, a gift from Mr. and Mrs. W. J. Hogan to the city in 1904. The fountain features the Greek nature god Pan and served as a watering spot for horses and dogs. We'll walk the loop counterclockwise to minimize any distraction from the slow-moving traffic. So, walk in the left lane, with the one-way lane for motorized vehicles on your right.

From Hogan's Fountain you'll have a nice long downhill until you pass both Dingle and Barrett Hill Roads on your right. At the intersection bear left (north) along the clearly marked Scenic Loop.

Your next turn will be another left (north) where Beargrass Road comes in on your right. Although you'll see a sign for the Nettleroth Bird Sanctuary, it has been fenced off to protect reforestation efforts. Woodcocks, colloquially known as timberdoodles, have been known to frequent this area. With long, slender bills and 360-degree vision, these birds tend to feed in the early evening by probing the soil for invertebrates. Woodcocks are also known for their elaborate mating rituals. Given that the females are much larger than the males, we can only guess who wins.

Stay on the Scenic Loop as it crosses Beargrass Creek several times, indicating you are nearing the halfway mark of your walk. At Ledge Road, bear left (southwest) at the Christensen Fountain, built in 1901 into the side of the hill. Even though the fountain was refurbished in 2002, the water is but a trickle and the stone Viking warship and its watering vessel (for riding and carriage horses) no longer serve their original purpose.

From here the Scenic Loop heads up to Baringer Hill, one of several hillsides the Louisville Metro Parks opens for sledding when snows are sufficient and proper equipment (that is, no old-car hoods or garbage-can lids) is used. Park staff will even light and maintain bonfires, supply first aid kits, and call emergency services if necessary. What more could you ask for your tax dollar? Grab a thermos of hot chocolate, and you're ready for some wintertime fun.

Your paved path then descends to Baringer Spring—although the water has nearly dried up, the surrounding stonework is worth the brief detour. From here you have only 0.4 mile of walking back to Hogan's Fountain.

Nearby Attractions

Now that you've hiked the Scenic Loop and have a better idea of the layout of Cherokee Park, be a little more adventurous and take one of the other shorter paved trails that run through the park or one of the many dirt paths that roam the woods. Unfortunately, it is difficult to turn any of these into meaningful loop trails without a good map, such as the Scenic Loop. But there is a very nice out-and-back paved trail that runs from Baringer Spring north to the Cochran Hill area. And the Big Rock area where Seneca Park Road enters the far east side of the park offers beautiful views of Beargrass Creek and several wooded walking paths. This is also a great section of the park for wildflower hunting in the springtime.

Directions

From Exit 8 off I-64, head southwest on Grinstead Drive. In 0.3 mile, bear left onto Cherokee Parkway and drive 0.5 mile. Turn left on Willow Avenue and then take an almost immediate left again on Cherokee Road for 0.4 mile; at the Daniel Boone monument traffic circle, take the third exit for Cherokee Park Road, which becomes the Scenic Loop. In 0.5 mile Hogan's Fountain will be on your left and several parking lots will be on your right.

THE CHRISTENSEN FOUNTAIN, BUILT IN 1901, WAS FASHIONED AS A STONE VIKING WARSHIP, AND ITS WATERING VESSEL SERVED RIDING AND CARRIAGE HORSES.

6 Falls of the Ohio Levee Trail

SCENERY: ★ ★ ★
TRAIL CONDITION: ★ ★ ★ ★ ★
CHILDREN: ★ ★ ★ ★ ★
DIFFICULTY: ★ ★ ★
SOLITUDE: ★ ★

THE DOWNTOWN LOUISVILLE SKYLINE, IMPRESSIVE DURING THE DAY, ONLY GETS BETTER AT NIGHT.

GPS TRAILHEAD COORDINATES: N38° 17.268' W85° 46.535'

DISTANCE & CONFIGURATION: 4-mile out-and-back

HIKING TIME: 1.5 hours

HIGHLIGHTS: Ohio River, Louisville skyline, historic-home site

ELEVATION: 451' at trailhead, with no significant elevation change

ACCESS: Trails are open (no charge) daily, 7 a.m.–11 p.m. Falls of the Ohio Interpretive Center open Monday–Sunday, 9 a.m.–5 p.m. (closed major holidays); see Directions for fees to enter the interpretive center.

MAPS: Available at the first website below and at the interpretive center

FACILITIES: Nature center, restrooms, playground

WHEELCHAIR ACCESS: Yes

COMMENTS: The paved trail is for pedestrians and bikers only. Dogs are permitted on leash. Swimming and wading are prohibited.

CONTACTS: Falls of the Ohio State Park, 812-280-9970; fallsoftheohio.org

Falls of the Ohio Levee Trail

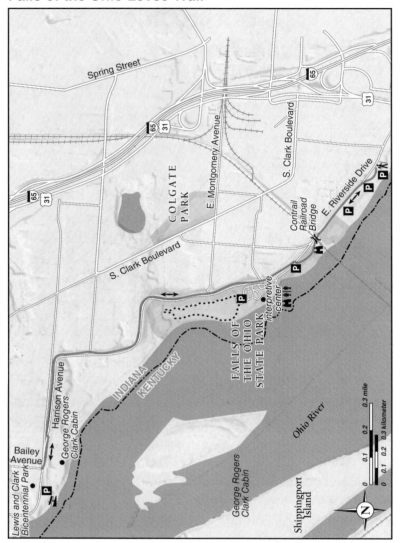

Overview

The paved Levee Trail is perfect for an after-work power walk, a sprint with the jogging stroller, or a leisurely saunter on a Sunday afternoon. The 2-mile (one-way) trail connects East Riverside Drive with Falls of the Ohio State Park and Lewis and Clark Bicentennial Park. Located just across the river from downtown Louisville, in southern Indiana, most of the levee trail runs atop the earthen-berm floodwall that protects the city of Clarksville from the mighty Ohio River.

Route Details

First things first: What's in a name? Both Louisville and southern Indiana are working like crazy to meet the growing demand for paved, multiuse trails. So now we have the Ohio Greenway Trail, the Ohio River Levee Trail, the Clarksville Heritage Trail, the Clarksville Discovery Trail, the Louisville Loop, and more! All this is good. But it's also confusing. To keep things simple, we're calling this hike the Falls of the Ohio Levee Trail because, well, it centers around the Falls of the Ohio State Park. But technically, we're talking about the Ohio River Greenway Trail that runs 7.5 miles (one-way) from Jeffersonville to New Albany, Indiana.

The Falls of the Ohio Levee Trail can be accessed from either end and at a variety of points along the way. Following the driving directions provided below, the route assumes you've left your car at the Ashland Park lot along East Riverside Drive. Regardless, your chances of getting lost in the Mall St. Matthews are much greater than getting lost here. There are lots of great trail signs, including mileage markers, placed right where you need them.

Beginning from the Ashland Park lot and walking north toward Falls of the Ohio State Park, the paved trail threads a line between the northern bank of the Ohio River and a popular playground area. The downtown Louisville skyline is clearly in view across the river. Ten minutes of walking will bring you to the underpass of the Contrail Railroad Bridge and a small overlook of the lowhead dam (also known as a fixed-weir dam) that forms the large pool of water just above the Falls of the Ohio. They're difficult to see from the overlook, but the shipping locks are behind the far island, on the Kentucky side of the river.

At this point, two islands divide the Ohio River into three distinct chutes of water. Nearest you, on the Indiana side of the river, is the Indian Chute (the "hero" route for early canoeists); on the far side, the Kentucky Chute holds the locks; and between the two is the Middle Chute. Goose Island, between the Indian and Middle Chutes, is protected as part of Falls of the Ohio State Park. The island contains several fossil beds and plays host to various habitats dominated by willow and cottonwood trees, and prairie grass. Access to the island is by private boat only.

Another 10 minutes (a total of 0.4 mile from the Ashland Park lot) of walking brings you to the Falls of the Ohio Interpretive Center and better views of the river below the dam. The pool of water formed by the dam obscures the falls, but the water spewing from the release valves provides for plenty of action as the river races along the bumpy riverbed. Occasionally you might see whitewater kayakers working on their eddy turns and peel outs in the swift current, or oar rigs practicing for a trip down the Colorado River. But be forewarned—this place is not safe for swimming, for man nor beast. Keep Fido on a short leash, and restrain yourself from lobbing that limb into the strong current.

Continue walking downstream along the paved Levee Trail, which now moves northwest and slightly away from the river. The sounds of the falls begin to fade as the wooded area insulates you from the riverbank. The trail takes on a comfortable pace as the trees continue to block the river views. Your eye may become slightly more voyeuristic as tidy backyards on the opposite side of the trail come into view.

Traffic on the paved trail follows the normal rules of the road: stay right, except when you want to pass, and watch for oncoming traffic, which could include cyclists, inline skaters, and runners pushing jogging strollers. Local neighborhood kids love to race their Big Wheels along the levee, and many a child has learned to ride a two-wheeler on the smooth paved surface.

As the paved trail begins to parallel Harrison Avenue (about 1.8 miles from the trailhead), views of the river appear once more. The hike officially ends at the old road that leads to the George Rogers Clark home site, near the entrance to the Lewis and Clark Bicentennial Park, and where Bailey Avenue dead-ends into Harrison. Known as Clarks Point, this land was given to George Rogers Clark (an older brother of William Clark, of Lewis and Clark fame) as part of a Revolutionary War land grant. In 1803 Clark built a small cabin here, which was later torn down; a replica was built in 2001. Call 812-280-9970 for a schedule of free cabin tours.

From the porch of the cabin, take in the skyline of downtown Louisville and try to imagine what Clark saw from this vantage point. And as you walk the 2 miles back to your vehicle, imagine running the falls in a dugout canoe while trying to keep your moccasins dry.

Nearby Attractions

From Lewis and Clark Bicentennial Park, you can walk another 1.25 miles (one way) to the **Loop Islands Wetlands.** But quite honestly, you may have better uses for your time and the soles of your shoes.

If hiking with younger kids, you might want to check out the short 0.7-mile **Woodland Loop Trail** that leaves from the Falls of the Ohio State Park's interpretive center. If you have time, head down the stairs behind the interpretive center to the fossil beds that adorn this side of the river. More than 650 fossil species have been found here, dating from the Devonian age 400 million years ago. It's hard to wrap your head around this, but these fossil beds at one time were located about 20 degrees south of the equator, lying lazily beneath a warm tropical sea, until continental drift brought them our way.

Falls of the Oho State Park also offers several special programs each month, such as fossil bed discovery hikes, a family nature club, and winter birds of Kentucky and Indiana. See their website for a complete list of offerings and an event calendar for dates and times.

Directions

From downtown Louisville, drive north on I-65 across the Ohio River and take Exit 0 toward Jeffersonville and Falls of the Ohio State Park. At the bottom of the exit ramp, turn left (west) on West Court Avenue. West Court will take you back under I-65; immediately turn left (south) on Missouri Avenue. Drive 0.2 mile and then turn right (west) onto West Market Street, which continues right onto East Riverside Street. Drive 0.3 mile; the Ashland Park lot will be on your left, just above the riverbank. Additional free parking is plentiful in the lots across from Widow's Walk Ice Creamery, at 415 East Riverside Drive.

Parking is also free and plentiful at the opposite (far western) end of the trail at Lewis and Clark Bicentennial Park, near the end of Harrison Avenue. To reach this lot from downtown Louisville, take I-65 North across the Ohio River into Indiana. Take Exit 1 north toward Jeffersonville/Clarksville. Turn left (west) on Stansifer Avenue and drive 0.4 mile. Turn right (north) on South Clark Road and drive 0.2 mile. Finally, turn left (west) on Harrison Avenue and drive 0.8 mile to the parking lot for the Lewis and Clark Bicentennial Park.

Parking at the Falls of the Ohio Interpretive Center costs $2 if you don't pay the entrance fee for the center ($9 for age 19 and older, with discounts for children.) This parking lot is about one-third of the distance from the Ashland Park trailhead to the far western trailhead at Lewis and Clark Bicentennial Park (see fallsoftheohio.org for detailed directions).

7

Goose Creek Loop at Tom Sawyer State Park

SCENERY: ★ ★ ★
TRAIL CONDITION: ★ ★ ★ ★
CHILDREN: ★ ★ ★
DIFFICULTY: ★ ★
SOLITUDE: ★ ★

GOOSE CREEK MAY HAVE BEEN NAMED AFTER WILLIAM GOOSE, AN 18TH-CENTURY WAGON-MAKER WHO LIVED IN THE AREA.

GPS TRAILHEAD COORDINATES: N38° 17.268' W85° 46.535'

DISTANCE & CONFIGURATION: 2.2-mile loop

HIKING TIME: 1 hour

HIGHLIGHTS: Diverse scenery, many special events

ELEVATION: 690' at trailhead, with no significant change in elevation

ACCESS: Daily, sunrise–sunset; free admission

MAPS: Online at tinyurl.com/GooseCreekLoop and displayed at the trailhead kiosk

FACILITIES: Restrooms, picnic tables, soccer fields, archery range, outdoor swimming pool, tennis and basketball courts, BMX track, and softball fields

WHEELCHAIR ACCESS: None on trail

COMMENTS: Pets must be leashed.

CONTACTS: E. P. "Tom" Sawyer State Park, 502-429-7270; tinyurl.com/sawyerpark

Overview

The Goose Creek Loop lies within the well-loved E. P. "Tom" Sawyer State Park, in northeastern Jefferson County. The trail winds around much of the 554-acre park, across open fields, and through lightly wooded areas along Goose Creek. Other trails traverse the park and are frequently utilized for cross-country practice and meets. The suburban park is extremely popular after work and on weekends and offers an excellent array of educational programs focusing on the great outdoors.

The park was named after Erbon Powers Sawyer (1915–69), a well-respected Jefferson County judge and the father of newscaster Diane Sawyer. The state bought the land from the Kentucky Department of Mental Health in 1969. Much of the property had been used as a farming operation for the mental hospital on the premises. Consequently, several outbuildings still stand on the property and many old farm roads crisscross the park.

Route Details

The Goose Creek Loop takes advantage of the small amount of wooded area within the park. The trailhead is just south of the large brown Activities Building, near the southwestern edge of the parking lot. This route combines portions of the 1.0-mile finely graveled Fitness Trail with the 1.25-mile Goose Creek Trail to create a 2.2-mile loop. The map displayed at the trailhead kiosk gives you a general feel for the layout of the park. You'll quickly notice that the multitude of cross-country trails, the Fitness Trail, and the profusion of gravel and paved farm roads create a spaghetti junction rivaling that found in downtown Louisville.

From the trailhead, walk almost due southwest from the kiosk to follow the 1.0-mile Fitness Trail counterclockwise. This portion of the trail follows the edge of several large open fields, with a pleasant array of trees and picnic tables providing some visual interest. The trail eventually veers left (south), and you'll come to an intersection with a gravel road, which leads to the model-airplane field. Leave the Fitness Trail by turning right (southwest) on the gravel road, and walk a short distance until you see a small dirt path on your left with a large sign indicating Goose Creek Trail. The trail then turns left (southwest) and approaches the far western edge of the park boundary. You may hear some road noise from Hurstbourne Parkway. A few smaller trails will come in on your right, leading to a small parking lot just off Hurstbourne and another trail called Goose Creek Walk. You can ignore all of these distractions.

Goose Creek Loop at Tom Sawyer State Park

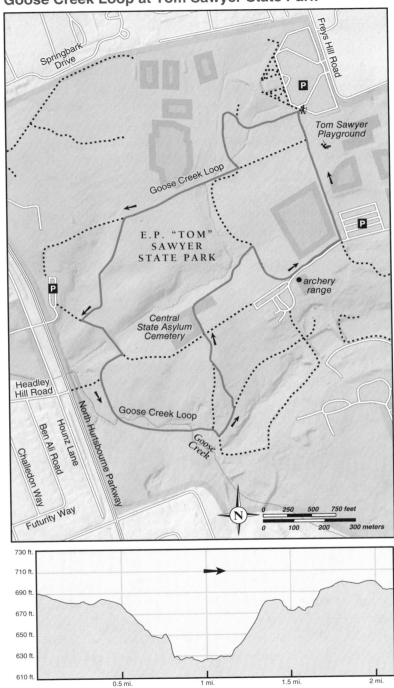

As the trail goes deeper into the lightly wooded area, Goose Creek will appear on your right, just south of the trail and a little less than a mile from the trailhead. The narrow, intimate creek is downright pretty in spots, with fish darting amid the shadows. The trail continues creekside for several hundred yards. At one point you'll see yet another rogue trail crossing the creek. Don't follow this path—instead, bear left (east), staying on the same side of the creek you started on.

Soon you will come to an intersection with a fine gravel trail. Bear slightly left here; in a few minutes you will see the hospital cemetery on your left and soccer fields on your right. Take the path that goes between these two open fields and the black wood plank fences that define them. At the end of the fencerow, the trail takes a sharp right-hand turn northeast. Another quick walk through the woods will bring you back out to the finely graveled Fitness Trail. Turn right once more and then left again (at the archery range), to stay on the Fitness Trail. It will bring you back to the starting point, the trailhead kiosk.

Before you get back in your car, note the array of classes and programs listed on the trailhead kiosk. The park offers an Outdoor Skills Series that includes classes on orienteering, knot tying and uses, and shelter and fire building. Other programs range from Leave No Trace principles to park geology, and how to play pickleball. The annual "In the Park After Dark" is "geocaching with a ghoulish twist"; using a GPS device, participants navigate the park from 8 p.m. to midnight. That might be easier than the trail gyrations I've described above.

Nearby Attractions

On the eastern side of Freys Hill Road, Tom Sawyer State Park operates a community garden. The park leases 20 x 20–foot plots for $40 each or $15 for a raised bed. Further information is available on-site or call 502-429-7270.

Tom Sawyer State Park also has one of only six Supercross BMX tracks in the country, and each year they host the National BMX Grand Championships. When not used for races, the track is open to the public March 1–October 31. Visit usabmx.com/tracks/1879 for more information.

Directions

From I-265 (KY 841/Gene Snyder Freeway), take Exit 32 and head west on Westport Road (KY 1447). Drive 0.5 mile and, at the second light, turn left (south) on Freys Hill Road. Drive another 0.4 mile. The dog park and community garden will be on your left; immediately after, the main park entrance will be on your right.

8

Harrods Creek Park

SCENERY: ★ ★ ★
TRAIL CONDITION: ★ ★ ★ ★
CHILDREN: ★ ★ ★
DIFFICULTY: ★ ★ ★
SOLITUDE: ★ ★ ★

WHAT A WONDERFUL PLACE FOR A GOOD BOOK AND A SACK LUNCH.

GPS TRAILHEAD COORDINATES: N38° 20.393' W85° 35.995'

DISTANCE & CONFIGURATION: 4.1-mile double-loop

HIKING TIME: 2 hours

HIGHLIGHTS: Limestone outcrops, views of Harrods Creek

ELEVATION: 452' at trailhead, ascending to 562' at high point, descending to 425' at low point

ACCESS: Daily, sunrise–sunset

MAPS: Available online and displayed at the trailhead kiosk

FACILITIES: Picnic tables, canoe launch

WHEELCHAIR ACCESS: None

COMMENTS: Pets are permitted as long as they are on leash or under control.

CONTACTS: Prospect City Hall, 502-228-1121; tinyurl.com/HarrodsCreek

Overview

Harrods Creek is a great example of a small neighborhood park, primarily frequented by those living within close proximity. While the scenery may not be stunning, the City of Prospect has done a good job maintaining and improving the 4-mile trail system that runs between Harrods Creek and a linear formation of limestone outcrops. The park is perfect for that early-morning or after-work brisk stroll, walking the dog during your lunch hour, or enjoying the delightful spring wildflowers that grow abundantly along the trail.

Route Details

The parking lot at Harrods Creek Park is rather small, holding 15–20 cars at most. Typically, that is never a problem, but you can also park on Montero Road and take the short, well-marked path to the trailhead. Either way, spend a few minutes reading the signs at the kiosk, which not only describe the trail you are about to embark upon but also tell of the other parks and trails owned and maintained by the city of Prospect.

The trail route described below begins just behind the kiosk and is basically a double-loop configuration, combining the blue, green, red, and orange trails. The city has generously placed several signs, including mileage markers and trail maps, throughout the park, so navigating your way is relatively easy. Start by going east along the Blue Trail (whereas walking north, up the hill, would take you to Montero Drive). Cross two small bridges, bearing left on the Blue Trail twice (do not take the Orange Trail). For the next 15 minutes of walking, the path winds through a deciduous forest of hardwoods and crosses the occasional seasonal creek. After a heavy rain, a few small waterfalls can be seen along the trail. Despite being nestled below suburban neighborhoods, the trail is amazingly quiet and has a feeling of seclusion.

To your left and just north of the trail, you will begin to notice a small limestone outcrop—mini palisades, if you will. Spicebush is also prolific here, identified by its clusters of greenish-yellow flowers in the spring, red berries in the fall, and fragrant aroma from lightly broken branches. Please observe the signs requesting you to not walk off-trail or intrude on adjacent private property, although the local deer population either cannot, or chooses not to, read the warnings.

Approximately 0.6 mile from the trailhead, bear left (north) to take the Green Trail. The limestone outcrop on your left will do the same, following you

Harrods Creek Park

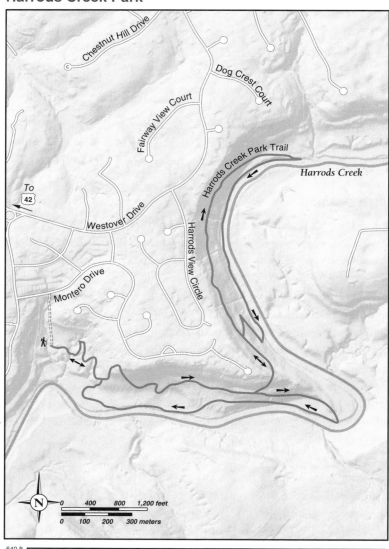

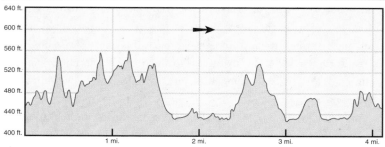

as you hike beneath a canopy of walnut, oak, and cherry trees. The forest floor is littered with luxurious moss-covered rocks and downed wood. For the most part the trail remains dry and relatively well maintained, even after a heavy rain.

As you get closer to the creek, there are a number of huge sycamore trees, complemented with a proliferation of wildflowers in the spring, including larkspur, sessile trillium, Dutchman's-breeches, and wood anemone. Where the 0.7-mile Green Trail ends close to the banks of Harrods Creek, bear right (south) on the Red Trail for another 0.6 mile. You will see several little, short paths leading to the stream, where you can get a good view of the creek and skip a few stones. The Red Trail then makes two hairpin turns as it slowly ascends the hill to once again join the Green Trail. Retrace your steps south on the Green Trail for just a few yards until it meets the Blue Trail once again. Whew, Roy G. Biv would be quite at home here.

Bearing left on the Blue Trail will take you southeast for 0.2 mile, before ending at the creek and transitioning into the Orange Trail. The openness of the Orange Trail is a nice yang to the yin of the shady forest trails. The trail begins a sharp ascent up a gravel path, but the greater the amount of sunlight that hits the gravel trail, the more prolific the lavender-colored aster blooms are in the fall. The city has also planted lots of new trees here, including birch, oak, cypress, dogwood, and sycamore, all of which are rapidly maturing.

As the gravel path becomes a country lane, multiple swinging benches provide an alluring invite to sit, perhaps read a book, and admire the creek. The Orange Trail ends after 0.8 mile, near the canoe launch, and just south of the parking lot.

Be sure to note all the Eagle Scout projects found at Harrods Creek Park, from the picnic tables to the mile markers, multiple benches, and the kiosk itself. It's nice to know that youth volunteerism keeps giving back. It may also be a good time to contemplate where your city taxes go.

Nearby Attractions

As mentioned previously, the city of Prospect owns several other parks, including **Putney Pond and Woodlands.** The 26-acre park was previously owned by Betty and Moseley Putney, who lived in the small log cabin that sat on the property. Sadly, their son died in a military training accident when his plane crashed. The pond was then named in his honor.

A series of short woodland trails wind their way through the property, across wetlands, around the pond, and past the State Champion Kentucky Coffee Tree. Putney Pond and Woodlands is located less than 3 miles from Harrods Creek Park. For directions and a trail map, go to tinyurl.com/PutneyPondPark.

Directions

From I-265 (Gene Snyder Freeway, Exit 37), head north on US 42 toward the city of Prospect. In 3.2 miles, turn right onto Hunting Creek Drive. Travel 0.9 mile; at the traffic circle, bear right onto Deep Creek Drive. Drive another 0.2 mile, then turn left onto Montero Drive. In a few hundred yards, you will see the sign for the park on your right and the small country lane that leads to the parking lot. If the lot is full, you can also park on Montero Drive.

HARRODS CREEK IS HOME TO SEVERAL GREAT BLUE HERON ROOKERIES.

9 # Iroquois Park Summit

SCENERY: ★ ★ ★ ★ ★
TRAIL CONDITION: ★ ★ ★ ★ ★
CHILDREN: ★ ★ ★
DIFFICULTY: ★ ★ ★
SOLITUDE: ★ ★

IROQUOIS PARK IS PERFECT FOR HIKING YEAR-ROUND.

GPS TRAILHEAD COORDINATES: N38° 10.113' W85° 47.140'

DISTANCE & CONFIGURATION: 4.4-mile balloon

HIKING TIME: 2.0 hours

HIGHLIGHTS: Paved path, views of downtown Louisville and Jefferson County

ELEVATION: 556' at trailhead, ascending to 746' at high point

ACCESS: Daily, 6 a.m.–11 p.m.; free admission. This is a gated paved road. Pedestrians and cyclists may use the road to the top of the summit daily throughout the year. Motorized-vehicle access is available Wednesday, Saturday, and Sunday, 8 a.m.–8 p.m., April 1–October 28.

MAPS: Available at olmstedparks.org USGS *Louisville West*.

FACILITIES: Picnic tables and shelters, playground

WHEELCHAIR ACCESS: Yes, but not for the faint of heart. There is a wheelchair-accessible path at the North Overlook.

COMMENTS: Pets must be leashed.

CONTACTS: Louisville Metro Parks, 502-456-8100; tinyurl.com/IROQPark

Iroquois Park Summit

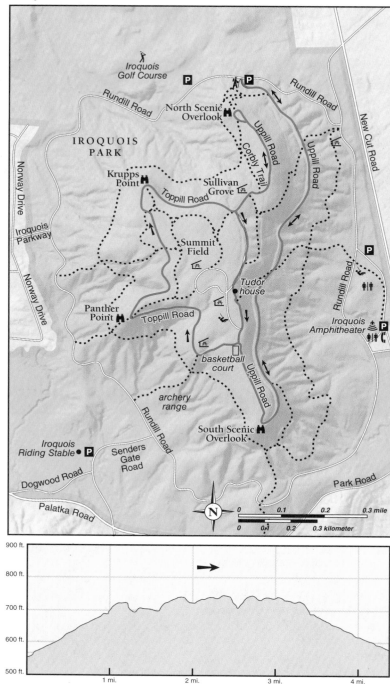

Overview

Iroquois Park is truly urban, completely surrounded by residential and commercial districts in southwest Louisville. Designed by Frederick Law Olmsted in 1897, Iroquois is among the 18 parks and six interconnecting parkways in Louisville attributed to him and his firm. Perched atop a heavily forested knob, the park offers commanding views of downtown Louisville and much of the surrounding countryside. The trail reaches the park summit by way of a paved road that is best hiked Monday, Tuesday, Thursday, or Friday, when the road is closed to vehicular traffic.

Route Details

The 725-acre Iroquois Park is extremely popular with walkers, joggers, and cyclists throughout the year. The east side of the park is home to the Sunnyhill Pavilion, the Iroquois Amphitheater, playgrounds, tennis courts, and a disc golf course. The Iroquois Golf Course is on the northern side of the park, and the southwestern corner is where Louisville Mounted Police horses are boarded and trained. All of these activities are connected by Rundill Road, which circles the perimeter of the park and is open for pedestrian and cyclists to use. Only a portion of Rundill Road allows vehicular traffic.

The heart of Iroquois Park can be reached via Uppill Road, as it winds around and up a large knob—a steeply sloping, often-cone-shaped hill common across much of central Kentucky. The top of the knob affords views in all directions, including the downtown Louisville skyline. Myriad dirt trails, the result of hikers, mountain bikers, and the resident deer population, crisscross the park. Unfortunately, these trails bear little resemblance to any published maps of the park and can be quite convoluted.

For the first-time summit hiker, walking Uppill Road to the top of the knob is the best assurance that you'll arrive where you want to be—and that you know how to get back down. As noted, the road to the summit is open seasonally on certain days of the week. I suggest that you avoid walking this paved trail when motorized traffic is present. Uppill Road will be gated and locked on the days it's closed. Simply walk to either side of the gate and continue up the road. Immediately you'll find yourself immersed in mature hardwood forests, with three or four robins to keep you company (since they all look the same, who knows if it's the same one?). The road is rather steep for a jogging stroller, but if you have the fortitude (and the calf muscles), it's not unheard of to see little tykes at the top. Cyclists and runners also use the ascent for training purposes.

The climb to the first overlook is 0.95 mile from the parking lot and leads you to the South Scenic Overlook, which faces, well, south. Enjoy the view while you catch your breath and snap a few pictures.

Continue up the road another 0.2 mile and congratulate yourself on reaching the top of the knob. A lonely basketball court stands to your left, torn nets twirling in the breeze. Any loose balls would surely plummet off the knob at breakneck speeds, only to wind up in Rupp Arena amid a sea of blue.

Just past the basketball court, turn left (west) and continue walking the road past the South and North Shelters (both are beautiful 1920s stone structures) to Panther Point, which is 1.55 miles from the parking lot below. You're now on Toppill Road. On this side of the knob you'll be facing due west, with views of rural Jefferson County (or what's left of it). Continue on Toppill Road as you circle the top of the knob and what is primarily an open meadow, referred to as Summit Field.

The Metro Park service periodically mows paths across these open fields. Here the bird populations, including meadowlarks, Eastern kingbirds, and even woodcocks, are always bustling. The small spring-fed ponds atop the knob provide fresh water for the wildlife that frequents these meadows.

Toppill Road continues circling the open fields until it reaches the next overlook, Krupps Point, which faces north toward the downtown Louisville skyline. Take time to notice the engraved stone set in the retaining wall. In the springtime, this side of the summit is a symphony of spring peepers, the latest generation living in the ponds atop the knob. Another 5 minutes (about 0.2 mile) of walking on Toppill Road will bring you back to Uppill Road. Bear left (north) here.

This dead-end section of Uppill Road leads you to the North Scenic Overlook, about 2.5 miles from the parking area. The views up here are fabulous, with 270-degree vistas of the city and surrounding countryside, plus the bluffs of southern Indiana. Spend a few minutes enjoying the scenery before heading back on Uppill Road the same way you came.

Taking the road back, you'll pass Toppill Road once more. Stay straight here, along Uphill Road. Shortly you will pass a historic stone structure with English Tudor architectural elements, named Jacob Lodge after the mayor of Louisville who was involved (purportedly illegally) in the original purchase of this land. The building includes a large, open-air covered pavilion, replete with stone fireplace and limestone mantel. Continue straight on Uppill Road, backtracking your steps when you get to the basketball courts. It's all downhill from here. Slowly work your way back down from the top of the knob, thinking about what these woods must have looked like when Frederick Law Olmsted first trekked up here.

Nearby Attractions

A unique Louisville landmark, the **Little Loomhouse** is just a few blocks from Iroquois Park, at 328 Kenwood Hill Road. On the National Register of Historic Places, the site consists of three wood cabins built in the 1860s and is dedicated to celebrating the life of Lou Tate and her passion for textiles and weaving. Lou inherited the property in the early 1900s and immediately began offering weaving classes to the women of Louisville and selling textiles to the public— including Eleanor Roosevelt, who placed an order for linens for the White House. Mrs. Roosevelt visited the Little Loomhouse several times in support of Lou's commitment to textile arts.

Visitors are welcome Tuesday–Friday, 10 a.m.–3 p.m.; Saturday 11 a.m.– 4 p.m. Historical guided tours are also available for $5; or your own private weaving lesson and take-home souvenir for $12. For more information, call 502-367-4792 or visit littleloomhouse.org.

Directions

From I-264 (Watterson Expressway), take Exit 9, head south on Taylor Boulevard, and drive 1.3 miles. To reach the trailhead parking lot, use the far northern entrance to Iroquois Park, where Taylor Boulevard turns into New Cut Road and Southern Parkway intersects from the northeast. Turn right (west) into the park and drive 0.2 mile. Turn right (northwest) on Rundill Road, toward the golf course, and drive another 0.3 mile. Before you reach the golf clubhouse, you'll see a small parking lot to your left, south of where Rundill and Uppill Roads intersect. Park here and get ready to hike up.

10 # Ohio River Levee Trail:
Farnsley-Moremen Landing

SCENERY: ★ ★ ★ ★
TRAIL CONDITION: ★ ★ ★ ★ ★
CHILDREN: ★ ★ ★ ★ ★
DIFFICULTY: ★ ★
SOLITUDE: ★ ★ ★

WALKING ATOP THE LEVEE AFFORDS COMMANDING VIEWS OF THE OHIO RIVER VALLEY.

GPS TRAILHEAD COORDINATES: N38° 5.793' W85° 53.661'

DISTANCE & CONFIGURATION: 1.0–7.4-mile (total) out-and-back, paved multiuse path

HIKING TIME: 2–3 hours

HIGHLIGHTS: Pastoral views of the Ohio River, historic home, steamboat landing, and chapel

ELEVATION: 477' at trailhead, with no significant elevation change

ACCESS: Daily, 6 a.m.–11 p.m. Free to hike; see riverside-landing.org for fees to tour historic Riverside, the Farnsley-Moreman Landing.

MAPS: Available at the website below or tinyurl.com/FarnMore

FACILITIES: Visitor center, restrooms, picnic area, historic-home tour

WHEELCHAIR ACCESS: Both the trail and the buildings are accessible.

COMMENTS: Drinking-water access is extremely limited along the trail. Dogs are permitted on leash.

CONTACTS: Louisville Metro Parks, 502-456-8100; tinyurl.com/LOUParks

Overview

The Ohio River Levee Trail is part of Louisville's ambitious plan to create 100 miles of multiuse paths around the city. The suggested out-and-back hike begins at the Farnsley-Moremen Landing, travels 3.7 miles to Riverview Park, then returns on the same paved trail. The path lies atop the levee and provides pastoral views of the Ohio River Valley. The trail is open to walkers, joggers, and cyclists. Alternately, walkers can also freely explore the grounds of the historic Riverside home and the limited-access paved road that goes from the trailhead to the historic Moremen Family Chapel, for a 1.0-mile round-trip.

Route Details

Our apologies to Don McLean if we're out of tune, but this hike will have you humming "Bye, bye, Miss American Pie / Drove my Chevy to the levee / But the levee was dry" the entire way. But what a great earworm to have as you walk atop the levee, with intermittent views of the Ohio River, tall grass wavering in the breeze, and butterflies fluttering back and forth.

The paved Ohio River Levee Trail begins at the Farnsley-Moremen Landing and runs north for 9.5 miles before joining several miles of bike lanes, which connect it to the 6.9-mile paved Riverwalk Trail. While cyclists can easily make the 19-mile round-trip ride on the Levee Trail, the average hiker wouldn't be interested in pounding his or her feet for that many miles. But shorter sections of the trail are popular with hikers and joggers. And it's not unusual to see parents walking the path pushing jogging strollers or following along as their kids ride their first two-wheelers. From Farnsley-Moremen, the levee trail also runs south for 2.8 miles (one way) to the Watson Lane Trailhead.

When is a good time to hike the Ohio River Levee Trail? For most walkers, spring and fall are ideal, when temperatures are well within reasonable ranges and breezes are gentle. The mixture of hardwoods along the river and the small knobs on the Indiana side provide nice fall color. In the peak of summer, however, the trail becomes less than ideal, as the humidity climbs and the pavement reflects all that heat back onto you. Wintertime hiking is also a challenge here, as the winds can be quite cold and biting; on the upside, you're guaranteed to have the place to yourself.

This hike begins at the Farnsley-Moremen Landing, where parking is plentiful and the scenes bucolic. Take a quick tour of the visitor center, hit the restrooms, and top off that water bottle or hydration pack—there's only one

Ohio River Levee Trail: Farnsley-Moremen Landing

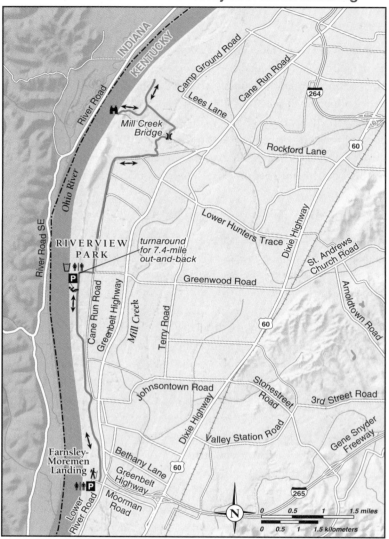

water fountain (open seasonally) between Farnsley-Moremen and Riverview, and no other facilities.

To reach the trailhead, walk to the northern end of the parking area, then turn right (east) and walk the way you drove into the park. At the top of the hill you'll see the trailhead sign and the paved path heading north from Moorman Road. You may have noticed the sign when you first entered the park off Lower River Road.

The Ohio River Levee Trail runs north atop the levee, parallel to the river and above Cane Run Road. In about 0.5 mile you'll see the historic Moremen Family Chapel (circa 1888), which originally stood at the corner of Bethany Lane and Dixie Highway. The chapel was moved to the new site and is currently being renovated.

The next 3.0 miles along the Ohio River Levee Trail consist of a peaceful walk with occasional views of the river to your left (west) and private homes to your right (east). The scenery is pleasant enough but changes only with the pace of your walk. Deer, rabbits, and turkey can be seen. On weekends, particularly during the summer, a golf cart carrying members of the Jefferson County Sheriff's Department may pass, ready to lend a hand to those in need.

About 3.7 miles from the trailhead, you'll see Riverview Park, also known as Greenwood Boat Ramp because of the facilities here. The park has picnic tables, both a traditional playground and a "spray ground" in the summer, and restrooms. Riverview is extremely popular with families, boaters, and anglers. Enjoy the lively activity here and the bucolic scenes of the riverfront. Take a last glance before retracing your steps south, back to the Farnsley-Moremen Landing.

Take heart and turn that hum into a whistle. Or, if no one else is within earshot, belt out a full-blown melody: "Them good ol' boys were drinkin' whiskey and rye. . . ." Try to remember as many verses as you can before thanking Don for his "American Pie" and for a wonderful day on the levee.

Nearby Attractions

Just north of the visitor center lies the historic home built in 1837 by Gabriel Farnsley. Rachel and Alanson Moremen bought the house and surrounding farmland in 1862, naming the site **Riverside**. Descendants of the Moremens sold the property to Jefferson County in 1988. The 300-acre Riverside park grounds are free to walk and are quite interesting, including the old boat landing on the Ohio River. Riverside is available for tours year-round (see riverside-landing .org for admission fees and hours). "A Family Exploration Guide of the Riverside Landing" is available free at the visitor center.

A limited-access paved road runs from Riverside to the Moremen Family Chapel (0.5-mile one-way or 1.0-mile round-trip). The chapel was moved here in 2006 and has been renovated, including new stained glass windows on the front and back, a courtyard, and changing rooms. The church is frequently rented out for events such as weddings. Otherwise, visitors are free to walk around the chapel.

Directions

Take I-65 South from downtown Louisville and turn right (west) on I-265 (KY 841/Gene Snyder Freeway). After about 9 miles, I-265 West becomes the Greenbelt Highway (KY 1934)—watch for a RIVERPORT sign. Drive 1.2 additional miles after the road changes; then, at the stoplight, turn left (south) on Lower River Road and drive 0.2 mile. Turn right (west) on Moorman Road, which ends in 0.2 mile at the Farnsley-Moremen Landing and the trailhead parking.

THE OHIO RIVER LEVEE TRAIL WILL BE PART OF THE 100-MILE PAVED LOUISVILLE LOOP.

11

Waverly Park Loops

SCENERY: ★ ★ ★ ★
TRAIL CONDITION: ★ ★ ★ ★ ★
CHILDREN: ★ ★ ★
DIFFICULTY: ★ ★ ★
SOLITUDE: ★ ★

THE TRAILS AT WAVERLY PARK ARE WELL MARKED AND EASY TO FOLLOW.

GPS TRAILHEAD COORDINATES: N38° 07.792' W85° 49.919'

DISTANCE & CONFIGURATION: 4.7-miles, with more or less mileage easily available

HIKING TIME: 2.0 hours

HIGHLIGHTS: Classic hardwood forest in suburban Louisville

ELEVATION: 530' at trailhead, ascending to 644' at high point

ACCESS: Daily, 8 a.m.–sunset; free admission

MAPS: Louisville Metro Parks, USGS *Louisville West*

FACILITIES: Picnic tables, grills, small fishing lake, playground, portable toilet

WHEELCHAIR ACCESS: None

COMMENTS: Pets must be leashed.

CONTACTS: Louisville Metro Parks, 502-456-8100; tinyurl.com/LOUWaverlyPark

Waverly Park Loops

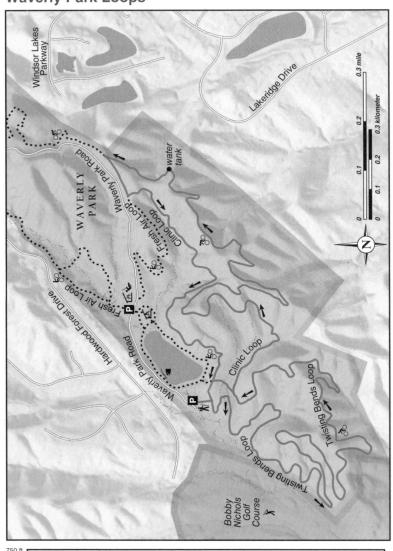

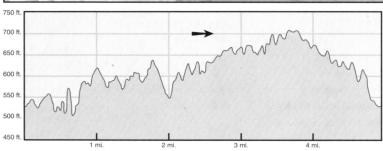

Overview

For many Louisville residents, Waverly Park, in southwestern Jefferson County, means two things: fishing and mountain biking. But the hiking here is top notch, and peaceful trails can be found during the week and off-season. The perfect after-work or weekend getaway, Waverly has three distinct trail loops, any of which can be combined to make a longer hike. These amoeba-shaped trails run through hardwood forests, winding their way over creeks, up ridges, and down moguls, and are well maintained. The proposed route combines the Twisted Bends and the Clinic Loops trails.

Route Details

The road through 300-acre Waverly Park ends at a small fishing lake and three distinct parking areas. The trailhead for this route can most easily be reached from the parking lot west of the lake, where the park road dead-ends. A short connector trail leads you on a short walk to the junction of the 2.2-mile Twisted Bends Loop and the 2.4-mile Clinic Loop.

Long a haven for the mountain-biking community, these trails have been faithfully maintained for years by the Kentucky Mountain Bike Association (KyMBA). The loops are tight and slightly technical singletrack, with the occasional wooden bridge traversing small creeks where needed. The Twisted Bends Loop earned its moniker honestly. In the spirit of sustainability, it packs a lot of trail into a small amount of acreage. For the most part, the trail is well drained despite the heavy clay content of the soil. The nine-hole Bobby Nichols Golf Course encircles much of the loop, buffering hikers from the suburban neighborhoods that surround the park.

Bear right (west) at the junction of the two trails to begin the Twisted Bends Loop through a beautiful hardwood forest of mature oaks, sweetgums, and beeches. The trail immediately takes on the graceful rhythm of a firefly on the wing. Ferns dot much of the forest floor, providing splashes of green year-round. Spring hikers will be greeted with an array of wildflowers, including cut-leaf toothwort and bluets. Early-blooming cornelian cherry dogwood (*Cornus mas*), a small multitrunked tree, is also plentiful along the hillsides. In July, the small, dainty yellow blooms of this dogwood mature into bright-cherry-red fruits that are quickly gobbled up by the resident squirrels and birds. In the summer there is enough shade and shadows at Waverly that the moss doesn't grow just on the north side of the huge white and red oaks along the trail. And fall hikers will enjoy the bright-yellow beech leaves as they contrast sharply with the reds and purples of the sweetgum trees.

After a little more than 2 miles of hiking, you'll find yourself back at the main junction, with the short trail to the parking lot straight ahead. Bear right (east) and follow the Clinic Loop uphill if you're ready for more hiking. The trail then follows a narrow ridge as it gains elevation. The Clinic Loop is considerably more strenuous than the Twisting Bends; the downhills are much faster and the uphills more challenging. KyMBA has built several moguls (short but steep hills), creating a roller-coaster effect along parts of the trail. One long downhill is affectionately referred to as the Luge.

About 3.5 miles from the trailhead (or 1.5 miles from where the Clinic Loop begins), the path joins the Fresh Air Loop, a 2.9-mile trail that runs on either side of the main park road. To stay on the Clinic Loop, bear left (south) and make a hairpin turn away from the Fresh Air Loop. At the 4.0-mile point, the trail is at its highest elevation and offers views of the small fishing lake below. From here you travel southwest before dropping toward the lake and back to the junction with the Twisting Bends Loop. Bear right (north) at this junction to return to the parking area.

At Waverly Park, bikers must give way to hikers, but sometimes practicality trumps courtesy. And given how much effort the biking community has put into trail building and trail maintenance, hikers should keep that in mind. In addition, mountain bikers typically ride the trails clockwise. The hiking directions given here suggest a counterclockwise rotation so hikers are "facing traffic," so to speak. When Waverly was developing into a cycling Mecca, few other alternatives existed. Now a multitude of good mountain-biking trails can be found in central Kentucky and southern Indiana. That has relieved some of the crowding at Waverly, as cyclists have more options, particularly on weekends.

Nearby Attractions

Waverly's wide, flat **Lake Loop** runs 0.4 mile on a mostly gravel surface. This is a great hike for young kids, who can race around the lake in no time.

The 3.1-mile **Fresh Air Loop,** at the park's northeastern end, covers a wooded terrain very similar to the two loops featured here. But because the Fresh Air Loop is much straighter than the Twisting Bends Loop and generally has fewer steep hills than the Clinic Loop, cyclists can build up a lot of speed.

The Fresh Air Loop can be accessed from either side of the park road, near the playground, and from the Clinic Loop.

The well-known **Waverly Hills Sanatorium** is located just west of Waverly Park. What started as a small private school in the late 19th century has been redeveloped and reimagined many times. The gothic-style building, constructed in 1926 just off Dixie Highway, originally served as a tuberculosis clinic and more recently as a nursing home before it was closed by the state in 1981. In danger of being torn down, the nonprofit Waverly Hills Historical Society now owns the property and offers various tours to support itself. For more information see therealwaverlyhills.com.

Directions

From the intersection of I-264 (Watterson Expressway) and Dixie Highway (US 31W/US 60), travel southwest out of Louisville on Dixie Highway 3.2 miles. Turn left (east) on St. Andrews Church Road (KY 1931). After 1.0 mile, turn right (south) on Arnoldtown Road. Drive 1.0 mile and turn left (west) on Waverly Park Road. In 1.2 miles, the park road dead-ends at a small parking lot, just west of the fishing lake.

WAVERLY PARK IS BEAUTIFUL ANY TIME OF YEAR.

Kentucky: South of Louisville and West of I-65

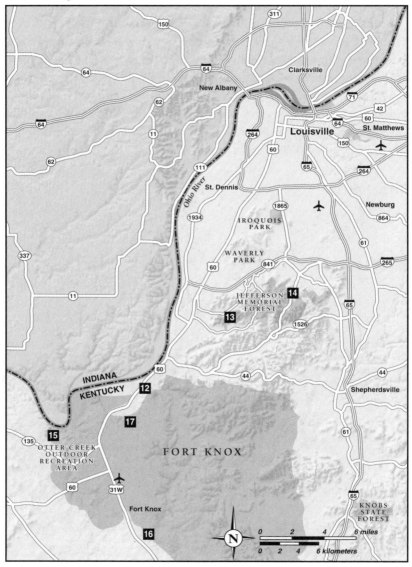

Kentucky: South of
Louisville and West of I-65

KENTUCKY HAS A LARGE NUMBER OF SPRING-FED CREEKS, INCLUDING SAUNDERS SPRINGS.
(See Hike 16, page 100.)

12

Fort Duffield

SCENERY: ★ ★ ★ ★
TRAIL CONDITION: ★ ★ ★ ★
CHILDREN: ★ ★ ★
DIFFICULTY: ★ ★ ★
SOLITUDE: ★ ★ ★ ★

THIS SWEET LITTLE PIECE OF REAL ESTATE CAN BE YOURS FOR THE ASKING.

GPS TRAILHEAD COORDINATES: N37° 59.505' W85° 56.729'

DISTANCE & CONFIGURATION: 3.0-mile loop; more mileage readily available

HIKING TIME: 2.0 hours

HIGHLIGHTS: Kentucky's largest earthen fortification, creekside trails

ELEVATION: 466' at trailhead, ascending to 712' at high point

ACCESS: Daily, sunrise–sunset; free admission, but donations are kindly accepted.

MAPS: Available at park trailhead kiosk; USGS *Vine Grove*

FACILITIES: Restrooms, picnic tables, and shelter

WHEELCHAIR ACCESS: A gated road leads to the top of the fort. Vehicle access to this road is limited to times when park volunteers are present.

COMMENTS: Dogs are permitted on leash.

CONTACTS: Fort Duffield Park and Historic Site, 502-922-4574; fortduffield.com

Overview

Fort Duffield offers views of the Ohio River Valley, the best-preserved earthen fortification in Kentucky, and 10 miles of hiking and mountain-biking trails. On reenactment weekends, the noise of cannon fire and musket balls can be heard over the sounds of derailleurs shifting and chain rings spinning. Consequently, the park attracts interesting combinations of outdoors aficionados. But on most days, hikers are left with tumbling creeks and quiet woods to roam and explore.

Route Details

Fort Duffield is the perfect place if you like your hiking served with a generous side-helping of history. As you approach the park, you cross the Louisville, Henderson, and St. Louis Bridge, a relic from the days when steamboats navigated the Salt River on their way to the Ohio River. Fort Duffield, authorized by General William Tecumseh Sherman and built at the mouth of the Salt River, sits atop a 300-foot bluff overlooking the Ohio River Valley. The fort was designed to protect both the Union's supply base at West Point, Kentucky, and the city of Louisville by monitoring activity along the surrounding waterways and railways.

After parking in the trailhead lot, stop at the kiosk and pick up a green trail map and tan fort brochure if you haven't visited before. The trail map shows a winding set of hiking and mountain-biking trails. In reality, if you hike beyond the fort, the trails are even more convoluted than shown. But take a close look at the map and you'll see some good boundary markers that can help guide your hike. The northern park boundary is constrained by a steep bluff that follows Dixie Highway and overlooks the Ohio River and the town of West Point. The eastern park boundary is constrained by another bluff, this one towering above the Salt River. Finally, the western boundary aligns with the entrance road to the park, and the southern boundary with an old roadbed and set of power lines.

As you face the kiosk, a paved road climbs steeply in front of you, to the north; the Duffield Memorial Cemetery Trail begins to your left (west); and the Fort Trail begins to your right (east). The quickest way to the fort is straight up the paved road; this may also be the best option for stroller access and those with disabilities. However, volunteers staff the park, and the gate blocking motorized access to this road may or may not be locked depending on who's working at the time.

Fort Duffield

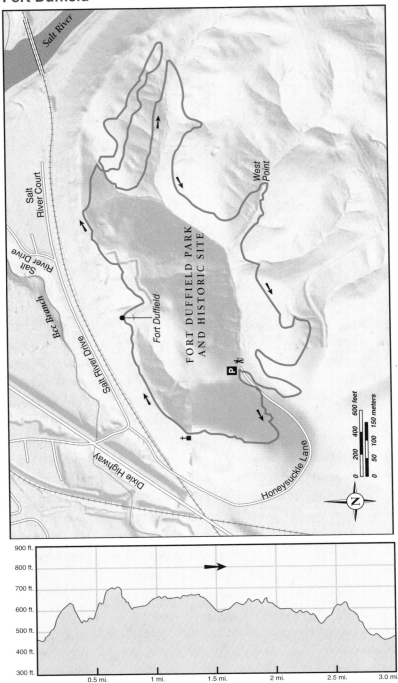

To walk the 3.0-mile loop clockwise, and to mix your history with your hiking, bear west out of the parking lot to begin the Cemetery Trail, just on the other side of the picnic shelter. This short but steep 0.25-mile climb leads you to the memorial grounds honoring 36 soldiers who died at Fort Duffield between 1861 and 1862, all members of the Ninth Michigan Infantry Regiment that served here.

Ionia Sweet. Miles Woods. Lafayette Porter. Isaac Columbus Tower. Philetus Bacon. Take time to read the names on the memorial markers and feel the gentle breeze blowing up the Ohio Valley. The views here are beautiful and the ambience serene, belying the skirmishes that took place nearby and the prevalence of disease that took lives so young.

The Cemetery Trail continues on the other side of the flagpole hoisting Old Glory, leading you along a wide gravel trail that descends back to the paved road leading to Fort Duffield. Continue walking straight on the merged road/trail another few minutes (about 50 yards). The fort sits just ahead, on the highest point of the bluff overlooking the Ohio River and the town of West Point. The earthen fortification took one and a half months to build and provided camping for 1,000 men. Rarely do today's defense contractors work that fast.

Several small wood cabins and a few other structures built more recently are used by the reenactment crowd and during living-history events. Likewise, young hikers with a need to play make-believe can use the cabins and lean-tos to battle Lord Voldemort or Darth Vader. It's difficult to believe that most of the trees on these hillsides had been cleared at one time to improve visibility to defend the fort from attack, and to provide wood for building, as well as heating and cooking fires.

After viewing the fort, the hiking trail continues on the far northeastern side of the earthen fortification and under several large walnut trees that grace the center of the fort, playing host to the mistletoe that thrives here. The trail quickly becomes a melting pot of red, yellow, and blue trail markers, all signed with a cyclist logo. Park volunteers have been working hard to clarify the signage and perform long-overdue trail maintenance. Fort Duffield receives only limited financial support from the city of West Point and Hardin County, so every dollar you drop into that donation box puts a smile on volunteers' faces and hope in their hearts.

The Red Trail is better maintained and stays more ridgetop, particularly on the eastern side with great views of the Ohio River Valley. However, the blue and yellow trails allow you to follow creek drainages (perfect for wildflower viewing in the spring) and tend to get fewer mountain bikers. You can't go wrong with any of these trails, but you do need to look sharp to make sure you're on the same trail you planned to be on.

To hike the Blue Trail, walk northeast for a few minutes along the bluff overlooking the Salt River. The trail will soon come in on your right, to the south of the bluff. Follow the Blue Loop Trail as it makes two large switchbacks through hardwood forest, including several large wild cherry and shagbark hickory trees. The Blue Trail then winds downhill, before meeting up with two different creek drainages, both offering an abundance of spring wildflowers, ferns, and deer habitat. Climbing the trail back up on the ridge, you may even see the "Outpost," which for now will be left up to your imagination.

Many of the trails at Fort Duffield were built and are maintained by members of the Kentucky Mountain Bike Association (KyMBA). These trails are primarily singletrack, technical, and fun. KyMBA built several ramps, moguls, and jumps for those wanting more than just creek crossing and log hopping. It's interesting how mountain bikers have continued to build earthen embankments and wood structures upon this land, just as their ancestors had done before them. Although bikers must always give way to hikers, one way to show our appreciation for the efforts of the biking community is to share the trail.

THE SERPENTINE EARTHWORKS OF THE UNION FORT ARE EXTREMELY WELL PRESERVED.

Nearby Attractions

Founded in 1796, the small town of **West Point, Kentucky,** can provide an interesting diversion for those with a little extra time. Located where the Salt River flows into the Ohio River, West Point earned its name for at one time being the westernmost outpost for those traveling down the river. West Point also proudly notes that it lies on the 38th parallel—the same dividing line between North and South Korea. (Someone in the chamber of commerce has been quite busy.)

West Point was the location of a pre–Civil War stagecoach stop, riverfront inn, and boat ramp, or embarcadero (Spanish for "embarking place"). It was at this embarcadero in 1806 that Thomas Lincoln loaded a flatboat of produce for his 60-day journey to New Orleans. The story goes that the trip was profitable enough that he was able to finalize his marriage plans to Nancy Hanks.

If the concept of a Sears and Roebuck house is new to you, be sure to visit the one built in 1899 across from the river landing. These "kit" houses were purchased from catalogs, shipped by rail, and assembled by local craftsmen. This particular house, at **201 Elm Street,** is in the "Three I" style, named for its popularity in Indiana, Illinois, and Iowa.

Are you a military history buff? If so, drive another 10 minutes farther south on Dixie Highway (US 31W) to the **General George Patton Museum.** Exhibits range from vehicles to weaponry to uniforms. Admission is free. See george patton.org for more information.

Directions

Fort Duffield is southwest of Louisville and just south of West Point, Kentucky. From the intersection of Dixie Highway (US 31W/US 60) and I-265 (KY 841/ Gene Snyder Freeway), drive west on Dixie Highway 7.5 miles. Just south of West Point, you'll see a sign for Fort Duffield on your right and the park entrance on your left. After you turn left (south) on Salt River Drive, the road immediately Ts, with the boat ramp to your left and the fort to your right. Turn right (southwest) on Honeysuckle Lane and drive 0.25 mile, being careful when crossing the railroad tracks. The road dead-ends into the trailhead parking lot.

Jefferson Memorial Forest:
Scott's Gap Trail

SCENERY: ★★★★
TRAIL CONDITION: ★★★★
CHILDREN: ★★★
DIFFICULTY: ★★★
SOLITUDE: ★★★★

TIME HAS A WAY OF ERASING THE PAST.

GPS TRAILHEAD COORDINATES: N38° 03.526' W85° 50.540'

DISTANCE & CONFIGURATION: 3.3-mile balloon (on a short string)

HIKING TIME: 1.5 hours

HIGHLIGHTS: Classic Kentucky hardwoods, a bounty of spring wildflowers, pastoral views

ELEVATION: 522' at trailhead, ascending to 802' at high point

ACCESS: Daily, 8 a.m.–sunset; free admission

MAPS: Louisville Metro Parks, Jefferson Memorial Forest Welcome Center and website, USGS Valley Station

FACILITIES: Picnic tables

WHEELCHAIR ACCESS: A 0.5-mile finely graveled loop trail is located at the trailhead parking lot.

COMMENTS: Dogs are permitted on leash.

CONTACTS: Jefferson Memorial Forest, 502-368-5404; Wilderness Louisville, memorialforest.com

Overview

In less time than it takes to drive the Henry Watterson Expressway, you could be hiking a beautiful trail in southern Jefferson County, complete with scenic overlooks, native hardwoods, and meandering creeks. And best of all, there's a good chance you won't have any company. This 3.3-mile trail is rated as moderate-strenuous by the staff of Jefferson Memorial Forest, due to its steep elevation changes. A 1.3-mile shortcut loop trail is also available.

Route Details

Scott's Gap Trail lies in the far southwestern reaches of Jefferson Memorial Forest (JMF), away from the more well-known (and crowded) Tom Wallace, Horine, and Paul Yost sections of the park. Louisville Metro Parks obtained the Scott Tract in 1982, and in contrast to some of the other trails in the JMF, horses are not permitted in this area. Consequently, trails tend to be singletrack and in better condition for hiking.

To begin the hike, walk north of the parking lot to the trailhead kiosk. The Scott's Gap Trail begins behind the kiosk on a finely graveled path. Scott's Gap trails are marked sequentially, beginning with an "SG" designation. A quick 30 yards of walking brings you to the intersection with the Siltstone Trail. Bear left (west at SG2) at this crossroad to keep on Scott's Gap Trail.

You'll soon come to another T-intersection, where the loop trail itself begins. Bear left (south at SG3) to hike the trail clockwise, steeply up and around a small balding knob, before going up to the ridgetop and then back again. The ups, downs, twists, and turns of this trail will challenge your sense of direction, but the trail is easy to follow and occasionally blazed with bright-red paint.

Less than 0.5 mile from the trailhead, you'll see a sign (SG4) indicating the shortcut loop, blazed in red and white, which reduces the total length of the loop trail to 1.3 miles. But to go the full 3.3 miles, bear left (west) here to stay on the main trail.

The surrounding forest is classic Kentucky hardwood, including black cherry, oak, sweetgum, hickory, and ash. Elusive wild turkeys like to haunt this area, and hopeful hikers wanting to catch a glimpse of Benjamin Franklin's choice for the national bird are cautioned to walk as lightly as possible and to talk even less—the quiet of the forest amplifies any noise. While not the smartest creatures, wild turkeys are extremely shy, albeit talkative.

Jefferson Memorial Forest: Scott's Gap Trail

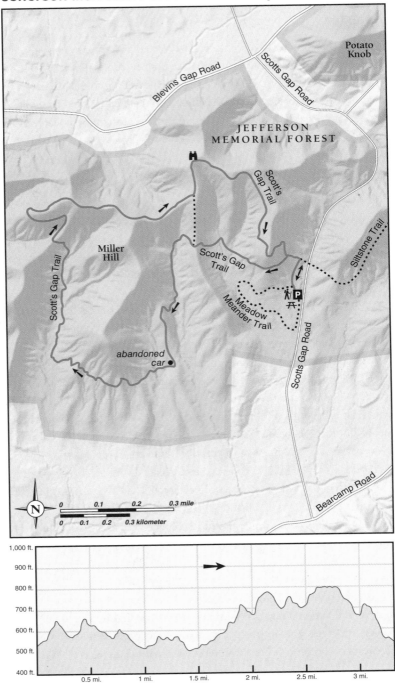

About 1 mile from the trailhead you'll come to the remains of an old car lying in the middle of a small stream, slowly washing farther down the creek-bed with each heavy rain. The passenger door has been left open, perhaps as an escape for the driver, who endured a spray of bullets that peppered the door on his or her side. It's easy to sit on the adjacent log and imagine all the scenarios that brought this twisted pile of metal to rest before your eyes.

This portion of Scott's Gap Trail winds along several creek drainages, promising a riot of wildflowers for spring hikers. A careful eye might detect jack-in-the-pulpit, trillium, toothwort, anemone, pussytoes, or dwarf crested iris. Cold-weather hikers will be greeted with Christmas, leatherwood, and maidenhair ferns.

About halfway around the loop, the trail ascends the ridgetop once again as it circles the base of Miller Hill. Lower-elevation sycamore and beech trees give way to the cedar and walnut that thrive above. As you walk this narrow ridge, notice the mature oak trees with their deeply creviced bark and thick, stubby arms. These oaks have survived many a fire, ice storm, and strong wind. The oldest trees in the forest are not always those with the largest girth, as the thin topsoil found here has restricted their trunk diameter.

The next mile is a repeat of the last as the trail descends into multiple seasonal creek drainages, wandering nomadically, before making another long ascent back to the ridgetop again. While the fall colors are spectacular atop the ridge, the pastoral views are equally beautiful after the leaves have dropped. At 2.5 miles, the trail once again intersects the shortcut loop—bear left (north) at this junction to continue on Scott's Gap Trail. Another 0.5 mile of walking will bring you to the top of the small bald knob you first viewed from below. A short descent completes the loop, as you continue right (south at SG3) to return to the parking lot.

Nearby Attractions

The 0.5-mile **Meadow Meander Trail** leaves due west from the same parking lot as Scott's Gap Trail. Strollers outfitted with rugged wheels can navigate this trail, if propelled by an able-bodied human machine. This loop circles a small open meadow that's home to many birds. A bat house and several birdhouses have been erected along the perimeter. A small pond, a drinking source for the local critters, is host to many a spring peeper and summer mosquito.

WHILE YOU'RE HIKING, LOOK UP AS WELL AS AHEAD.

If you're interested in a longer hike, the **Siltstone Trail** is 6.7 miles one way and leads to Tom Wallace Lake and the JMF Welcome Center. From the Scott's Gap Trailhead, follow the finely graveled path just behind the kiosk to the first trail intersection. Bear right (east) at this intersection, and you'll soon cross a small bridge and the road you drove in on. The Siltstone Trail is quite popular with local hikers training for longer adventures and can be accessed from a variety of trailheads. Unfortunately, a loop configuration is not available, forcing hikers to do either an out-and-back or set up a shuttle. A map for the Siltstone can be obtained from tinyurl.com/ScottsGap, or you can use the USGS *Valley Station* map.

Directions

Scott's Gap Trail is southwest of Louisville, in the Jefferson Memorial Forest. Traveling on I-265 (KY 841/Gene Snyder Freeway), take Exit 3 and head south on Stonestreet Road, which becomes Blevins Gap Road. After 2.7 miles, turn left (south) on Scotts Gap Road. Trailhead parking will be less than 1 mile ahead, on your right.

Jefferson Memorial Forest:
Yost Ridge to Mitchell Hill Lake

SCENERY: ★ ★ ★ ★
TRAIL CONDITION: ★ ★ ★ ★ ★
CHILDREN: ★ ★ ★
DIFFICULTY: ★ ★ ★
SOLITUDE: ★ ★ ★

CAN YOU IMAGINE A MORE TRANQUIL LOCATION THIS CLOSE TO DOWNTOWN LOUISVILLE?

GPS TRAILHEAD COORDINATES: N38° 5.083' W85° 46.032'

DISTANCE & CONFIGURATION: 3.4-mile balloon

HIKING TIME: 1.5 hours

HIGHLIGHTS: Ridgetop trail descending to Mitchell Hill Lake

ELEVATION: 593' at trailhead, ascending to 868' at high point

ACCESS: Daily, 8 a.m.–dusk; free admission

MAPS: Louisville Metro Parks, Jefferson Memorial Forest Welcome Center and website, USGS *Valley Station*

FACILITIES: Restrooms at Welcome Center, open Monday–Saturday, 8:30 a.m.–4:30 p.m.; Sunday, 10 a.m.–3 p.m.

WHEELCHAIR ACCESS: None

COMMENTS: Dogs are permitted on leash.

CONTACTS: Jefferson Memorial Forest, 502-368-5404; Wilderness Louisville, memorialforest.com

Jefferson Memorial Forest:
Yost Ridge to Mitchell Hill Lake

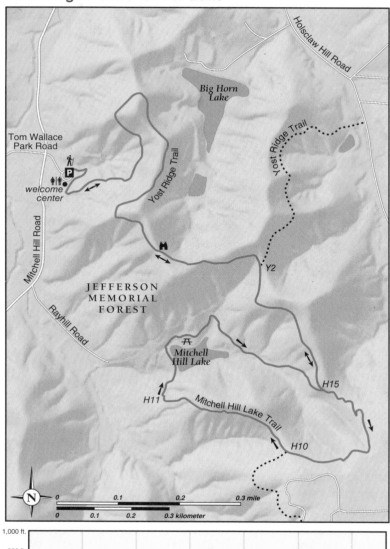

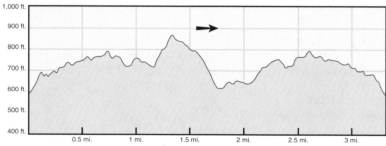

Overview

Yost Ridge and Mitchell Hill Lake lie within the Paul Yost Recreation Area and the adjacent Horine Reservation, both part of the Jefferson Memorial Forest, just southwest of Louisville. The trail leaves from the welcome center, climbs Yost Ridge, and then descends to Mitchell Hill Lake. This hike is popular on weekends during late spring and early fall, summer days, and after work when the days get long. Otherwise, you may find you have the trail to yourself for relaxing and enjoying the beauty of a hardwood forest.

Route Details

After parking, meander around the Jefferson Memorial Forest Welcome Center and grab a hiking stick before you hit the trail. The welcome center offers a variety of maps, a small selection of gifts, and a few outdoor activities for the kids.

To reach the trailhead, circle to the back of the center to find the trail marked YOST RIDGE TRAIL (Y1). (A handy tip: trails in the Yost Recreation Area begin with Y, and those in the Horine Reservation begin with H.) As you walk around the center, you'll see evidence of Zipline Kingdom, which is closed until further notice.

Adjacent to the trailhead, you may see a spindly woody plant with sharp thorns protruding from its slender trunk in all directions—the devil's-walking-stick. While it's bereft of any leaves in winter, in late spring small panicles of creamy-white flowers appear. In the fall, the long, narrow leaves turn an attractive bronze-red with a yellow tinge on the outer edges. If you keep a sharp eye out, you'll find more devil's-walking-sticks all along the trail as you climb Yost Ridge.

And climb you will. From the welcome center, the trail ascends 200 feet in a little more than 0.5 mile. About 0.7 mile from the trailhead, the trail begins to flatten, and in the winter you get great views of the downtown Louisville skyline—about 13 miles away as the crow flies.

Around 0.8 mile from the welcome center, the trail intersects the Mitchell Hill Lake Trail, marked as Y2. To reach the lake, bear right (south) and follow the trail to the ridgetop. Although the path may not be wide enough for Dorothy and her three buddies, you can easily lock arms with your BFF as you walk under a canopy of hardwood trees and the occasional cedar.

The trail then begins a short descent to the Mitchell Hill Lake Trail, which makes a loop about 1.25 miles from the trailhead, at trail marker H15. From here you can hike either way on the loop, but clockwise is the preferred route, so bear left (southeast) at this intersection. The next 0.2 mile involves a strong vertical ascent. If you find yourself getting short of breath, you can always stop after about 100 yards and admire the large oak. Or stop in another 100 yards to look at the large woodpecker holes. Or stop in the last 100 yards to inspect the three large shagbark hickories growing magnificently along the path. And voilà! You're at the top of another ridge.

Over the next 0.4 mile, the trail descends once more among clouds of white dogwoods and pink redbuds rising off the forest floor in the spring, or the spectacular fall colors of the oaks, sugar maples, and paw paws in midautumn. At trail marker H10, continue right (northwest) on the trail to reach the lake.

The trail then proceeds atop a small earthen berm that forms Mitchell Hill Lake. To circumvent the creek that serves as overflow for the lake, bear left across the small wood bridge, then circle to the right to follow the lakeshore. On the far northern side of the lake, two picnic tables offer a respite at the water's edge. An old bat house stands as testimony to the mosquito populations that thrive here in the summer. You're now about 1.9 miles from the trailhead, and many leagues from civilization.

Once you've soaked up the peaceful sights, follow the trail to the north side of the small lake and along the drainage that feeds the bottomlands. In the spring, blooming cutleaf toothwort, rue anemone, and bluets will be scattered across the forest floor.

The trail then heads south (east), past several small waterholes and the delightful cacophony of spring peepers that inhabit these overgrown puddles. In no time, you'll have completed the loop and be back to marker H15. Head left (north) and hike back up to Yost Ridge, bearing left (west) at marker Y2. The ridgetop breezes here are quite welcome after you've ascended past the rocky, scruffy scree found along this section of the trail. Finally, make your way back down the ridge to the welcome center.

Nearby Attractions

If this type of hiking appeals to you, you can choose from a number of other trails in the immediate vicinity. As alluded to previously, the Jefferson Memorial Forest consists of four sections: Horine Reservation, Tom Wallace Recreation Area, Paul Yost Recreation Area, and the Scott's Gap Section. The Horine Reservation offers the **Red Trail** (a 4.8-mile mostly loop trail) and the shorter **Orange Trail** (a

2.0-mile loop). While the Paul Yost Recreation Area also serves equestrian riders, the trail system is in good condition and includes more than 20 miles of hiking options. Finally, the Tom Wallace Recreation Area hosts both the 6.7-mile (one-way) **Siltstone Trail** and a variety of shorter hikes such as the **Lake Loop** and the **Purple Heart Trail** (logging in at 0.5 mile and 2.0 miles, respectively).

How lucky we are to have so many fine hiking choices. Please support Louisville's City of Parks initiative, including the Floyds Fork Greenway Project and the Louisville Loop (a shared-use path of more than 100 miles), the Parklands of Floyds Fork, Wilderness Louisville, Parks Alliance of Louisville, Olmsted Parks Conservancy, and a host of other park projects.

Directions

From I-265 (KY 841/Gene Snyder Freeway), take Exit 6 and turn south on New Cut Road (KY 1865), which becomes West Manslick Road. After 1.4 miles, turn right (west) on Mitchell Hill Road. Drive 1.5 miles to the Jefferson Memorial Forest Welcome Center, on your left.

THE 6,600-ACRE JEFFERSON MEMORIAL FOREST HAS MORE THAN 35 MILES OF HIKING TRAILS, A STOCKED LAKE FOR FISHING, AND A BEAUTIFUL FORESTED CAMPGROUND.

Otter Creek Loop Trail

EVIDENCE OF RIVER OTTERS AND BEAVERS CAN BE SEEN ALONG OTTER CREEK.

GPS TRAILHEAD COORDINATES: N37° 56.422' W86° 2.934'

DISTANCE & CONFIGURATION: 7.7-mile loop

HIKING TIME: 3.5 hours

HIGHLIGHTS: Creekside hiking, panoramic views of the Ohio River, wildflowers

ELEVATION: 398' at trailhead, ascending to 691' at high point

ACCESS: Wednesday–Saturday, sunrise–sunset; closed Monday and Tuesday, except for holidays. Daily entry fee, $3 per person; free for children under 12. See website below for additional fees.

MAPS: Available at the park entrance gate or tinyurl.com/OtterCreekMap; USGS *Ekron*

FACILITIES: Portable toilets, picnic shelters and tables, campground, disc golf; archery, rifle range

WHEELCHAIR ACCESS: None

COMMENTS: Dogs are permitted on leash. Trails are closed in wet or muddy conditions (call 502-942-5052 to check trail status). The recreation area is closed during firearms deer-hunting season (check website below for a full list of hunting seasons).

CONTACTS: Otter Creek Outdoor Recreation Area, 502-942-9171; tinyurl.com/OtterCreekPark

Overview

While many hikers complain about paying three bucks to hike Otter Creek, it's about the same price as a cheap hamburger and infinitely more satisfying. This loop trail heads north to Morgan's Cave; east atop a bluff high above the Ohio River; south along Otter Creek; and then north once more under a magnificent hardwood canopy. Views here are panoramic and wildlife is plentiful. The key to happy hiking at Otter Creek is deciphering the trail signage and avoiding both the hunting season and the heat of summer.

Route Details

The history of Otter Creek Outdoor Recreation Area is an interesting one. In 1934 the National Park Service bought 3,000 acres of land in Meade County, southwest of Louisville, to provide outdoor recreational opportunities for residents of the surrounding area. The park was opened in 1937, and a year later property was leased to the YMCA to form Camp Piomingo. In 1947 the federal government gave the park to Louisville in recognition of the city's service during World War II.

In 2008, however, Louisville closed the park as part of citywide budget cuts. Otter Creek was essentially abandoned until the Kentucky Department of Fish & Wildlife reopened it in 2011. After land swaps with Fort Knox (which lies south and east of the park), the Otter Creek Outdoor Recreation Area now covers about 2,600 acres. Camp Piomingo continues to operate on the premises.

The transition from park to outdoor recreation area resulted in a more elaborate land-use management plan. Otter Creek is stocked with trout and is open for hunting. Horseback riding is permitted, and the mountain-biking community spins its gears on many of the trails. Daily fees vary by type of activity; annual-use permits are available.

Many hikers are hesitant to share horse paths, but the trails at Otter Creek are in excellent condition. The park has very strict rules on use during wet or muddy conditions, and most of the trails are covered with fine gravel or a mixture of sand and clay soil. Thankfully, there is very little evidence of damage to the trails by hikers, horses, or mountain bikers.

One of the best ways to hike the area is to take the Otter Creek Trail from the trailhead (described below) and make a big, clockwise loop, using parts of the Red Cedar Trail. But let's talk nomenclature because there's a bit of a disconnect between the official park map and the trail signs.

Otter Creek Loop Trail

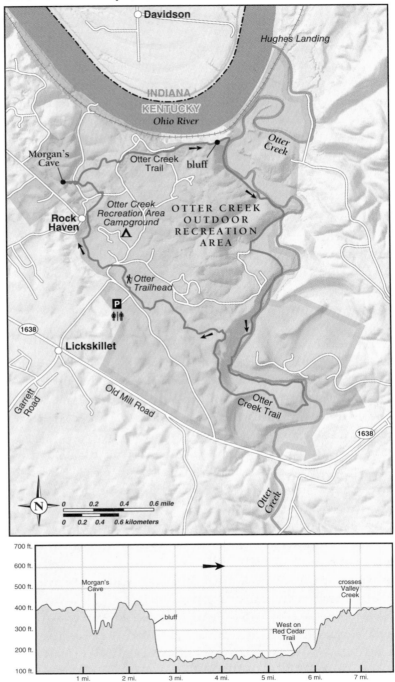

The first thing to know is the colors on the park map are not always the same as the trail blazes. Second, the trail signs use abbreviations that are not used on the map. So, let's get a few trails straight: the Otter Creek Trail (indicated in both solid black and dashed red on the park map) is blazed in sky blue, and the trail markers read "OCT." The Red Cedar Trail (indicated in solid red, orange, dashed red, and dashed purple on the park map) is blazed in red, and the trail markers read "RCT." The Valley Overlook Trail (indicated in solid purple on the park map) is blazed in purple, and the trail markers read "VOT." If you're a tad confused, you're not the only one.

In addition, the park uses small, round metal signs to indicate approved uses: green with a hiker means it's a hiking trail; blue with a mountain biker means it's a biking trail; and red with a horse means it's approved for horse riding. A black slash through any of these signs indicates that the trail is not approved for that use.

After passing through the entrance gate, proceed for 1.0 mile until you see a gravel lot on your left with signs for disc golf (west of the road). Just past this on your right (east of the road) is another gravel lot (marked "Nature Center Lane" on Google Maps.) Turn right and park here. The trailhead is due north, across the grassy area, at the treeline. You want to follow the trail straight (north) into the woods, marked with OCT and approved for both hiking and mountain biking.

For the next several miles the trail follows the OCT in a clockwise loop, which is blazed with sky-blue paint. You'll see all kinds of other signs and colors . . . but just stay on the OCT with sky-blue blazes.

In no time the trail crosses several paved roads with white crosswalk lines. Stay on the OCT for about 1.2 miles until you see a sign for Morgan's Cave, a short out-and-back trail, that goes past an old limestone quarry and down into a nice creek drainage. At the creek crossing, look to about one o'clock to follow the trail up the hill. While the opening to the cave is gated off, this area is excellent for wildflower viewing in the spring and worth the detour.

From here, hike back to above the quarry and turn left (north) on the OCT. For the next 1.25 miles the OCT travels through a mature hardwood forest, with glimpses of the Ohio River and pastoral views to the north. But look sharp where the trail disappears atop a steep bluff (about 2.5 total miles into your hike). Confusingly, a connector trail comes in on your right, blazed in purple and sky blue. You want to continue straight (east) here and scramble down the rocks that form the narrow edge of the bluff. Yes, you are still on the OCT with more sky-blue blazes. At the bottom of the descent, the trail Ts close to Otter Creek. A left (northeast) turn will take you along the railroad tracks and down to the Ohio River. But bear right (southwest) to continue our loop hike. Continue to follow signs for the OCT and look for the sky-blue blazes, as this section of trail actually merges with the Red Cedar Trail.

For the next 3.0 miles the OCT/RCT follows the west bank of Otter Creek. The eastern cottonwood trees grow huge along the floodplains of the creek, with some trunks 10–12 feet in diameter. You'll also see 3-foot-tall scouring rush or horsetail, used for cleaning iron skillets or eaten young like asparagus shoots, growing prolifically along the creek banks. This entire stretch is ideal for spring wildflowers, from hepatica and violets to Solomon's seal.

You can follow the OCT all the way back to your vehicle, but you do get quite a bit of road noise. Alternately, about 5.6 miles into your hike, the Red Cedar Trail (marked in orange on this section of the park map), bears right (west) and follows a 2.0-mile diagonal trajectory across the southern part of the park to reach the parking lot. The RCT will cross the VOT several times, but follow the red blazes and RCT signs. Even though this section of the trail is open to horses, it is in amazingly good condition, thanks to the diligent Otter Creek management team and responsible riders.

Nearby Attractions

If you like to fly-fish, Otter Creek is stocked with 7,500 rainbow trout each year; another 7,500 rainbows and 500 brown trout are stocked upstream on the Fort Knox side of the bridge. The daily creel limit within the Otter Creek Recreation Area is eight trout—only one may be a brown that must be 16 inches or longer. A Kentucky fishing license and trout stamp are required, but fishing on the Fort Knox side requires special permits that are difficult to obtain.

Trout fishing in Otter Creek is best from late fall to early spring. Hopeful anglers may want to focus on the run adjacent to the Garnettsville Picnic Area or the Blue Hole (marked on the park map). Usually, #14 or #15 pheasant tails and hare's ear nymphs will do the trick. If not, consider a #14 or #15 Adams or #20 WD40s and zebra midges.

During the warm summer months, the trout become stressed and fishing turns to smallmouth bass and the small children who like to play in these waters. During this time of year, anglers may want to turn their attention elsewhere.

A VARIETY OF BASS, SUNFISH, AND TROUT SWIM THE WATERS OF OTTER CREEK.

Directions

Take I-265 (KY 841/Gene Snyder Freeway) to Exit 1, turn south on Dixie Highway (US 31W/US 60) toward Fort Knox, and drive 13.2 miles. Turn right (west) on KY 1638 and drive 2.7 miles. The entrance to Otter Creek Outdoor Recreation Area will be on your right. From the park entrance gate, drive about 1.2 miles until you see a small gravel parking lot on your right. If you see the turnoff for Lick Skillet Road (don't you just love that name?), you have gone too far.

SCENERY: ★ ★ ★ ★
TRAIL CONDITION: ★ ★ ★ ★
CHILDREN: ★ ★ ★
DIFFICULTY: ★ ★
SOLITUDE: ★ ★

SAUNDERS SPRINGS NATURE PRESERVE HAS 26 ACRES OF HIKING AND BIKING TRAILS.

GPS TRAILHEAD COORDINATES: N37° 51.285' W85° 56.319'

DISTANCE & CONFIGURATION: 2.2-mile loop, with more mileage readily available

HIKING TIME: 2 hours

HIGHLIGHTS: Cascading streams, 1880s log cabins, two small lakes

ELEVATION: 746' at trailhead, descending to 467' at low point

ACCESS: Daily, sunrise–sunset; free admission, but donations are gratefully accepted

MAPS: Posted at multiple trailheads, but paper copies may not be available

FACILITIES: Visitor center, restrooms, water, picnic tables, and pavilions

WHEELCHAIR ACCESS: Very limited access

COMMENTS: Dogs are permitted on leash.

CONTACTS: Radcliff Tourism Office, 270-352-1204; tinyurl.com/TiogaFallsTR

Overview

Don't let the relatively short 2.2-mile suggested route fool you. With a 200-foot elevation variance, there are more than 900 steps embedded on the 11 trails that crisscross this nature preserve. But every step takes you farther along cool, rushing streams; past prolific wildflower displays; and around spring-fed lakes. Four 19th-century log cabins have been reconstructed on the property, and the remains of an old mill provide additional grist for many a discussion. Adjacent to this 26-acre preserve is the 73-acre Saunders Springs Annex, offering an additional 8 miles of hiking and mountain biking trails.

Route Details

You can leave your Fitbit at home for this hike and skip the StairMaster the next time you're at the gym. To reduce erosion and help you navigate the steep changes in terrain, the City of Radcliff and the Radcliff Forestry and Conservation Board have your back. Or at least the arches of your feet. Yes, there are some steep sections along these trails, but the workout can leave you feeling better than when you arrived.

There is a lot packed into this little nature preserve and something for everyone. While the wooded areas and cascading streams are undoubtedly picturesque, the multitude of springs located on the preserve account for the rich history of the area. It is believed that both Union and Confederate soldiers camped in the vicinity, and Saunders Springs was the site of the original water reservoir for what was then called Camp Knox.

If you haven't been here before, your first stop should be the Vincent Kieta Welcome Center (open limited hours), repurposed from a 1920s one-car brick-and-timber garage that stood on the property. In addition to a map and informational brochures, the center has several photographic displays to peruse. Although the four log cabins reconstructed on the preserve are only open for special events, each has a story to tell.

Honestly, with its multitude of named trails, connectors, and switchbacks, Saunders Springs is meant to be wandered rather than hiked. At the nature preserve, it's so easy to be distracted by a charming lake view, the sound of a cascading stream, or a log cabin window just waiting to be peered through, that you may not want to have an agenda here. This is particularly true if you have kids along, as they are rarely linear hikers to begin with.

Saunders Springs Nature Preserve

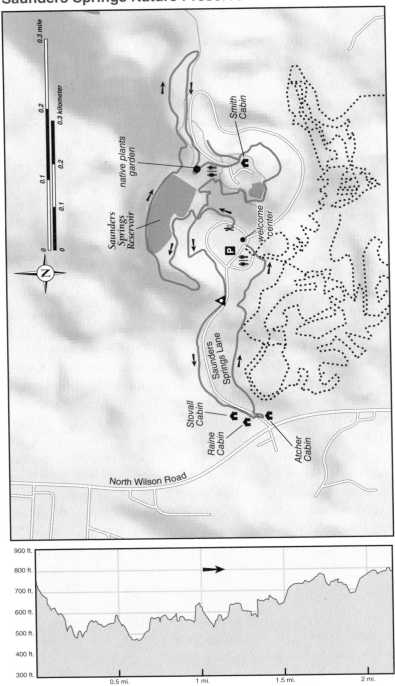

But if you feel like you need some direction, park near the welcome center and, from the east side of the park road, hike down the Eagle Trail. Immediately you'll begin a steep descent down a set of steps made from old railroad ties, secured into the hillside. The sound of a rushing stream will be on your right, and glimpses of the spring-fed and well-stocked High Lake reservoir are ahead of you. Bear left (west) on the Tranquility Trail, which will connect you to the Lake Trail as you circumnavigate the small lake clockwise.

On the other side of the reservoir, bear left (east) on the Cascade Trail and descend to the lower parking area and picnic pavilion. The "Hidden Trail" (signed but not marked on the map) loops downstream of the reservoir outflow before bringing you back to the picnic area. Take a few minutes to explore the Native Plants Garden and the Stith cabin. From here you can pick up the short out-and-back Comeback Trail (chock-full of wildflowers in the spring), before winding your way around the Fern Trail and the small reservoir fed by Saunders Spring, which flows directly out of a small cave.

Return to the larger reservoir via Tranquility Trail, then take the Canyon Trail to the main road and overlook. From here follow the North Cabin Trail west toward the Stovall (circa 1873), Raine (built 1836), and Atcher (about 1873) cabins at the front entrance to the park. The South Cabin and Wilderness Trails will take you back to the welcome center.

All of these directions and trail names hide the real beauty of the nature preserve. Scattered around the park are a multitude of signs identifying the six different ferns found at Saunders Springs. Plus, signs that point to old beaver activity, a small bladdernut shrub, bluestar flowers, and swamp milkweed. And signs adorn each cabin explaining who built the structure, where it originally stood, and the fact that log cabins built after 1850 typically have square rough-hewn logs rather than round ones.

Notably, the wildflowers here are magnificent in spring. Perhaps one trail should have been named Hepatica Heaven.

Nearby Attractions

Serving the greater Fort Knox area, the town of **Radcliff** offers a tantalizing array of restaurants, from Korean to German and Caribbean. But barbecue is also big here, as are steaks and burgers. And if all that hiking has left you thirsty, try the **Boundary Oak Distillery,** which produces small-batch bourbon and moonshine. Free self-guided tours are available (also open to those under the age of

21); tastings are $8 with proof of age. Located at 2000 Boundary Oak Drive in Radcliff, the distillery is open Monday–Saturday, 10 a.m.–6 p.m., and Sunday, noon–5 p.m. For more information, visit boundaryoakdistillery.com.

If staying on the cutting edge is important to you, **Red Hill Cutlery** (Kentucky's largest cutlery dealer) is located just next to Boundary Oak Distillery. For those less informed, we're not talking silver place settings here. We're talking hunting knives, filet knives, multitools, axes, whetstones, and much, much more. You can't miss the store, located at 92 Bourbon Trace in Radcliff, as the world's largest pocketknife—made from 6,200 pounds of American steel and featuring a 17.5-foot blade—is visible from the highway. Open Tuesday–Friday, 10 a.m.– 6 p.m.; Saturday, 10 a.m.–4 p.m.; closed Sunday and Monday; redhillcutlery.com.

Directions

Take I-265 (KY 841/Gene Snyder Freeway) to Exit 1, then turn south on Dixie Highway (US 31W/US 60) toward Fort Knox. Drive a little more than 19.0 miles. Turn left (east) on Redmar Boulevard and drive 0.4 mile. Then turn right (south) on North Wilson Road and drive 0.3 mile. Finally, turn left (east) on Saunders Spring Lane and into the preserve parking area by the welcome center.

THE ATCHER CABIN, BUILT AROUND 1875, HAS SQUARE ROUGH-HEWN LOGS AND A FULL SECOND FLOOR.

17 Tioga Falls and Bridges to the Past

SCENERY: ★ ★ ★ ★ ★
TRAIL CONDITION: ★ ★ ★ ★ ★
CHILDREN: ★ ★ ★
DIFFICULTY: ★ ★ ★
SOLITUDE: ★ ★

THE TURNPIKE, COMPLETED ABOUT 1838, WAS USED BY BOTH UNION AND CONFEDERATE SOLDIERS DURING THE CIVIL WAR.

GPS TRAILHEAD COORDINATES: N37° 58.125' W85° 57.671'

DISTANCE & CONFIGURATION: 4.7 miles (two out-and-back trails, each 2+ miles in length)

HIKING TIME: 3 hours

HIGHLIGHTS: Multiple waterfalls, historic sites, stone bridges

ELEVATION: 453' at trailhead, ascending to 655' at high point

ACCESS: Sunrise–sunset; free admission

MAPS: Unofficial maps can be found online.

FACILITIES: picnic tables

WHEELCHAIR ACCESS: Limited accessibility on the Bridges to the Past paved road.

COMMENTS: Tioga Falls and Bridges to the Past are owned by the U.S. Army Fort Knox and trails are occasionally closed for military training or during certain hunting seasons. You may want to call the Radcliff Tourism Office to confirm if the trails are open. Dogs are permitted on leash.

CONTACTS: Radcliff Tourism Office, 270-352-1204; tinyurl.com/TiogaFallsTR

Tioga Falls and Bridges to the Past

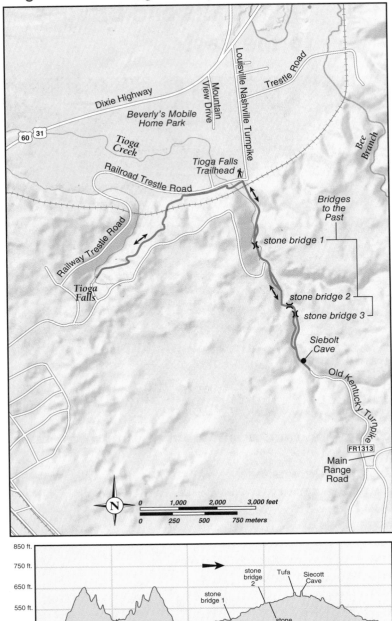

Overview

Both Tioga Falls and Bridges to the Past leave from the same trailhead, so you can hike each trail separately, or combine them into one 4.7-mile outing. The 2.4-mile hiking trail to Tioga Falls shadows an old wagon roadbed, until it reaches the base of the 130-foot waterfall. The 2.3-mile Bridges to the Past trail is paved and follows a preserved section of the old Louisville and Nashville Turnpike. The original road was completed in 1838 and features several old bridges with beautiful stonework.

Route Details

Naturally, the best time to visit Tioga Falls is in the spring when the wildflowers are a riot of color and cool water is tumbling down the hillside from Tioga Springs. But weekends can get hectic here, so plan your visit accordingly. Cold winter days may bring ice formations to the falls and solitude to your hike.

Since we're talking about the falls, why don't we hike that way first? The trail leaves from the kiosk and almost immediately crosses the East Fork of Tioga Creek via a wooden footbridge. But then the path abruptly hits U.S. Army property and briefly doglegs onto a quiet country back road, yet everything is well signed and easy to follow. So, take the road past the River of Life Church on your right and the mysterious brick building on your left and up the hill to the railroad tracks. Carefully cross the tracks and continue following the old wagon road that serves as your trail. On beautiful days you'll meet lovers lugging picnic baskets, youngsters merrily skipping along, and pooches out for a Sunday afternoon stroll. It's only 1.2 miles from the trailhead to the falls, so enjoy your walk beneath this hardwood canopy.

The top of Tioga Falls has two distinct "horsetails," so named as the water fans out as it cascades over each ledge, while retaining contact with the limestone layer below. Horsetail-style waterfalls are younger than plunge-style waterfalls, in which the rock beneath the upper lip of a plunge-style fall has eroded away over time. The name Tioga comes from the North American tribes who lived here before the colonists arrived and means "at the forks."

After leisurely spending time at the falls, walk back to the trailhead, but be sure to note the carefully stacked stone wall that forms the foundation of the road you've been so placidly walking upon. What a work of art! Once back at the parking lot, simply turn right to walk the Bridges to the Past road.

While Tioga Falls can get slammed with people during early spring and the dog days of summer, Bridges to the Past can seem relatively quiet. While the paved road frequently is covered with leaves and greenery at the margins, the old turnpike leads hikers through another life, another time. As a reminder, you are a guest of Fort Knox. Please stay on the road, with the exception of short sections provided for up-close viewing of the stone bridges, as being conscripted into the army may not be part of your career plans.

Over the years, the turnpike has carried way more famous people than you or me, including President Andrew Jackson; Swedish opera singer Jenny Lind on her tour across America in 1851; and a multitude of Civil War–era regiments on their way to do battle. You'll see signs along the road indicating the site of an early 19th-century mill and an old limestone quarry dug to build the turnpike.

Hikers will quickly come upon the three stone bridges that allowed early travelers using the turnpike to cross the East Fork of the Tioga Creek. The bridges were built using an arch-and-keystone design, engineered for maximum strength and longevity. The turnpike was closed to the public in 1919, but interestingly, the bridges were repaired for army use by German POWs in World War II.

The creek itself is a perfect example of the karst topography, accountable for so many caves and subterranean streams prevalent across Kentucky. Even after a rainy day, the creekbed is dry, as the water quickly goes underground before reappearing later downstream. It's not until the area gets several days of hard rain that the creekbed fills and can become a raging torrent as evidenced by its deeply cut and eroded banks.

Immediately before the road ends at a clearly marked fence, look to your right (west of the trail), to the stream that flows from the small cave in the hillside. In particular, note the gorgeous tufa that has formed where, over the years, the mineral-rich waters have slowly trickled out from deep within the earth to build a large mound. Carefully touch the pyramidal structure of the tufa—while it appears quite spongy, the minerals have precipitated out of the water and hardened to calcium carbonate or limestone.

As you walk back to the parking lot, imagine driving winding country highways with no guardrails, no flashing lights, no liquor stores, and no fast-food chains. But be sure to take note of the white walnut (butternut) and cottonwood trees, the dazzling spring wildflowers, and the peacefulness of just being. The road gives one pause as to where our footsteps fall relative to our ancestors.

Nearby Attractions

Located at the confluence of the Ohio River and the Salt River just north of West Point is **Kulmer Beach Reserve,** a 28-acre linear park owned by Jefferson County/Louisville Metro Parks. A 1.0-mile trail runs the length of the reserve, sandwiched between the Ohio River on one side and the Pacific Nashville Railroad on the other. Although the park is in need of a little TLC, both the views of the river and the birding opportunities along this section of the Mississippi Flyway may be worth the stop.

The first time you walk this trail, you may ask yourself, "Why am I hiking this?" The noise from Dixie Highway is irritating, let alone the cacophony created by a passing train. Was this land given to Jefferson County as a tax write-off? The land as valued for development is minuscule. But for a small price, what are we preserving? As population pressures continue to threaten our flora and fauna, perhaps these linear reserves, squeezed by development on all sides, will truly protect more than we will ever realize.

Directions from Tioga Falls trailhead: Drive back north on the Louisville Nashville Turnpike until you reach Dixie Highway once again. Turn right (north, toward Louisville) on US 31W. Drive 3.1 miles. Turn left (west) onto Abbotts Beach Road, which dead-ends shortly into the park. The reserve is open 6 a.m.– 11 p.m. For more information, see tinyurl.com/KulmerReserve or tinyurl.com /KulmerBeach. An online map may be found at tinyurl.com/KulmerMap.

Directions

Take I-265 (KY 841/Gene Snyder Freeway) to Exit 1, then turn south on Dixie Highway (US 31W/US 60) toward Fort Knox. Drive a little more than 9.0 miles. Turn left (south) on the Louisville Nashville Turnpike (a small brown sign with white lettering announcing both Tioga Falls and Bridges to the Past gives you a small advance warning of the impending turn). In 0.7 mile you will see the large, triangular-shaped parking area on your right.

Kentucky: South of Louisville and East of I-65

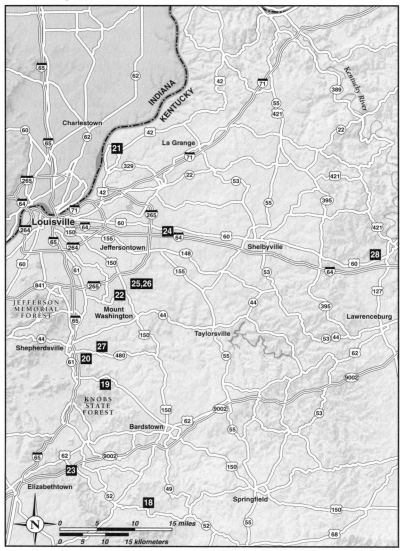

Kentucky: South of Louisville and East of I-65

FOR A TRANQUIL HIKE, VISIT THE ABBEY OF GETHSEMANI. *(See Hike 18, page 112.)*

Abbey of Gethsemani

SCENERY: ★ ★ ★ ★ ★
TRAIL CONDITION: ★ ★ ★ ★
CHILDREN: ★
DIFFICULTY: ★ ★ ★ ★
SOLITUDE: ★ ★ ★ ★ ★

THE ABBEY OF GETHSEMANI GENEROUSLY ALLOWS HIKERS THE USE OF ITS TRAILS AND BACK ROADS.

GPS TRAILHEAD COORDINATES: N37° 39.771' W85° 31.856'

DISTANCE & CONFIGURATION: 6.9 miles

HIKING TIME: 5 hours

HIGHLIGHTS: Historic Trappist Monastery, multiple lakes, knob-top views

ELEVATION: 560' at trailhead, ascending to 1,035' at high point

ACCESS: Daily, sunrise–sunset

MAPS: Available at the entrance gate and the welcome center

FACILITIES: Bathrooms, gift shop, retreat house, abbey

WHEELCHAIR ACCESS: None on the trail

COMMENTS: Dogs are permitted on leash.

CONTACTS: Abbey of Gethsemani, 3642 Monks Road, Trappist, KY, 502-549-3117; monks.org

Overview

For some, hiking can be a spiritual journey, and the Abbey of Gethsemani generously allows you to roam 1,500 of its 2,200 acres any time of the year. From short, easy hikes to strenuous all-day exploits, the variety and scope of trails at the monastery have something for everyone. The hike described below will carry you up and over two different knobs, beside several lakes and ponds, past St. Enoch's stone house, and along the Trail of Statues.

Route Details

Founded in 1848, the Abbey of Our Lady of Gethsemani is considered the motherhouse of all Trappist and Trappistine monasteries in the United States and is the oldest monastery still operating in the country. Noted for prayer, labor, and silence, the monks operate a working farm, including cutting timber, growing hay and corn, and producing much of their own food. A retreat house with private rooms is available for those seeking quiet contemplation and study. The abbey also receives the proceeds from the written works of Thomas Merton, the well-known author, social activist, mystic, and scholar of comparative religion. Merton lived at Gethsemani from 1941 until his death in 1968.

After turning onto the grounds of the monastery, your first stop should be the welcome center, which includes a gift shop and a running video describing the history and the mission of the monastery. The shop offers a large selection of books, religious iconography, and foodstuffs made at Trappist monasteries around the world, including coffee, biscotti, hot sauce, and Gethsemani's own bourbon fruitcake and fudge. You can also pick up a free map of the hiking trails and access the public restrooms.

To hike at Gethsemani, visitors are asked to park in the main lot by the welcome center. Hikers must then cross Monks Road to access the trails. To follow the route described below, walk back to the entrance gate and carefully cross the road at the caution light to begin walking west on Hanekamp's Road. The yellow-colored brick Family Guest House sits atop a small hill on your right, just north of the road. Although Hanekamp's begins as a paved road, it quickly turns to a gravel-and-dirt farm lane.

In 0.5 mile you will have intermittent views of St. Elmond's Lake as the farm lane leaves the row-cropped fields and enters a forest of mixed-deciduous hardwoods. In another 0.25 mile you will see your first numbered sign (18) on your left (south) of the road and another trail bearing off to your right (to the

Abbey of Gethsemani

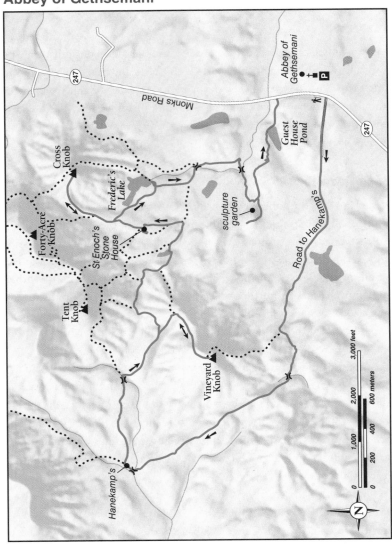

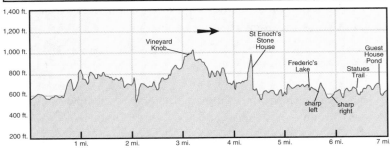

north). These numbered signs can be found on the free trail map and will help you navigate the first half of this hiking route.

Continue walking on Hanekamp's Road for the next 1.25 miles. Two miles from the trailhead, Hanekamp's makes a sharp right (northwest) turn just after it crosses a small creek. From here you will see a variety of other trails and old farm roads crossing your path. This is where the sign numbering system is invaluable. At this juncture you should see sign 1 with an arrow pointing the same direction you will be walking, directing you to the abbey.

Follow the old farm lane, passing signs numbered 2–5. At sign 5, you are 2.7 miles from the trailhead. Bear right (south) on the small out-and-back trail signed for Vineyard Knob. The trail to the knob ascends straight up and is not for the timid. But the deer prints in the soft clay indicate that you are not the only one hoofing it up to the top. It's 0.4 mile from the main trail to the top of the knob—and another 0.4 mile back down. The breezes up here are always heavenly, but what else would you expect at a monastery? Naming this Vineyard Knob must be an insider's joke to entice you to make the climb through the woods. Yet when the leaves are off the trees, the view is fabulous.

Once back on the main trail, continue hiking east, passing signs numbered 6–8, until you see Slate Pond (a small monk-made reservoir) on your left, just north of the trail. At sign 10, bear left (north) on the trail indicating the way to St. Enoch's stone house. Built in 1967, this small retreat cottage is pure midcentury modern with its angled roof line and endearing boxy construction. Be sure to go inside, light some incense found on the fireplace mantel, read the prayers left behind by others, and perhaps write your own. After leaving St. Enoch's, continue walking north on the trail for another 5 minutes or so. You will then see a sign indicating the trail to Cross Knob, but importantly do not take the trail marked SCENIC ROUTE. So, bear right (northeast) and hike the 0.3 mile it takes you to get to Cross Knob.

At almost 850 feet of elevation, Cross Knob is not quite as high as Vineyard, but a view of the abbey and farm can be seen far below. After enjoying the sight, retrace your steps back down to the main trail. Bear left (southeast) following the signs to Dom Frederic's Lake—a right (southwest) would take you back to St. Enoch's. Frederic's is the largest lake on the property and also serves as a reservoir.

Continuing on the main trail past Frederic's, you will come to a T. Bear left (east) here. You should cross over a small creek that drains Frederic's, with the main trail taking a right (south) turn once again. Notice the large grove of cypress here, bony knees protruding, just right (west) of the trail. Take an immediate right at the sign for TO THE STATUES.

The Trail of Statues features a combination of religious statuary and three large sculptures created by Walker Hancock and dedicated to Jonathan Myrick Daniels, a civil rights worker killed in 1965 in Haynesville, Alabama. The trail is a short out-and-back that also passes the Family Guest House Pond. The end of this route takes you back to Monks Road, north of where you originally crossed at the caution light. Carefully cross the road and walk south between the pavement and the stone wall of the abbey garden. A quick walk through the cemetery will take you back to the parking lot.

Nearby Attractions

Sisters of Loretto Motherhouse, one of the first Roman Catholic communities of women established in the United States, is located 20 minutes east of Gethsemani. The 788-acre farm has been home to the Loretto Community since 1824. The property houses the Loretto Heritage Center, an art gallery (featuring the work of renowned sculptor and multimedia artist Sister Jeanne Dueber), a historic chapel, and an outdoor sculpture garden. At the time of publication, public concerts have been curtailed and seminars limited to Zoom. For more current information, go to lorettocommunity.org/about/motherhouse. Their physical address is 515 Nerinx Road, Nerinx, Kentucky, 40049.

Directions

From downtown Louisville, drive south on I-65 and take Exit 105. Turn left (south) onto KY 61 S; drive 4.1 miles. Turn right (west) onto US 62 W; drive 1.0 mile. Turn left (east) on KY 52 E; drive 11.2 miles. In New Haven, take a quick right on North Main Street (US 31E) and then a quick left on KY 52 E. Drive another 4.3 miles, then turn left (north) onto Monks Road (KY 247). The abbey will be on your right.

From east Louisville, you may want to take US 150, through Bardstown. Either way, it is about a 50-minute drive from the Gene Snyder Parkway to Gethsemani.

19 Bernheim Arboretum:
Elm Lick Trail

SCENERY: ★★★★
TRAIL CONDITION: ★★★★★
CHILDREN: ★ ★
DIFFICULTY: ★★★★
SOLITUDE: ★★★★

THIS SYCAMORE TREE SERVED AS THE INSPIRATION FOR THE COPPER LEAF DRAWING ON DISPLAY AT THE BERNHEIM VISITOR CENTER.

GPS TRAILHEAD COORDINATES: N37° 54.412' W85° 37.296'

DISTANCE & CONFIGURATION: 5.0-mile balloon

HIKING TIME: 2.5 hours

HIGHLIGHTS: Ridgetop views, Elm Lick Creek, wildflower displays

ELEVATION: 806' at trailhead, ascending to 893' at high point, and descending to 559' at low point

ACCESS: Daily, except Thanksgiving, Christmas, and New Year's Days; trails are open 7 a.m.–7 p.m.; $10 suggested donation, per vehicle

MAPS: Available online and at the entrance gate

FACILITIES: Bathrooms, restaurants, gift shop, playgrounds, and more

WHEELCHAIR ACCESS: None on the trail

COMMENTS: Dogs are permitted on leash.

CONTACTS: Bernheim Arboretum and Research Forest, 2075 Clermont Road, Clermont, KY, 502-955-8512; nature@bernheim.org, bernheim.org

Bernheim Arboretum: Elm Lick Trail

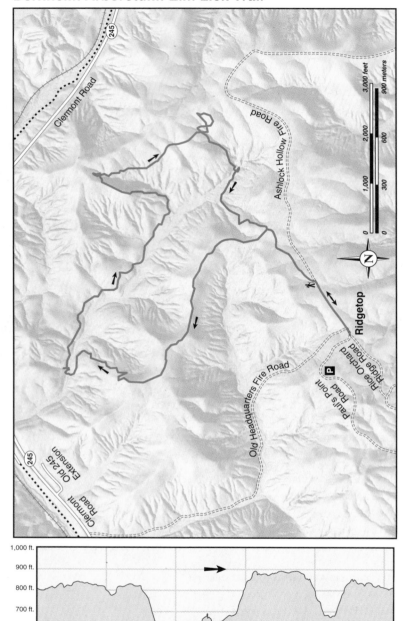

Overview

Elm Lick Trail is the second-longest hiking trail at Bernheim, only after the Millennium Trail. If you're looking for an excellent workout, this one will make you sweat as you traverse the undulations of the Elm Lick watershed. The best time to hike Elm Lick is in the fall, when colors are at their peak and temps are cooler, or in the spring, when the wildflowers are out. In addition to Elm Lick Creek, other highlights include an old grain tower and a homestead site.

Route Details

Elm Lick Trail is one of the most popular backcountry trails at Bernheim due to its length, which hits a sweet spot for many dedicated hikers. That said, on weekends and holidays you might find the parking lot rather full, whereas midweek you might only see one or two other vehicles. Other factors make this a desirable trail—dogs are permitted on leash on Bernheim, and this particular trail has several steep ascents and descents, which make for a great training hike.

After finding a place to park in one of the many smaller parking lots off the far side of Paul's Point Road (see directions on page 121), make your way to the Ashlock Hollow Fire Road. It's a bit confusing—you must hike 0.25 mile along this gravel road to get to the Elm Lick Trailhead, but this distance (out-and-back) is included in the total 5.0 miles of Elm Lick Trail. So, from Paul's Point Road, hike northeast along the fire road until you see the official trailhead on your left. Here you will find a nice kiosk with a permanent map affixed and other trail information.

From the kiosk, Elm Lick Trail continues northeast for another 0.25 mile until you get to the loop portion of the trail. It's a toss-up to decide which direction to hike, but the commentary below assumes you turn left (northwest) to hike the loop clockwise. For the next mile, the red-blazed trail gently rolls along a ridgetop under an oak-hickory and beech-maple canopy and is in excellent condition. From early spring through late fall, these ridges are a mycologist's dream. The mushrooms found here are rich in color and texture and grow profusely along the trail. From the orange and yellow chicken of the woods to the creamy coral fungus and the scarlet elf cups, the variety of mushrooms found at Bernheim is amazing.

After about 1.5 miles of hiking, the trail begins dropping into the Elm Lick creek drainage via a 0.5-mile series of switchbacks, resulting in a 300-foot descent to the creekbed. At the point where the trail crosses the Elm Lick creek, a large American sycamore stands astraddle the water flow. This tree served as the inspiration for a copper leaf drawing that is part of an interactive installation by 2020 artist-in-residence Lee Emma Running, which can be seen at the Bernheim Visitor Center.

After crossing the creek, the trail turns southeast and follows along beside the water. Hiking another 0.4 mile will bring you to the base of an abandoned grain storage tower and an old stone foundation. Continue walking another 5 minutes or so, and a small rogue trail comes in on your left, leading to the remains of an old homestead. If you have ample time and curiosity, consider this short diversion.

Shortly after the intersection, you will see a small sign on your left indicating a sharp left turn as Elm Lick Trail begins a short but steep ascent to the next ridge. At the far end of this ridge, you can take a shortcut trail, marked with a sign for an easy exit that brings you out on Ashlock Hollow Fire Road. But continue straight on the Elm Lick Trail as it drops once again into the upper reaches of the creek drainage. The 200-foot descent soon turns into a 200-foot ascent back out of the drainage.

From here it's a quick hike back to the start of the loop. Bear left (southwest) under the huge persimmon tree that graciously drops its sweet fruit in mid-October. You only have a 0.25-mile walk back to the official Elm Lick Trailhead and then a quick right turn on Ashlock Hollow Fire Road as you continue hiking southwest to the parking area.

Nearby Attractions

Remember the **Millennium Trail?** Well, it's the Big Kahuna of all hiking trails at the Bernheim Arboretum and Research Forest. Clocking in at 13.75 miles, only fit, experienced hikers should attempt this trail—so use the Millennium wisely to train for a multiday backpacking trip or simply to keep in excellent shape. While no single stretch of the Millennium Trail is exceptionally difficult, the sheer length of the trail and the constant ups and downs make for a long, strenuous day. Hikers must sign in at the visitor center and, depending on the time of year, be able to complete the trail well before nightfall. Water is also scarce along the trail, so be sure to bring plenty.

Directions

From downtown Louisville, drive south on I-65. Take Exit 112 and turn left (east) at the bottom of the ramp on Clermont Road (KY 245 South). The park entrance will be 1.0 mile ahead, on your right. After passing through the entrance gate, continue driving for less than 1.0 mile to get to the visitor center. Bear left (east) on Bernheim Forest Road. Drive 2.0 miles, then turn left (north) on Paul's Point Road (toward the Canopy Walk). After turning onto Paul's Point Road, in 0.7 mile you will see signs for Elm Lick Trail and several parking areas. Paul's Point Road is a one-way loop, so if you miss your parking area, you will have to go around the loop again.

EVIDENCE OF THE AGRICULTURALISTS WHO WALKED HERE BEFORE WE DID

Bernheim Arboretum:
Forest Giants Trail

SCENERY: ★ ★ ★ ★ ★
TRAIL CONDITION: ★ ★ ★ ★ ★
CHILDREN: ★ ★ ★ ★ ★
DIFFICULTY: ★ ★
SOLITUDE: ★ ★

MAMA LOUMARI HAS A NORDIC MYTHICAL VIBE, THANKS TO HER DANISH CREATOR.

GPS TRAILHEAD COORDINATES: N37° 58.080' W85° 39.479'

DISTANCE & CONFIGURATION: 2.0-mile balloon

HIKING TIME: 2.0 hours

HIGHLIGHTS: The giants!

ELEVATION: 543' at trailhead, descending to 507' at low point

ACCESS: Daily, except Thanksgiving, Christmas, and New Year's Days; trails are open 7 a.m.–7 p.m.; $10 suggested donation, per vehicle

MAPS: Available online and at the entrance gate

FACILITIES: Bathrooms, restaurants, gift shop, playgrounds, and more

WHEELCHAIR ACCESS: Limited

COMMENTS: Dogs are permitted on leash.

CONTACTS: Bernheim Arboretum and Research Forest, 2075 Clermont Road, Clermont, KY, 502-955-8512; nature@bernheim.org, bernheim.org

Overview

Pack the kids in the backseat, tuck Grandpa in the front, and head out for a fabulous day of family fun—the sprawling Bernheim Arboretum and Research Forest has something for everyone. The easy 2.0-mile Forest Giants Trail ducks through the woods, crosses open fields, pays homage to three giants, and was designed for the kid in all of us.

The trail surface varies from paved, to crushed gravel, to dirt trail, to wooden bridges. Strollers are a common sight, as are physically challenged hikers, determinedly walking with a cane or staff in hand. Everyone wants to see the giants!

Route Details

Isaac Wolfe Bernheim, a German immigrant, arrived in America in 1867 with less than $4 in his pocket and even fewer English words in his vocabulary. After a short stint peddling dry goods and various sundries, Bernheim's horse died and he was forced to find a new line of work. Bernheim then moved to Kentucky in 1868, where he became extremely successful in the wholesale liquor and distilling industry. Grateful for the opportunities his adopted home afforded, he bequeathed 14,000 acres of redeveloped farmland for the people of Kentucky to enjoy.

If you've never been to Bernheim, your first stop should be the visitor center. After entering the park, head straight back on the main road and follow the signs. The visitor center was the first certified Platinum LEED Green Building in a multistate region. Inside you'll find lots of nature-themed activities for the kids, including giant floor puzzles, two sizable aquariums, and a "Please Touch" table. The large glass windows and cozy southern exposure make the kid-size willow furniture inviting for Hobbits and munchkins alike. The small bookstore, gift shop, and reasonably priced café all deserve a second glance.

The Forest Giants Trail showcases three giant sculptures created by Danish artist Thomas Dambo, using recycled and repurposed materials. The family of giants consists of Mama Loumari; her children (Little Nis and Little Elina), and her third baby giant, who is currently living in Mama's belly. If you are interested in the entire fairy tale, it can be viewed at tinyurl.com/Valley-of-Giants. Originally commissioned in celebration of Bernheim's 90th anniversary, these sculptures have proven to be the park's most popular attraction in history, as evidenced by entrance fee proceeds, expanded parking lots, and the proliferation of children's grins.

Bernheim Arboretum: Forest Giants Trail

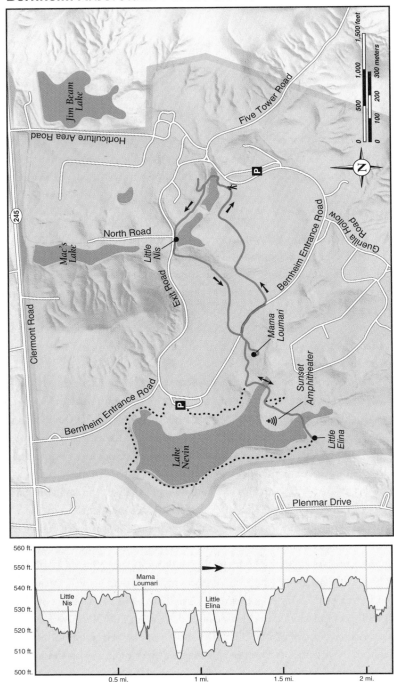

The trail begins at the back (southern side) of the visitor center. The ubiquitous signs and yellow-painted giant's feet easily show you the way. A 5-minute walk brings you to the Olmsted Ponds, named after Frederick Law Olmsted, the father of American landscape architecture.

Turn right (northwest) along the paved walk for your first viewing of Little Nis, who is continuously amazed by his reflection in the pool of water. There is a great little overlook for picture taking. However, feel free to walk right up to Little Nis and give him a big hug.

Follow the signage another 0.35 mile to Mama Loumari, who is lying contently beneath a large tree, enjoying some downtime, and oblivious to all the attention. The shady area surrounding Mama is more of a giant's living room with lots of things for the kiddos to explore and role-play.

Then walk another 0.35 mile as the trail crosses two branches of Lake Nevin, including a cypress-tupelo swamp. Turtles are frequently seen in the calm waters below, as are smallmouth bass and bream. The last forest giant is Little Elina, who in 2021 received new wooden locks that are frequently adorned with native flowers.

From Little Elina you must retrace your steps back past Mama Loumari to Arboretum Way (a paved road). Bear right (southeast), using the walking/bicycle path, before heading left (northeast) across the Big Prairie. Continue following the signs until you cross the Olmsted Ponds again and are back to the visitor center. While this may all sound confusing, the signage is immensely clear and helpful.

Bernheim has a clear winner with the Forest Giants Trail. The new sculptures have brought in many, many visitors who had never been to the park before and have exposed more children to the wonders of nature. It's amazing how many kids can walk 2 miles when motivated!

The park has also done an excellent job placing the statues in various locations to keep the kids entertained while they hike. Crossing the pond boardwalks is always a popular diversion to simply walking the trails. Plus many of the trees and shrubs are identified with name plates, including dragon's eye pine, devil's-walking-stick, and possum haw (a native deciduous holly). And it's fun to read the little enviro-signs Bernheim has planted along the way (such as BERNHEIM PRODUCES 102 BILLION LBS OF OXYGEN PER YEAR and BEING IN NATURE AT BERNHEIM = 55% LOWER RISK OF MENTAL HEALTH DISORDERS). All this easily lends itself to conversation and banter with your hiking mates.

Finally, upon returning to your car, you may see the quote by Isaac Wolfe Bernheim in 1939: "My vision embraces that all will be welcome and treated with an equal consideration with no distinction related to wealth or race." May we all share and propagate that vision.

Nearby Attractions

The Forest Giants Trail provides an overview of what the park has to offer. Other popular kid activities include the **Canopy Walk, I Spy Trail** (for a list, see bernheim.org/ispy/), and a stroll through the edible garden.

With a strong focus on education, Bernheim offers plein-air-painting workshops, photography classes, Eco Kids Discovery Days, stargazing, full-moon hikes, OWLS (Older Wiser Livelier Seniors) outdoor experiences, and lots more. And there are almost another 40 miles of trails to explore!

Directions

From downtown Louisville, drive south on I-65. Take Exit 112 and turn left (east) at the bottom of the ramp on Clermont Road (KY 245 South). The park entrance will be 1.0 mile ahead, on your right. After passing through the entrance gate, continue driving for less than 1.0 mile to get to the visitor center, where the trail starts.

FLOWER NECKLACES FREQUENTLY ADORN LITTLE NIS.

Creasey Mahan Nature Preserve

SCENERY: ★★★★★
TRAIL CONDITION: ★★★★★
CHILDREN: ★★★★
DIFFICULTY: ★★
SOLITUDE: ★★★

LET YOUR WORRIES MELT AWAY AS YOU PASS THROUGH THE GATE.

GPS TRAILHEAD COORDINATES: N38° 24.026' W85° 35.392'

DISTANCE & CONFIGURATION: 1.5-mile out-and-back, with more mileage available

HIKING TIME: 45 minutes

HIGHLIGHTS: Nature center, children's programs, frog pond, woodland garden

ELEVATION: 701' at trailhead, descending to 581' at low point

ACCESS: Preserve is open daily, sunrise–sunset. The nature center hours are limited. All events are free; donations welcome.

MAPS: Available at the preserve and the website below; USGS *Prospect*

FACILITIES: Picnic tables and shelter, restrooms, swings, recreational fields, nature center, field house

WHEELCHAIR ACCESS: None on trails

COMMENTS: Leashed, well-behaved pets welcome

CONTACTS: Creasey Mahan Nature Preserve, 502-228-4362; creaseymahannaturepreserve.org

Creasey Mahan Nature Preserve

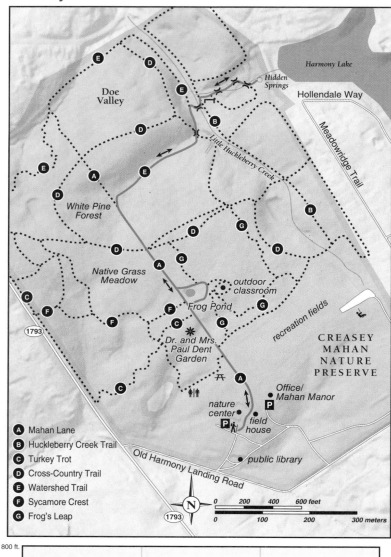

Harmony Lake

Hollendale Way

Hidden Springs

Doe Valley

Little Huckleberry Creek

Meadowridge Trail

White Pine Forest

Native Grass Meadow

outdoor classroom

Frog Pond

recreation fields

Dr. and Mrs. Paul Dent Garden

CREASEY MAHAN NATURE PRESERVE

(1793)

Office/ Mahan Manor

nature center

field house

public library

Old Harmony Landing Road

(1793)

Ⓐ Mahan Lane
Ⓑ Huckleberry Creek Trail
Ⓒ Turkey Trot
Ⓓ Cross-Country Trail
Ⓔ Watershed Trail
Ⓕ Sycamore Crest
Ⓖ Frog's Leap

| 0 | 200 | 400 | 600 feet |
| 0 | 100 | 200 | 300 meters |

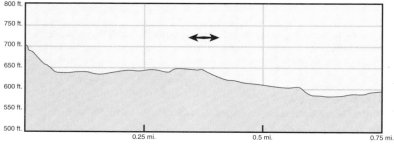

Overview

While Creasey Mahan Nature Preserve may be quiet during the week, most weekends are filled with activity, laughter, and fun. The staff provides a welcome that's warm enough to melt the fleece on your back and put a smile on your face. Under their energetic leadership, the trail system has been enlarged and a new woodland garden has been developed. Dedicated to recreation, education, conservation, and preservation, Creasey Mahan appeals to everyone from trail runners to curtain crawlers.

Route Details

If this is your first time to the Creasey Mahan Nature Preserve, a quick glance at its calendar of events (find it online at creaseymahannaturepreserve.org) may influence your planning. The preserve offers a variety of programs each month, such as Snakes!, National Squirrel Appreciation Day, and tree identification and care. The small campground and fire pit are rented out most weekends by local Boy Scout troops. Workshops are frequently offered, ranging from wildflower identification to raptor rehabilitation to master gardening.

Inside the nature center, four life-size dioramas are filled with taxidermic delights, showcasing Kentucky's woodlands, wetlands, fish, and early Native American life. Herons, waterfowl, owls, sandhill cranes, bears, and foxes are among the species represented. Neatly displayed Indian artifacts include incense burners, a hair roach, and an eagle pipe. A bird blind with two-way glass overlooks a wildlife-habitat garden, testing visitors' knowledge of spicebush, passionflower vine, sneezeweed, and other native plants. The bird-nest collection is outstanding, particularly the nests of the chimney swift and mud barn swallow. Who needs Netflix with all this fun?

But even with all of these goings-on, Creasey Mahan is a hiking destination as much as it is a community center, with 8.5 miles of trails ranging from open meadows to woodland forests to creekside strolls. A good hike for the younger ones begins at the nature center, travels past the Dr. and Mrs. Paul Dent Garden and Frog Pond, then follows Little Huckleberry Creek before ending at Hidden Springs. At about 0.75 mile one-way (1.5 miles round-trip), this hike provides lots of interesting diversions to keep the kids engaged.

Beginning at the parking lot, walk northeast between the nature center and the field house, and pass under the wooden trellis, before turning left (northwest) along Mahan Lane (labeled as Trail A on the preserve map). As you pass under a canopy of wild cherry, the picnic area will be to your left (just west of the trail) and the recreational fields to your right (east). Just ahead, another wooden arch leads to the hiking trails.

Shortly after you pass under the second wooden arch, the new Woodland Fern Garden will be on your left (west). Scores of new native trees and thousands of native wildflowers and ferns have been planted here, complemented by a small arched bridge and tumbling creek. Feel free to take a side trip through this woodland wonderland.

Mahan Lane continues past the Woodland Fern Garden to the Frog Pond, on your right. Take time to quietly circle the pond and catch a glimpse of the bullfrogs, red-eared sliders, or widow skimmers that reside here. Multiple benches provide a quiet respite for reflection or a staging area for a quick snack.

As you continue down Mahan Lane, the canopy diversifies from cherry into locust and cedar before descending a small hill through a patch of white pines. At the bottom of the hill, about 0.4 mile from the trailhead, turn right (northeast) onto the Watershed Trail (Trail E on the preserve map). This trail doglegs left (north), down a short but steep hillside to a small waterfall, over a small bridge, and across Little Huckleberry Creek. In just a few yards, turn right (northeast) and cross the small wooden bridge that traverses the creek. This short stretch of trail immediately Ts into the Huckleberry Creek Trail. A quick left and then a right will take you to Hidden Springs. You'll pass three more bridges and a small set of benches. The springs are just ahead, bubbling below an earthen berm that supports a small pond.

From this point you can retrace your steps back to the parking lot, completing your 1.5-mile walk; more-adventurous hikers can take a variety of other trails back to the starting point. Either way, your day at Creasey Mahan will have left you a little more relaxed and a little more appreciative of what nature has to offer.

Nearby Attractions

If you're looking to lengthen your hiking day, **Morgan Conservation Park** is just 20 minutes from Creasey Mahan, north of La Grange. The park's 4.3 miles of trails wind among a 252-acre tract of primary and secondary successional woods, wetlands, and old agricultural fields. In springtime, the Creekside Trail, a short path connecting to the 2.2-mile Primary Loop Trail, offers an impressive wildflower and waterfall display.

To reach the Morgan Conservation Park from Creasey Mahan, turn left (east) on US 42 and drive 13.4 miles. Hang another left (north) on KY 524, which becomes 18 Mile Creek Road; the park will be 1.3 miles ahead, on your right. (*Note:* There are two turnoffs onto KY 524 from US 42. If you took the first one, onto KY 524/Westport Road, you turned too soon.) For more information, contact Oldham County Parks & Recreation, 502-225-0655; tinyurl.com /MorganConPark.

Directions

From the intersection of I-71 and I-265 (KY 841/Gene Snyder Freeway), drive north on I-265 for 2.2 miles. Turn right (north) on US 42 toward Prospect. After 6.0 miles, turn left (north) at the large water tower onto KY 1793, and drive 1.0 mile. Turn right (east) on Old Harmony Landing Road. The preserve is 0.3 mile ahead, on your left.

CREASY MAHAN LETS HIKERS BURN OFF ENERGY WHILE TAKING TIME TO REFLECT.

SCENERY: ★ ★ ★ ★ ★
TRAIL CONDITION: ★ ★ ★ ★
CHILDREN: ★ ★ ★
DIFFICULTY: ★ ★
SOLITUDE: ★ ★ ★ ★

A SMALL TRIBUTARY OF FLOYDS FORK FORMS THE 40-FOOT FAIRMOUNT FALLS.

GPS TRAILHEAD COORDINATES: 38° 5.506' W85° 34.728'

DISTANCE & CONFIGURATION: 1.1-mile balloon

HIKING TIME: 45 minutes

HIGHLIGHTS: Waterfall, spring wildflowers

ELEVATION: 612' at trailhead, ascending to 694' at high point

ACCESS: Park is open daily, 8 a.m.–sunset. Admission is free, but to visit you must secure a permit in advance by calling Jefferson Memorial Forest at 502-368-6517.

MAPS: Available at the website below; USGS *Mount Washington*

FACILITIES: Picnic table at trailhead

WHEELCHAIR ACCESS: None

COMMENTS: Once you've completed the permit process, your information is kept on file, making subsequent visits easy. Dogs are permitted on leash.

CONTACTS: Jefferson Memorial Forest, 502-368-6517; tinyurl.com/FFalls

Overview

Just outside Louisville, this hidden gem provides a quick respite from the city. Dropping from a height of 40 feet, Fairmount Falls is frequently touted as "Louisville's tallest natural waterfall" (though it should also be noted that the competition is pretty slim). The falls are easy to reach from the trailhead—just 10 minutes away. The short trail is perfect for teaching young children the joy of hiking and providing instant gratification for those with short attention spans. Multiple creek drainages provide an ideal ecosystem for abundant spring-wildflower displays.

Route Details

While this hike requires a bit of pretrip planning, your odds of getting a permit are considerably better than picking a Kentucky Derby trifecta (see "Access" and "Contacts" for details). Jefferson Memorial Forest keeps visitors capped at three vehicles per day. Relatively few people know of this park, but wet springs and glorious wildflower shows can nonetheless result in full capacity on weekends.

Your permit comes with a key code that unlocks the gate at the park entrance. Follow the instructions, lock the gate behind you, and leave your permit on the dash of your vehicle. At the far end of the parking lot, you'll see the trail sign leading to Fairmount Falls.

The trail winds behind the parking lot and past several large boulders before picking up on the other side of Hidden Creek Lane (a private drive). As soon as you cross the road, you can hear the falls, drawing you deeper into the woods. Several short trails take you to the rim of a small gorge, cut by Fairmount Creek as it winds down to Floyds Fork. While the rim provides excellent vistas for photo ops, a short scramble down the rim will allow you a closer look from the base of the falls.

Spring visitors will frequently be treated with tumbling water and cool spray, while winter hikers can watch the falls as if in stop motion. However, from midsummer to late fall, the creek frequently dries up as mosquitoes and gnats take center stage. Timing is everything.

Just above the falls, the trail crosses the creek to the other side of the small gorge. As you read this, you've probably drawn two very important conclusions: One, the more fortunate you are to see a heavy flow of water falling over the lip of the gorge, the wetter your boots will get as you cross the creek. Second, given that the trail crosses about 10 feet from the edge of the 40-foot

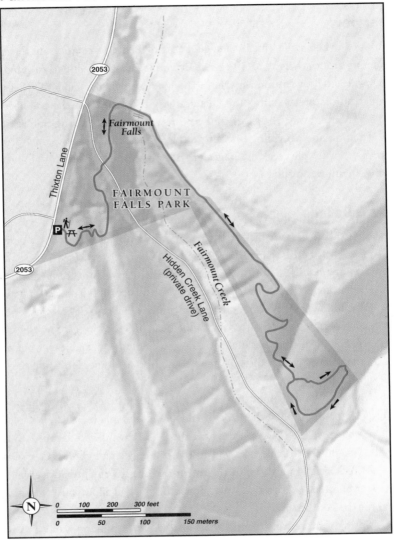

falls, one wrong step could be disastrous. Keep children and other loved ones close at hand.

After crossing the creek, you'll be walking southeast on the wooded trail, with a small subdivision on your left and Fairmount Creek far below on your right. In 0.2 mile, the trail splits into a small loop, rendering the trail like a small balloon with a very long tail. It's easier to take the loop clockwise, so bear left (east) at the junction.

The loop brings you down to another smaller creek drainage. Fairmount Falls is popular with spring hikers due to the abundance of wildflowers here. Trillium, wild yam, bloodroot, wild ginger, and mayapple abound. Wild columbine and fern tend to prefer the rocky crags of the boulders casually strewn about, while a second creek coming in on your left provides plenty of moisture year-round. The rich environs also provide a perfect habitat for viewing mushrooms.

After completing the loop, turn left (west) on the trail and retrace your steps back to the falls and the parking lot. Break out that picnic basket you packed and think about making a four-part montage of the falls for your photo album, with one picture taken in each season.

On your way home, stop by your favorite local bookstore and finally spring for that book on wildflowers you've been lusting over. Store it in your day pack, preloaded for your next hike at Fairmount Falls.

Directions

From Louisville, head south on Bardstown Road (US 150 East/US 31 East). Three miles south of I-265 (KY 841/Gene Snyder Freeway), turn right (west) on Thixton Lane (KY 2053) and drive 1 mile. Just before the road makes a sharp right turn, you'll see a small gravel lot to your left, almost hidden behind some trees. Park in front of the cable gate. Using the key code that came with your permit, unlock the cable. Pull inside and park, then relock the gate behind you. Reverse these steps upon departing.

23 # Hall Hill/Vernon-Douglas State Nature Preserve

SCENERY: ★ ★ ★ ★
TRAIL CONDITION: ★ ★ ★ ★
CHILDREN: ★ ★
DIFFICULTY: ★ ★ ★
SOLITUDE: ★ ★ ★ ★

CAN YOU IDENTIFY KENTUCKY'S STATE TREE AT THE PRESERVE?

GPS TRAILHEAD COORDINATES: N37° 44.003' W85° 42.469'

DISTANCE & CONFIGURATION: 3.6-mile balloon

HIKING TIME: 1.5 hours

HIGHLIGHTS: Second-growth forest, birding, spring wildflowers

ELEVATION: 474' at trailhead to 823' at high point

ACCESS: Daily, sunrise–sunset; free admission

MAPS: Available at the website below

FACILITIES: None

WHEELCHAIR ACCESS: None

COMMENTS: No pets are permitted.

CONTACTS: Kentucky State Nature Preserves Commission, 502-573-2886; tinyurl.com/vernondouglasnp

Overview

The Hall Hill/Vernon-Douglas State Nature Preserve, just south of the ever-popular Bernheim Arboretum and Research Forest (see Hikes 19 and 20), rarely sees a hiker. Donated to the Audubon Society of Kentucky in 1972 and now managed by the Kentucky State Nature Preserves Commission, this 730-acre tract protects a large second-growth forest in the Knobs region of central Kentucky. The trail traverses low-lying creeks and dry rocky ridges, supporting a wide variety of flora and fauna. Pileated woodpeckers and hooting owls drown out the occasional road noise from the Martha Layne Collins Bluegrass Parkway.

Route Details

The trail kiosk is hidden behind the trees at the rear of the parking lot, in what is known as Burns Hollow. Visitors frequently seem to find two or three sturdy hiking sticks, left by past hikers, leaning up against one large tree or another. It's a welcoming sign.

This land once belonged to siblings Eleanor and Ollie Douglas and had been in their family since the early 1900s. Determined that the land never be logged again, Ollie practiced conservation techniques to protect and preserve the area for future generations to come. Ollie got a little sidetracked when he planted kudzu for erosion control and Virginia pines on the ridgetops, but we don't hold that against him.

The forest comprises magnificent pignut hickory, sweetgum, beech, buckeye, sassafras, and tulip poplar—Kentucky's state tree. Now about that last one. . . .

Not to digress too much, but the tulip poplar was designated Kentucky's state tree in 1956 until Joe Creason, a well-liked columnist for the Louisville *Courier-Journal* for more than 30 years, launched an all-encompassing campaign to have the Kentucky coffee tree named the state tree. Two years after Creason died, the state legislature acquiesced. But the poplar vs coffee tree wars didn't end there: in 1994, the legislature reversed itself again and restored the tulip poplar—also known as the yellow poplar and the tulip tree—as Kentucky's official tree.

Anyway, back to hiking. After taking a minute to read the information posted at the kiosk, follow the trail straight ahead (south) as it climbs the side of a small knob. At this point you may be wondering if you'll hear the sounds of the Martha Layne Collins Bluegrass Parkway the entire hike. Thankfully, on

Hall Hill/Vernon-Douglas State Nature Perserve

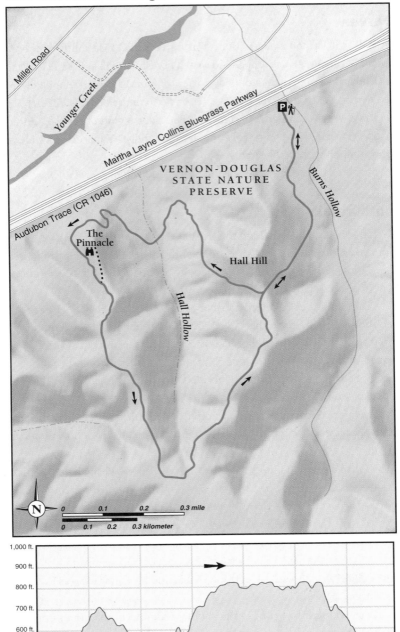

the back side of each knob a large sound eddy forms, sheltering your ears from the noise of civilization. After about 0.6 mile, the trail splits and forms a loop. Walking the loop counterclockwise is your best bet.

Turning right (west) at this junction takes you down a spiny ridge along an old roadbed through Hall Hollow. The trail flattens a bit as it crosses a shallow creek, which offers the finest opportunity along the trail to see a spectacular spring-wildflower display. Keep an eye out for trillium, bloodroot, columbine, rock cress, and mayapple.

The trail climbs quickly again to the top of a second knob. This is a good time to look for the multitude of 'shrooms and other "fun guys" that populate this preserve. (If you still haven't bought that mushroom-identification book, don't put it off any longer.)

Before you reach the top of the ridge, you'll see a clearly marked trail coming in on your left (you're now about 1.5 miles from the trailhead). This short spur leads you to what locals call the Pinnacle. At 800 feet, the hilltop faces north and overlooks Youngers Valley. In the summer and early fall the views are greatly obstructed by the tree canopy, but at other times of the year you can catch glimpses of distant pastoral landscapes.

The main trail continues along the ridgetop for another 1.5 miles. Here the soils are quite thin and the undergrowth quite sparse. Past ice storms, lightning strikes, and heavy winds have taken their toll, giving the local woodpecker population a perpetual feast. Birds of prey frequent these ridgetops, as do wild turkeys and owls. Halfway along the ridgetop trail, the preserve skirts adjacent farmland, where local agrarians raise corn and cell phone towers to make ends meet.

Once again, the trail quickly descends back to the junction with the out-and-back stem of the balloon. These steep, rocky spines are a good place to spot crinoids, the fossils of ancient marine animals. In some places along the trail, the crinoids are so plentiful they look like pennies tossed across a parking lot. (Leave them where you find them, though.)

Bear right (north) at the junction to walk the final 0.6 mile back to the parking area. If you've borrowed a hiking stick, be sure to return it for the next hiker. And be sure to murmur a word of thanks to Ollie and Eleanor for their vision and passion.

EVEN "FUN GUYS" ENJOY CONDO LIVING.

Nearby Attractions

If you still have the energy to hike, **Freeman Lake Park** in Elizabethtown is only a 15-minute drive away. The park offers a 4.7-mile paved loop trail, which circumnavigates the lake. Or if antique cars appeal to you, check out **Swope's Cars of Yesterday Museum**, located just across Dixie Highway from Freeman Lake, at 1100 North Dixie Avenue. Swope's showcases more than 60 cars, from a 1914 Model T to a 1956 Thunderbird, and better yet it's free. For more information on either of these options, see elizabethtown.org.

Directions

From Louisville, head south on I-65. From the intersection of I-65 South and I-265 (KY 841/Gene Snyder Freeway), drive 20.0 miles; at Exit 105, turn left (south) on KY 61 and drive 4.1 miles. In the small town of Boston, bear right (west) on US 62 West and drive 3.8 miles. Turn left (south) on Youngers Creek Road (KY 583). In another 2.0 miles you'll cross the Martha Layne Collins Bluegrass Parkway. Take an immediate right onto Audubon Trace (County Road 1046). Drive another 0.5 mile and you'll see a small sign on your right for the nature preserve. Park in the small, unmarked gravel parking lot, on your left.

24 The Parklands of Floyds Fork: Coppiced Woods

SCENERY: ★ ★ ★
TRAIL CONDITION: ★ ★ ★ ★
CHILDREN: ★ ★ ★
DIFFICULTY: ★ ★
SOLITUDE: ★ ★

ANGLERS LAKE AS SEEN FROM THE COPPICED WOODS TRAIL.

GPS TRAILHEAD COORDINATES: N38° 13.834' W85° 28.073
DISTANCE & CONFIGURATION: 2.0-mile loop
HIKING TIME: 1 hour
HIGHLIGHTS: Overlook of Floyds Fork, multiple lake views
ELEVATION: 586' at trailhead, ascending to 713' at high point
ACCESS: Daily, sunrise–sunset
MAPS: Available at the website below
FACILITIES: Picnic tables, restrooms, potable water
WHEELCHAIR ACCESS: None
COMMENTS: Pets are permitted on leash.
CONTACTS: The Parklands of Floyds Fork, 502-324-4231; theparklands.org

Overview

Opened in November 2012, Coppiced Woods was the first "soft" (unpaved) trail at the Parklands of Floyds Fork. The trail, located on the northern side of Beckley Creek Park, wanders around two of the William F. Lakes before dipping into

141

The Parklands of Floyds Fork: Coppiced Woods

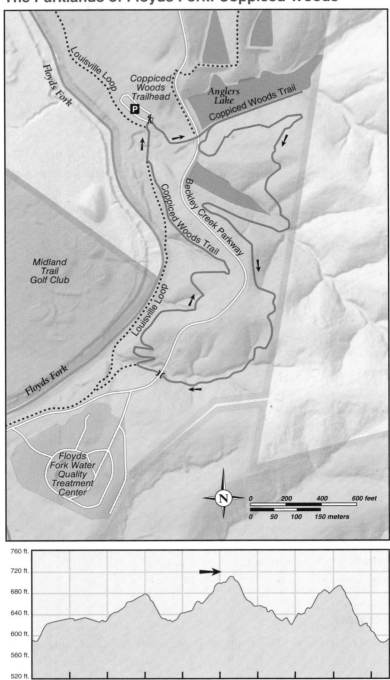

the woods. While Coppiced Woods is also open to mountain bikers, it is used more for hiking, as the off-road cyclists tend to gravitate to the southern side of the Parklands. Although hikers have the right-of-way over bikers, it's always good to be on the lookout.

Route Details

The Coppiced Woods Trail can be easily accessed from the North Beckley Paddling Access parking lot. Otherwise, you will have to park in the lot by the William F. Miles Community Garden and walk to the trailhead via the paved multiuse Louisville Loop. From the east side of the paddling access lot, carefully cross the Beckley Creek Parkway and head toward Anglers Lake. The trail does an out-and-back on the southern side of the lake, before retracing its steps back to the parkway. Once back at the road, the Coppiced Woods Trail once again heads east along a small meadow before entering a stand of hickories and oaks, with a few maples and eastern red cedars mixed in. Most of the oaks here are bur (alternately spelled *burr*) or mossy-cup oaks, easily distinguished in the fall by their furry little caps.

As for trivia, coppiced wood is an old forestry-management tool in which every 20–25 years trees are cut stump-high and the wood harvested, typically for poles. The remaining stump then regenerates new branching, and the cycle begins again. There is some evidence that this management can be beneficial for certain kinds of woodland creatures, though it's not a popular or common strategy anymore.

After a scant 0.2 mile, the trail makes a short switchback up to the other side of the small meadow you first saw from below. The summer crop of black-eyed Susans and Queen Anne's lace is supplemented with yellow goldenrods and purple asters later in the year. The trail descends gradually along the drainage that forms a small pond, one of many water sources for the resident deer population. Quiet footsteps and silent voices might reward the vigilant hiker with a brief glance at the six-point buck that lives in these parts.

The trail then slips between several old barbwire fencerows before bearing left (east) and roughly paralleling the eastern side of Beckley Creek Parkway, heading southeast. About 1.0 mile from the trailhead, you'll cross three shallow creekbeds before the trail ducks under a stone-clad bridge carrying cars overhead on the Beckly Creek Parkway. You're now walking on the opposite (west) side of the parkway, heading toward Floyds Fork.

A few yards past the bridge underpass, the trail turns abruptly right across the creek and travels east once more. After a heavy rain, this creek rumbles along quite noisily, and a 6-foot waterfall flows just downstream from where you crossed.

A few more gentle switchbacks along the trail bring you to a small ridge overlooking Floyds Fork. The views are best from late fall to early spring, when most of the leaves are young or off the trees and the white bark of the sycamores reflects in the water below. In the spring, the blooms of white dogwood and pink redbuds dot the forest. You have several good vantage points to choose from along this ridge, so walk slowly and enjoy the sights.

Periodically along the trail you may see several old deer stands, as evidenced by dilapidated two-by-fours still nailed, yet hanging precipitously, to the crotches of mature trees. The profusion of oaks guarantees the nonstop barking of the gray squirrels that thrive in these woods.

Soon the trail leaves the overlook and descends gently to the paved Louisville Loop that follows Floyds Fork. At 1.9 miles, you will see the parking lot just north of the trail.

Nearby Attractions

The **William F. Miles Lakes** are stocked spring and fall with channel cats, largemouth bass, bluegill, and rainbow trout. The occasional crappie might also make an appearance. The lakes here are quite popular among local anglers on weekends and after work.

Paddlers might also enjoy a trip down **Floyds Fork.** In addition to the watercraft launch at North Beckley, there are several other paddling access points, including Creekside, Fisherville, Cane Run, Seaton Valley, Broad Run Valley, and Cliffside. For more detailed information see tinyurl.com /PaddlingAccess.

Directions

From I-265 (KY 841/Gene Snyder Freeway), take Exit 27, heading east on US 60 (Shelbyville Road). Drive 2.0 miles and, just past the Valhalla Golf Club, turn right (south) on Blue Heron Road (Miles Parkway). Drive another 0.6 mile to the small parking lot on the left (east) side of the road. Start here to walk the loop trail clockwise.

25 # The Parklands of Floyds Fork: Favorite Shorts

SCENERY: ★ ★ ★ ★ ★
TRAIL CONDITION: ★ ★ ★ ★
CHILDREN: ★ ★ ★
DIFFICULTY: ★ ★
SOLITUDE: ★ ★

AN EXAMPLE OF INSPIRING HARDSCAPES FOUND AT THE MOSS GIBBS WOODLAND GARDEN

GPS TRAILHEAD COORDINATES: Moss Gibbs Woodland Garden N38° 06.957' W85° 32.008'

DISTANCE & CONFIGURATION: 3 individual hikes, each 1.0–1.6 miles in length

HIKING TIME: 4 hours

HIGHLIGHTS: Creative garden hardscape and stonework, small gorge, wildflowers

ELEVATION: Trails have only modest changes in elevation.

ACCESS: Daily, sunrise–sunset

MAPS: Available online and some displayed at the trailhead kiosk

FACILITIES: Picnic tables, potable water, and restrooms at Moss Garden only. Portable toilets elsewhere.

WHEELCHAIR ACCESS: None

COMMENTS: No dogs are permitted at Moss Gibbs. Pets are permitted on leash elsewhere.

CONTACTS: The Parklands of Floyds Fork, 502-324-4231; theparklands.org

The Parklands of Floyds Fork: Favorite Shorts

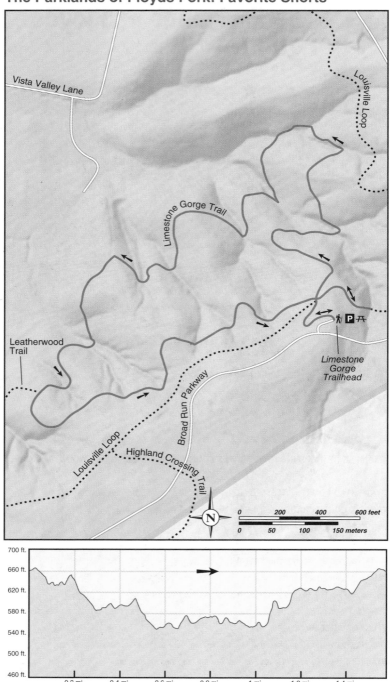

Overview

All of us probably have our favorite shorts—hiking pants, cutoff jeans, or pressed khakis. Or our favorite short films, from documentaries to animations to experimentals. But some of us have our list of favorite short trails at the Parklands too. This set of short hikes focuses on the Moss Gibbs Woodland Garden, the Limestone Gorge Trail, and the Wild Hyacinth Trail. Each hike can be done individually or strung together to make a longer day of it. These hikes are also great for children and other hikers with less stamina because you get to have nice breaks between each hike, and you might not realize you have walked 4 miles!

Route Details

Moss Gibbs Woodland Garden *(1.0-mile loop; 45 minutes' hiking time; N38° 06.957' W85° 32.008')*

The Moss Gibbs Woodland Garden is located just north of the Cliffside Center, at the far southern end of Broad Run Park. The best place to begin is at the Big Vista Overlook, with commanding views of what was once an ancient lake. Despite the visual clutter of the power lines, the Brown-Forman Silo Center is clearly visible off in the distance. From the northwest edge of the parking lot, continue walking west just a short distance to find the trailhead for the gardens. A map of the 1.0-mile loop trail can be found at tinyurl.com/MossGibbs, but be patient, as it takes a while to load.

The woodland garden has been planted with thousands of native floras, including wildflowers and trees. But some of the real beauty lies in the overall design of the gardens, which has divided the space into various rooms and small alcoves. Multiple stone paths, frequently linked with steps, meander through the woods, taking you past the Redbud Rondel, through the Glade and Glen Gardens, and on farther until you reach the Kentucky Coffee Tree Rondel at the far western edge of this green oasis.

The stonework at Moss Gibbs is an inspiring collection of flagstone walkways, huge limestone slab steps, a gorgeous rock bridge accompanied by a touching plaque of dedication, and whimsical creek-hoppin' steps. Bring a book. Bring a lunch. Bring your gratitude for the designers who labored here.

Limestone Gorge Trail *(1.6-mile loop; 60 minutes' hiking time; N38° 06.041' W85° 32.159')*

After walking in the Moss Gibbs Garden, get back in your car and drive less than a mile to the Limestone Gorge Trail (see directions on page 150). This

1.6-mile loop trail takes you over a multitude of seasonal creeks and a spring wildflower display.

The parking lot at Limestone Gorge is quite small but offers picnic tables and trail access. Begin hiking by following the sidewalk down the short hill until you reach the paved multiuse trail, the Louisville Loop. Watch yourself, as the Louisville Loop is heavily used by cyclists, particularly on weekends. Turn right (northwest) for a 5-minute walk to the bridge overlooking the gorge. Layers of limestone, the result of the water continually eroding the creekbed, have created a beautiful and intimate gorge. This will be your best (and only) view of the gorge.

Retrace your steps back to the point where the Louisville Loop met the sidewalk from the parking lot; bear right at the trail sign for the Limestone Gorge Trail and descend the short set of stone stairs. Hiking the rugged loop trail in the winter brings solitude but icy conditions where the trail crosses various small streams. Spring hikers will see purple swirls of larkspur, white clouds of dogwood blooms, and wide swaths of mayapple. By midsummer the trail dries out and fall brings wonderful autumnal color.

A little less than a mile from the trailhead, the steep Leatherwood Trail descends to your right. Bear left here (south) to stay on the Limestone Gorge Trail and return to the parking lot.

Wild Hyacinth Trail *(1.5-mile balloon; 60 minutes' hiking time; N38° 07.235' W85° 32.197')*

If you have the energy, let's do one more hike along the Wild Hyacinth Trail. Following the directions on page 150, drive 2.0 miles to the Ben Stout House and parking lot and the Wild Hyacinth Trailhead. Dating back to the early 19th century, the 18-inch-thick stone walls of the Ben Stout House, built from locally sourced limestone, remain impressive.

The 1.5-mile Wild Hyacinth Trail begins behind the kiosk on the far eastern side of the parking lot. Follow the short trail that also leads to the Boone Bottoms Trail, but carefully traverse Ben Stout Road at the crosswalk to pick up the Wild Hyacinth Trail.

The Wild Hyacinth Trail follows Turkey Run Creek, before it empties into Floyds Fork. Perhaps the best time to walk this trail is in the spring, when the white or pale blue wild hyacinths are in bloom and blanket the forest floor. This is a good hike to bring that native wildflower book to be sure you can tell the difference between wood anemone and bloodroot, and "real" versus false Solomon's seal.

About 0.6 miles from the trailhead, the Wild Hyacinth Trail crosses the paved Louisville Loop. Continue straight (east) another 0.1 mile until the trail forms a 0.7-mile loop that goes past several old stacked-stone walls, an indication of the agrarian life that once held strong here, and crosses Turkey Run Creek twice. Be sure to read the sign about legacy trees, also evidence that much of this land had been farmed. After completing the loop, head west again on the Wild Hyacinth Trail and the final 0.6 mile back to the parking lot.

Nearby Attractions

The 1.2-mile **Boone Bottoms Trail** mentioned above is an interesting contrast to the Wild Hyacinth Trail. While the latter displays some vestiges of what the land looked like in its former agrarian life, Boone Bottoms has transitioned from farm to fallow land in much more recent times. Hiking Boone Bottoms clockwise from the kiosk at the Ben Stout House parking lot, the level trail follows Turkey Run Creek south for about 0.4 mile before turning north along Floyds Fork for another 0.5 mile.

All the area east of Floyds Fork is proverbial bottomland that was cropped not so long ago. But there is widespread evidence of Floyds Fork leaving its bank, flooding the bottomlands, and depositing rich silt, both destroying and promising future crops. However, recent management practices have allowed some of this land to naturally revert, while a larger portion has been planted with more than 3,000 trees, in particular sycamores, which like to keep their feet wet, as part of a reforestation project.

Several short trails lead to the edge of the creek and Mussel Shoals, a gravel bar popular for fossil hunting. Once you leave Floyds Fork, walk east another 0.3 mile to return to the parking lot.

Directions

To get to Moss Gibbs Woodland Garden: From the intersection of Billtown Road and I-265 (Gene Snyder Freeway, Exit 19), head southeast on Billtown Road 0.8 mile. Turn right (west) onto Seatonville Road; drive 0.5 mile. Turn left (south) onto Broad Run Road and drive another 2.4 miles. Turn right (south) onto Fairmount Road; drive 0.3 mile. Finally, turn left (south) onto Broad Run Parkway and drive 0.3 mile. The parking lot for the Big Vista Overlook will be on your right.

To drive from Moss Gibbs to the Limestone Gorge Trailhead: Turn left (east) out of the Big Vista Overlook parking lot. Drive 0.8 mile on Broad Run Parkway. The trailhead parking lot is marked and will be on your right.

To drive from the Limestone Gorge Trailhead to the Wild Hyacinth Trailhead: Turn right (east) out of the Limestone Gorge parking lot and drive 0.8 mile. Take a slight right onto Fairmount Road. Then take a sharp right onto Broad Run Road and then an immediate left onto Stout Road. Drive 0.9 mile. The trailhead parking lot (and the Ben Stout House) will be on your left.

THE WILD HYACINTH TRAIL AT THE PARKLANDS IS IDEAL FOR SPRING WILDFLOWER VIEWING.

26

The Parklands of Floyds Fork: Turkey Run

SCENERY: ★★★★★
TRAIL CONDITION: ★★★★
CHILDREN: ★★
DIFFICULTY: ★★★★
SOLITUDE: ★★

A CLIMB TO THE TOP OF THE 60-FOOT SILO OFFERS 360-DEGREE VIEWS OF THE PARKLANDS OF FLOYDS FORK.

GPS TRAILHEAD COORDINATES: N38° 06.957' W85° 32.008'

DISTANCE & CONFIGURATION: 5.4 miles, double loop

HIKING TIME: 3.5 hours

HIGHLIGHTS: Historic silo, deep woods, Turkey Run Creek

ELEVATION: 660' at trailhead, ascending to 670' at high point, descending to 558' at low point

ACCESS: Daily, sunrise–sunset

MAPS: Available online and displayed at the trailhead kiosk

FACILITIES: Picnic tables, potable water, restrooms, agrarian outbuildings

WHEELCHAIR ACCESS: None on the trail

COMMENTS: Dogs are permitted on leash.

CONTACTS: The Parklands of Floyds Fork, 502-324-4231; theparklands.org

The Parklands of Floyds Fork: Turkey Run

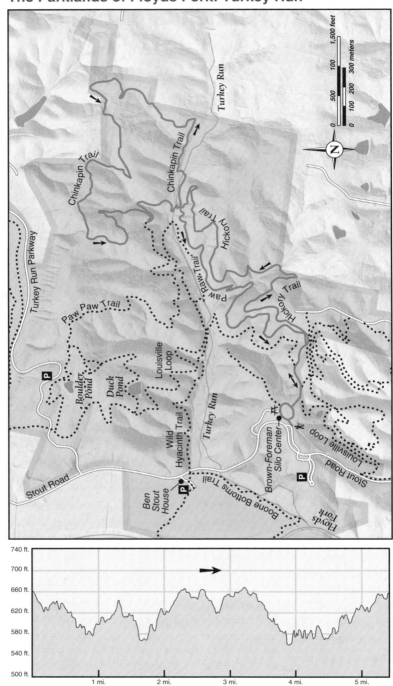

Overview

It's difficult to find an unpaved hiking trail at the Parklands of Floyds Fork that is longer than 1.5 miles. It's impossible to find an unpaved hiking trail longer than 2.0 miles that is not also open to mountain bikers. We love mountain biking, but this is simply one of the challenges of creating multiuse trails in a linear park.

That said, the trails at Turkey Run Park can be strung together so the avid hiker can get in well over 5 miles of backwoods hiking. The route begins at the Brown-Forman Silo Center and meanders through the forest using the Hickory, Chinkapin, and Paw Paw Trails.

Route Details

The multiple parking lots at the Brown-Forman Silo Center can really get crowded, particularly on weekends or if an event is scheduled. But there are several parking spaces, and perseverance is your friend. The described route begins at the northeast corner of the parking lot closest to the Silo Center, where the sidewalk leads to the central lawn. (Note: The Silo Center is frequently rented out on Saturdays from early spring until late fall. You may want to call ahead to confirm or schedule for another day.)

If you have not been to the Silo Center yet, take plenty of time before or after your hike to fully explore the area. Yes, they have real bathrooms here, as well as potable water. But definitely climb those 100-plus steps to the top of the 60-foot-tall silo and soak up the 360-degree view it freely offers up. Also walk around the Hockensmith Barn, the Pignic Barn, and the Farmer's Table. Unless the space has been previously reserved, it's not unusual to see a family laughing or a couple conversing over a picnic basket of fine eatin' victuals, with a small cooler of bubbly on the side.

To begin this hike, follow the sidewalk that runs southeast between the silo and the Pignic Barn. At the bottom of the small hill, you will see an information kiosk and the paved Louisville Loop. Turn left (east) here and walk past the Silo Center Bike Park on your right. Just past the main gate to the bike park, you will see a small brown sign for all three trails: Paw Paw, Hickory, and Chinkapin. This trail almost immediately connects with the Hickory Trail. To hike counterclockwise, bear right, following the signs to the Hickory Trail.

Let's stop a moment and talk about right-of-way. Bikers, runners, and hikers all use the aforementioned trails. But hikers always have the right-of-way and bikers must always give way. That leaves runners with right-of-way over bikers, but they must give way to hikers. However, if you are hiking and have time to get off the path, in this writer's estimation that is the kind and friendly thing to do.

The relatively level Hickory Trail runs just a little over 1.4 miles, through a pleasant hardwood forest. The trail meanders a bit and crosses several small creeks that frequently run dry in the summer months. While there are 10 different species of hickory native to Kentucky, the shagbark and shellbark are the most common. Belonging to the walnut family, hickory wood is valued for its robust and shock-resistant nature and is used for baseball bats, drumsticks, golf clubs, and, of course, walking sticks. While all hickories produce nuts, it is the drupe from the shellbark that is most prized for its sweet meat, hence earning itself the moniker king nut.

Just before you cross Turkey Creek, the Hickory, Paw Paw, and Chinkapin Trails all intersect. Turn right (east) on the Chinkapin, a large 2.2-mile loop trail that crosses Turkey Run Creek on a small wood bridge, before winding its way through more hardwood forest. Observant hikers have an excellent chance of spotting several white-tailed deer, which are almost as prolific as the acorns scattered across the forest floor.

The Chinkapin Trail ends where it Ts into the Paw Paw Trail. Bearing right (north) will take you to Turkey Run Parkway and Seaton Valley, but you will want to turn left (south) to head back to the Silo Center. The Paw Paw Trail will once again cross Turkey Run Creek and then switchback up a steep hill before returning to the intersection of the Hickory and Chinkapin Trails you previously encountered. Stay right (west) to return on the Paw Paw Trail.

Pawpaws are ubiquitous across much of Kentucky, and their fruit has frequently been described as a cross between a mango and a banana. But actually finding a fruiting pawpaw is easier said than done. The trees typically reproduce asexually via runners underground (thus forming large colonies) but can also reproduce sexually via their large seeds scattered by animals. Interestingly, pawpaw trees are considered trioecious, having separate female, male, and hermaphroditic plants, but they are not self-pollinating. Since bees have no interest in the flowers, the old-time method of getting pawpaw flowers to fruit is by hanging dead meat (from roadkill to slices of raw bacon) on the tree branches to attract flies and some beetles, the trees' primary pollinators.

By the time you can read and digest that last paragraph, you will have finished walking the final 1.5 miles of the Paw Paw Trail and will find yourself back at the Silo Center Bike Park. Retrace your steps back to the Brown-Forman Silo Center. If it's approaching sunset, be sure to climb the silo steps once again to watch the evening draw to a close after another great day in the woods.

Nearby Attractions

The Parklands at Floyds Fork offers a variety of educational programs geared toward kids, including Wee Wednesday Wonders, Junior Explorers, and various school-break camps. The Field & Fork fundraisers, seasonal farmers' markets, and everything from 5K to half-marathon footraces also attract large and diverse crowds.

The **Brown-Forman Silo Center** is available to rent for private parties, weddings, music events, and more. The former dairy farm includes the repurposed pig barn, Pignic, which can be reserved (for a fee) or is freely available on a first-come, first-served basis.

The Parklands has a host of other indoor and outdoor venues available for reservation. Check out the Parklands website for more detailed information on all of these options.

Directions

From the intersection of Billtown Road and I-265 (Gene Snyder Freeway, Exit 19), head south on Billtown Road 0.8 mile. Turn right (west) onto Seatonville Road; drive 0.5 mile. Turn left (south) onto Broad Run Road and drive another 2.4 miles. Turn left (north) onto Stout Road. In another 0.5 mile you will see the Brown-Forman Silo Center on your right. There are parking lots on both sides of Stout Road.

27

Pine Creek Barrens Nature Preserve

SCENERY: ★ ★ ★
TRAIL CONDITION: ★ ★ ★ ★
CHILDREN: ★ ★ ★
DIFFICULTY: ★ ★
SOLITUDE: ★ ★ ★ ★ ★

THE TRAIL FOLLOWS PINE CREEK FOR A GOOD PORTION OF YOUR HIKE.

GPS TRAILHEAD COORDINATES: N37° 58.823' W85° 37.553'

DISTANCE & CONFIGURATION: 2.5-mile loop

HIKING TIME: 1.25 hours

HIGHLIGHTS: Barrens and glade; views of Pine and Cedar Creeks

ELEVATION: 557' at trailhead, descending to 456' at low point

ACCESS: Daily, sunrise–sunset; free admission

MAPS: Posted on kiosk at trailhead

FACILITIES: Portable toilet

WHEELCHAIR ACCESS: None

COMMENTS: No pets allowed

CONTACTS: The Nature Conservancy, 859-259-9655, kentucky@tnc.org; tinyurl.com/Pine-Creek-Barrens

Overview

The Pine Creek Barrens Nature Preserve protects several rare and endangered plant species, including Kentucky glade cress, which is only found in small pockets scattered across Bullitt and Jefferson Counties. Glade cress is a member of the mustard family and thrives on the limestone/dolomite barrens that form the heart of the preserve. The wooded loop trail provides views of the barrens and accompanying glade, native prairie, and both Cedar and Pine Creeks.

Route Details

Officially opened in 2017, Pine Creek Barrens is a relative newcomer to Kentucky's growing collection of nature preserves. But the preserve has already attracted a small but extremely loyal following of local hikers who frequent its environs. And although located just minutes away from the ever-popular Bernheim Forest, most hikers have never heard of Pine Creek Barrens, rendering the parking lot almost empty even on beautiful spring days. If you're hiking during the week or the off-season, there is a good chance no one else will be on the trail.

While the Nature Conservancy claims 3.0 miles of hiking, the official loop trail is only 2.5 miles at best. After parking, be sure to read the information signs on the west side of the lot. The trailhead also begins here, giving hikers the option of traveling either clockwise or counterclockwise. The directions below assume hiking the loop in a counterclockwise progression.

Facing the aforementioned signs, bear to the right (north) toward the picnic table. From here the trail continues in a generally northern direction. One of the first things you might notice is how young the forest appears—in part due to development activity prior to the formation of the 158-acre preserve. But equally if not more important, the tree canopy remains severely constrained due to the thin soil structure that sits atop the barren rock and the periodic prescribed burns conducted here.

Five minutes of hiking brings you to another information sign explaining how the Nature Conservancy uses these prescribed burns to protect the preserve. Prior to settlement, much of south-central Kentucky was covered by native prairie, with few of the towering, mature trees that many people might expect. Occasional fires, induced by Mother Nature and essential for their rejuvenating powers, burned large swaths of grasslands. Now prescribed burns keep the understory at bay, allowing the grasses and other flora to grow and prosper.

Pine Creek Barrens Nature Preserve

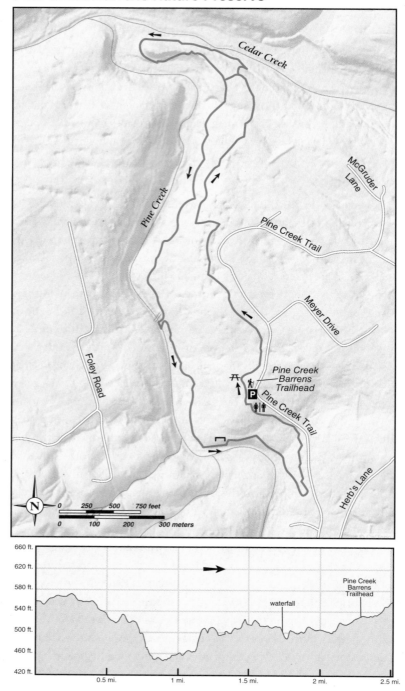

Continuing north along the loop, the trail crosses a small barren, where frequently seen deer prints remind us that we are not alone. From here the trail begins a gentle descent into the Cedar Creek drainage. Although the soil has a heavy clay content, the trail is well drained and hiking is easy. A crossover trail soon appears on your left, leading to a small bench. Continuing straight down the hill, about 0.8 mile from the trailhead, the path joins Cedar Creek, whose waters flow quietly, even after a heavy rain.

After another 5 minutes of walking, the trail approaches the confluence of Cedar and Pine Creeks. The path loops back on itself, then threads uphill between some interesting limestone formations, before heading south up the Pine Creek drainage. The proliferation of limestone and karst resulted in many of the sinkholes you'll see along the way.

When the leaves are out in full swing, only glimpses of the creeks are available to hikers. But when the leaves have fallen off the trees, the beauty of both creeks, as well as the limestone formations that form the drop edge of the barrens, are clearly in view. Winter hiking is also desirable here, as the limestone ledges create a variety of icy stalagmites and stalactites seen along the path.

The crossover trail leading to the bench reappears on your left this time. Continuing south as the trail follows the Pine Creek drainage, spring flowers can be found in abundance. Almost 1.75 miles from the trailhead, the sounds of a small, cascading waterfall can be heard to your right. The trail continues up the Pine Creek drainage for another 0.25 mile, before reaching another bench.

Again, the trail loops back on itself, reversing its direction to north once more. The barrens are in plain view and the thin soils that lie atop the limestone and dolomite rock of the preserve create a rich environment for the glade cress, blazing star, coneflower, Indian grass, and little bluestem that flourish here. Kentucky glade cress grows low to the ground (only 2–4 inches in height), with small four-petaled flowers ranging from white to lilac. Needless to say, be careful where you step.

Another information sign is located here, further describing the role of grasslands in early Kentucky. Hiking an additional 5 minutes leads you back to a large persimmon tree, standing sentry at the edge of the parking lot. Harder than either maple or oak, persimmon wood is still used in many golf club heads. But in the fall, a juicy, sun-sweetened persimmon can be heaven to the taste buds.

THE PRESENCE OF BOTH PINE AND CEDAR CREEKS ENSURES A GOOD WILDFLOWER DISPLAY IN THE SPRING.

Nearby Attractions

If you have an interest in rare and endangered plants, both the Nature Conservancy and the Office of Kentucky State Nature Preserves own several parcels of land that are open to the public. Frequently, these parcels are small and relatively unknown, offering up quiet, secluded hiking, away from the crowds. For more information, see the websites of the Nature Conservancy (tinyurl.com/TNC-KY) and the Office of Kentucky State Nature Preserves (tinyurl.com/KY-SNP).

Directions

From downtown Louisville, take I-65 South. From the intersection of I-65 South and I-265 (KY 841/Gene Snyder Freeway), drive 9.0 miles; at Exit 116, turn left (east) on KY 480, also known as Cedar Grove Road. Drive 4.5 miles; just past the Marathon on your right, turn left (north) on Pine Creek Trail. Drive another 0.7 mile. The parking lot and sign for the preserve will be on your left, on the west side of the road.

Salato Wildlife Education Center

28

SCENERY: ★ ★ ★ ★ ★
TRAIL CONDITION: ★ ★ ★ ★ ★
CHILDREN: ★ ★ ★ ★ ★
DIFFICULTY: ★
SOLITUDE: ★ ★

CONSTELLATIONS OF SPOTS DAPPLE THESE WHITE-TAILED FAWNS.

GPS TRAILHEAD COORDINATES: Main Trail, N38° 10.670' W84° 55.392';
Pea Ridge Trail, N38° 10.712' W84° 55.585'

DISTANCE & CONFIGURATION: 1.5-mile double loop (includes both a paved figure-eight path around the wildlife exhibits and an unpaved loop trail combining the Habitrek and Prairie Trails). An additional 2.5 miles of hiking utilizing the Pea Ridge Trail are also available.

HIKING TIME: 1.5 hours (generously estimated for short toddler strides)

HIGHLIGHTS: Indoor education center and outdoor exhibit area of native flora and fauna

ELEVATION: 855' at trailhead, descending to 784' at low point

ACCESS: Open March–late November, Tuesday–Saturday, 9 a.m.–4 p.m. Closed on state holidays and seasonally (see website below for details). Free to hike; see website for fees to enter the education center. Hiking the Pea Ridge Trail is free and includes daily access, sunrise–sunset.

MAPS: Available at the website below and at the education center

FACILITIES: Restrooms, picnic tables and shelters, small fishing lake

WHEELCHAIR ACCESS: Yes, with 0.5 mile of paved trail in the outdoor exhibit area

COMMENTS: Check the website for special events such as wildflower walks, live-owl shows, and native-plant sales. Salato is also popular for school groups and summer camp outings. Sorry, no pets are permitted.

CONTACTS: Kentucky Department of Fish & Wildlife Resources, 502-564-7863; tinyurl.com/SalatoCenter

Salato Wildlife Education Center

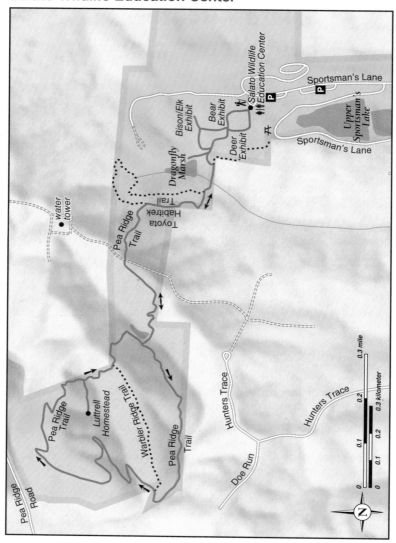

Overview

This one has "kids" written all over it. Pack up the little taters and give them a taste of native Kentucky. Both indoor and outdoor exhibits showcase the flora and fauna of the Bluegrass. Owned by the Kentucky Department of Fish & Wildlife, Salato gives the kids a chance to run with wild abandon while teaching many of the lessons only Mother Nature can offer. Big kids will also enjoy hiking the Pea Ridge Trail for its history and scenic beauty.

Route Details

Before hiking, you may want to start your adventure at the main building of the education center. The information desk can provide maps, an Animal Tracks Audio Tour, and all kinds of wildlife pamphlets and paraphernalia.

The education center alone can be a destination on cold or rainy days when you don't want to hike. Just past the information desk, stuffed owls, geese, hawks, and other avian critters dangle from the ceiling as you walk past exhibits showcasing the variety of Kentucky's ecosystems. At the end of the hall, the hanging sculptures change to flying fish such as muskellunge, stripers, rainbow trout, and largemouth bass.

Both cold and warm freshwater tanks let you see native fish up close in their natural habitats. While the serpentarium cases might make some guests squirm, the collection of stuffed raccoons, deer, beavers, foxes, and other mammals are a taxidermist's delight. There are also several learning stations where kids can "catch" catfish, count the points on a buck, or observe flying squirrels sleeping soundly.

The large glass doors at the end of the hall lead to the outdoor exhibits. From here a wide paved trail takes you past live exhibits of bald eagles, black bears, wildcats, bison, deer, wild turkeys, and elk. A waterfall and creek exhibit features live fish.

Ramps provide access for strollers and wheelchairs, and benches are scattered generously around the path. It's not unusual to see grandparents pushing strollers while passing along a bit of nature appreciation to the next generation.

While the paved trail is basically a 0.5-mile figure-eight configuration with several spurs shooting in various directions, kids tend to zigzag across the area, going back again and again to see their favorite animals. Patches of wildflowers and grasses native to the Bluegrass, including black-eyed Susan, purple coneflower, and butterfly weed, link the live-animal exhibits.

After you've seen the fauna, young hikers may want to try a short dirt trail. Close to Dragonfly Marsh, a well-marked wooded walkway leads to both the Habitrek and Prairie Trails. Together, these trails form a 1.0-mile loop of relatively flat terrain. Given enough time and encouragement, very young children can complete these trails. Even in the dry of summer, moist areas showcase deer and raccoon prints, and finches can be seen feasting on cone-flower seeds.

Hardier hikers can take the 2.5-mile Pea Ridge Trail, a balloon that follows several creek drainages and low rock walls before ambling past the old Luttrell homestead. From the middle of the Habitrek Trail, turn left (west) onto the out-and-back portion of the Pea Ridge balloon. In less than 0.5 mile, you reach the loop part of the trail (which in turn is bisected by the Warbler Ridge Trail).

At the loop intersection, turn left (southwest) to follow the Pea Ridge Trail clockwise. In the spring, this area is populated with wildflowers, including trilliums, wild ginger, Virginia bluebells, trout lilies, fire pinks, and Jacob's ladder. In 0.45 mile, the Warbler Ridge Trail bisects the loop. If you take Warbler Ridge, your hike will be shortened by 0.6 mile. Alternately, you can stay on the Pea Ridge Trail to drop down into another creek drainage before climbing to a high spot along Pea Ridge itself. This is a good place to spot wild turkeys, box turtles, and deer roaming free.

The Luttrell family homesteaded this land before the Civil War, and many of their descendants still live in the area. You'll observe evidence of their farming operations along several portions of the trail. Stone fences are the remnants of fields that were cleared before plowing. In other places, huge piles of rocks were stacked within creek drainages to reduce erosion and capture running water.

A spur takes hikers a short distance off the Pea Ridge Trail to the site of the old Luttrell log cabin. All that remains are several stone structures, a large notched beam, and several vernal pools formed in depressions where the outhouse and an outbuilding were located.

Returning to the Pea Ridge Trail, you'll pass a small pond in a few hundred yards, alerting you to the intersection of the loop and the out-and-back section. Turn left (southeast) back onto the main stem of the Pea Ridge balloon to get back to the Habitrek Trail and the education center.

Nearby Attractions

If the weather is good, bring a picnic basket and ye olde fishing pole. Salato's small lake is well stocked, and fishing is free for kids under age 16, but it's BYOB—bring your own bait.

Hungry? Turn right (west) on US 60 upon leaving Salato and travel 20 miles to feast at **Claudia Sanders Dinner House** in Shelbyville (3202 Shelbyville Road; 502-633-5600). Colonel Harland Sanders's wife didn't miss a trick in learning how to make finger-lickin' chicken. Visit claudiasanders.com for menus and hours.

Directions

From Louisville, take I-64 East toward Frankfort about 42 miles. At Exit 48 (Lawrenceburg/Graefenburg), turn left (north) on KY 151. Drive 1.1 miles and turn right (east) on US 60. Drive 4.2 miles and turn left (north) onto Sportsman's Lane, formerly known as Game Farm Road (*Note:* many GPS units and online mapping services still use the old name). The education center and parking area are at the rear of the property.

EVIDENCE OF THE LUTTRELL FAMILY, WHO HOMESTEADED THIS AREA BEFORE THE CIVIL WAR

Indiana: North of Louisville and West of I-65

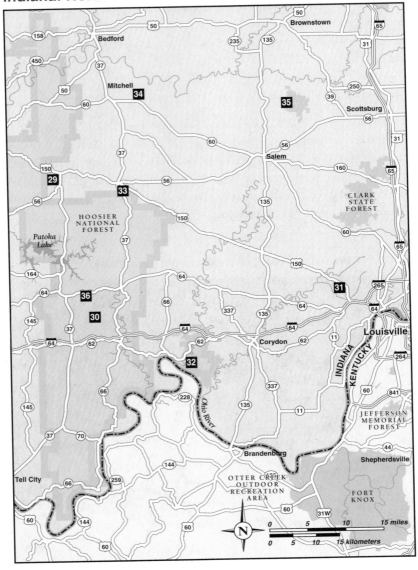

Indiana: North of Louisville and West of I-65

MOUNT ST. FRANCIS OFFERS HIKERS OPPORTUNITIES FOR BOTH SOLACE AND CONTEMPLATION. *(See Hike 31, page 178.)*

29

French Lick Loops

SCENERY: ★ ★ ★ ★
TRAIL CONDITION: ★ ★ ★ ★ ★
CHILDREN: ★ ★
DIFFICULTY: ★ ★ ★ ★
SOLITUDE: ★ ★ ★ ★

BEAR ENJOYS HIS OWN PERSONAL SPA ALONG THE TRAILS OF FRENCH LICK.

GPS TRAILHEAD COORDINATES: N38° 33.438' W86° 37.528'

DISTANCE & CONFIGURATION: 8.4-mile balloon loop, with less mileage easily available

HIKING TIME: 4 hours

HIGHLIGHTS: Ridgetop trail to creekside hiking

ELEVATION: 482' at trailhead, ascending to 873' at high point

ACCESS: Daily, sunrise–sunset; free admission

MAPS: Available at tinyurl.com/FrLickLoop and at the Valley Link Golf Shop

FACILITIES: Bathrooms and water at the parking lot

WHEELCHAIR ACCESS: None

COMMENTS: Dogs are permitted on leash.

CONTACTS: French Lick Resort, 888-936-9360; frenchlick.com

Overview

In addition to blackjack tables, swimming pools, an award-winning golf course, and an upscale spa . . . did you know that the French Lick Resort also has down-and-dirty hiking and mountain bike trails? It's probably a safe bet that many of you reading this book have never considered hiking French Lick, but this might change your mind. The proposed route combines Trails 2 and 3 to form a rugged 8.4-mile loop, with lesser mileage readily available.

Route Details

The original French Lick Springs Hotel was built in 1845 and catered to the wealthy elite seeking the medicinal sulfur springs found on the property. Since that time the resort has grown to a 3,000-acre complex, including two historic hotels, three golf courses, upscale restaurants offering culinary events, and a casino with more than 13,000 slot machines.

Gambling at the resort has an interesting history. By the 1920s French Lick had developed a reputation for illegal gambling. But developments in more recent years changed the roll of the dice for the resort. A gaming license that was originally intended for property at Patoka Lake was transferred to French Lick in 2006. At the time, Indiana law mandated only water-based gaming, so the original casino at French Lick was designed as a boat, surrounded by water (hence the well-earned nickname "boat in a moat"). But in 2008 the moat was filled in and French Lick Resort became the state's first land-based casino.

In an effort to expand its appeal to a wider audience, the French Lick Resort maintains three hiking trails: Trail 1 is 1.5 miles and leads to a small overlook of a golf course; Trail 2 is open to both hikers and mountain bikers and runs 5.1 miles in length; and Trail 3 is 3.8 miles. But there are two caveats to hiking loop trails 2 and 3. First, hikers must walk 0.4 mile (one-way) from the parking lot to the trailhead that serves both loops (0.8 mile round-trip). Second, you can only hike Trail 3 by hiking Trail 2 first. Consequently, the proposed route combines both loops 2 and 3 to keep you away from the risky roulette wheel and onto more solid ground.

All trails start behind the Valley Links Golf Shop, sandwiched between the northern side of the resort and the Valley Links Golf Course. Leaving from the parking lot, follow the paved road up the small hill to the golf shop and walk west past the crisply painted red-and-white sign for Trail 1. At 0.2 mile, make a sharp right-hand turn and head east on the gravel path that leads to a

French Lick Loops

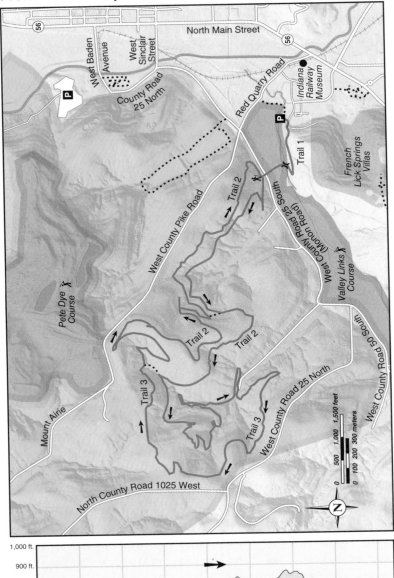

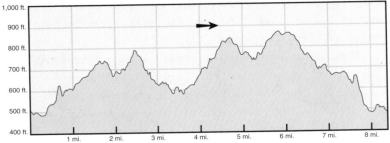

wooden bridge with a bright-red metal roof, taking you across the creek to the golf course. After crossing the bridge, continue walking straight on the gravel path that threads between two golf fairways. The gravel path ends at Monon Road. Carefully cross the pavement to find the large trailhead sign announcing the Buffalo Trace Trails. Yes, bison once roamed these grounds and congregated here for the salt licks, which were also valuable to early settlers.

One of the things you'll notice at the trailhead is a large map of the trail system and the start of trail mile markers. French Lick Resort does a good job maintaining these trails, and everything is very well signed. We'll start by hiking the first half of Trail 2 clockwise, hike the entire Trail 3 clockwise, and then return on the second half of Trail 2 (also clockwise). As you can see from the map, there are two different shortcut trails if at any point in time you want to ditch this hike and get to the craps table or soak in the spa.

From the trailhead, turn left (west) to begin walking Trail 2 clockwise. The mile markers are spaced every 0.25 mile and are numbered consecutively as you hike the loop clockwise. As you climb the hillside, you'll notice the scent of freshly crushed pine needles emanating from beneath your feet. Passing mile marker 1 indicates that you have come 0.25 mile from the trailhead. Between mile markers 4 and 5, the shortcut trail comes in on your right, essentially cutting Trail 2 in half.

Between mile markers 7 and 8, Trail 2 joins Trail 3. Stay left (bear west) here if you want to hike the entire 8.4 miles. The mile markers on Trail 3 run consecutively from 21 through 35. After more ridgetop hiking and mile marker 25, the trail dips into several pretty creek drainages where the wildflowers are best in the spring. After crossing the creek at mile marker 29, the trail climbs once again. There are no huge waterfalls here or stunning rock arches—just beautiful woodland scenery.

After completing the 3.8-mile Trail 3 loop, you will rejoin Trail 2 by bearing left (east) at the junction. You have about 3.0 miles of twisting and turning trail before arriving to the trailhead once again. Carefully cross Monon Road and make your way back to the golf shop and your vehicle.

Nearby Attractions

One mile north of French Lick Resort is the **West Baden Springs Hotel,** part of the same complex. The current West Baden Springs Hotel was built in 1902, which at the time had the longest free-spanning dome in the world. The 200-foot dome that sits atop the atrium is gorgeous and certainly worth seeing.

If one of the 243 luxury rooms at the West Baden Hotel is out of your price range, their website offers virtual tours of the atrium, lobby, and indoor pool. The 1.0-mile paved, multiuse Ferguson Trail runs between the French Lick Resort and the formal gardens just south of the West Baden Hotel. For more information, contact French Lick Resort, 888-936-9360; frenchlick.com.

For more casual fare, try the **Bagel Bistro** in West Baden, 812-936-9222, or **French Licks** (that's the name of it!) for your fill of ice cream, coffee, and artisan pizza. They are located at 469 South Maple Street, 812-936-3131.

If you're looking for something a little stronger, **French Lick Winery** has a tasting bar and offers retail sales. Visit them at 8145 West Sinclair Street, West Baden, 812-936-2293; frenchlickwinery.com.

Directions

From downtown Louisville, take I-64 West into Indiana. At Exit 79, turn right (north) toward French Lick. Follow IN 37 north 7 miles, then continue straight on IN 64 west 1.1 miles. Finally, follow IN 145 north for the last 16.2 miles. Continue straight into French Lick resort, then follow the curving road right and head to the Valley Links Golf Shop. Park in the lot just east of the shop, at the bottom of the hill.

DESPITE THE ABUNDANCE OF SPRINGS, THE TRAILS AT FRENCH LICK REMAIN DRY AND WELL MAINTAINED.

30 Hemlock Cliffs Nature Preserve

SCENERY: ★ ★ ★ ★ ★
TRAIL CONDITION: ★ ★ ★ ★
CHILDREN: ★ ★ ★
DIFFICULTY: ★ ★ ★
SOLITUDE: ★ ★

THE ROCK HOUSE AT HEMLOCK CLIFFS IS SIMPLY MAGNIFICENT.

GPS TRAILHEAD COORDINATES: N38° 16.642' W86° 32.346'

DISTANCE & CONFIGURATION: 1.5-mile loop

HIKING TIME: 1 hour

HIGHLIGHTS: Large rock houses, imposing cliffs, lush wildflower habitat

ELEVATION: 838' at trailhead, descending to 671' at low point

ACCESS: Anytime year-round; free admission

MAPS: Available online and at the trailhead using a QR code, which points to a georeferenced map

FACILITIES: None

WHEELCHAIR ACCESS: None

COMMENTS: Although kids love this trail, please hike with care, particularly along the cliff overhangs and rock houses. Dogs are permitted on leash.

CONTACTS: Hoosier National Forest, 866-302-4173 or 812-275-5987; tinyurl.com/HemCliffs

Hemlock Cliffs Nature Preserve

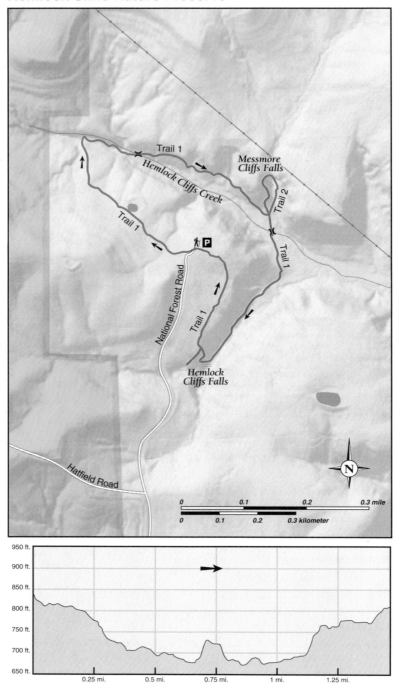

Overview

Hemlock Cliffs is one of the most spectacular natural areas in southern Indiana. The trail quickly takes you into a magical world of rock houses, filtered sunlight, verdant ferns, and running water. The most popular time to visit is spring, when the wildflowers generously litter the trail and cling to the cliffs. But the trail is equally stunning in the fall and winter, as it brings better views of the cliffs and rock houses. You can even find a place to park and solitude on the trail. Regardless, tread lightly—the ecosystem is as fragile as it is beautiful.

Route Details

One complaint you're likely to hear about Hemlock Cliffs is that there just isn't enough of it to go around. The short 1.5-mile loop trail is about one-third woodland wonder, one-third creekside oohing and aahing, and one-third jaw-dropping scenery as the path travels under cliffs and rock houses. You could spend 2 hours here and still want to hike the loop a second time.

Unfortunately, the natural beauty of Hemlock Cliffs draws large numbers of hikers from all over, and sometimes solitude is hard to find, particularly during spring weekends. But the area is equally beautiful during other seasons. The high cliffs shelter visitors from the hot summer sun, and multiple caves and springs push cool air into the small gorge. The fall offers an array of color from the beeches, maples, and hickories found here, while winter brings dripping ice formations that hang from the cliffs above.

The loop trail can be walked either clockwise or counterclockwise, and both directions have their advantages. Walking the trail clockwise provides a gradual immersion into the small gorge, while going the other direction gives you immediate access to the main waterfall.

To walk the trail clockwise, begin on the west side of the parking lot, opposite the kiosk. A number of small signs identify trees along the way: red, black, and white oak; pignut hickory; sassafras; red and sugar maple; blackgum; and more. The path travels northwest until it takes a gentle hairpin curve back to the right (southeast). The trail then runs roughly parallel to a broad but shallow seasonal creek and crosses a small footbridge. Be on the lookout for yellow ladyslippers amid the wide variety of ferns that thrive here.

Past the bridge, about 0.6 mile from the trailhead, the trail forks. Heading left (north) on the loop will lead you up a set of wooden stairs, past white-plumed false Solomon's seal, jack-in-the-pulpit, and wild stonecrop. The trail then takes you along a wide shelf that runs under a large rock house. If heights or drop-offs make you nervous, stop here, enjoy the view, and retrace your steps to the start of the loop. But if you're the adventurous type, continue on the trail—the views up here are wonderful.

The rock house is basically a work of art in action. The trickling water falling from the small creek gently carves various layers of sandstone and limestone, each eroding at different rates. Eventually, long after this book has turned to dust, the rock house will erode until a natural arch is formed, similar to the many natural arches found in eastern Kentucky. Enjoy your time up in the cool rock shelter, watching how the trees filter the light in different patterns and noticing how the weathering of the iron ore has honeycombed the rock. Carefully continue around the inner perimeter of the rock house and work your way down the rocks to finish the loop back to the main path.

Now back where the trail forked, bear left (south) to continue working your way creekside to the bottom of a small gorge lined with iron-stained cliffs on either side. Both false and true Solomon's seal grow here, along with star chickweed, crested iris, phacelia, white trillium, and alumroot. Wild ginger, the rare wintergreen, sweet woodruff, and a variety of ferns grow almost year-round. A few namesake hemlocks accent the forest canopy, and a sweet breeze always seems to be blowing through here as the cooler air falls, pushing the warmer air higher. An abandoned campsite lies on the other side of the creek, testimony to when rock climbers were permitted to scale and rappel from these cliffs. (Hemlock Cliffs is part of the Hoosier National Forest, and camping is permitted as long as sites are 300 feet from the nearest trail, water source, or rock house.)

After crossing a second footbridge 1.2 miles from the trailhead, the trail climbs another set of wooden steps. From this vantage point a large seasonal waterfall appears, falling from the cliffs above. Several rogue trails are evident where previous hikers have explored this and the adjacent creekbed and stone formations. While you may be tempted to leave the main trail, do so with caution—the fragile ecosystem balances on a delicate fulcrum between use and misuse. This place deserves reverence, and all visitors must stay on the trails as much as possible.

The main trail continues to climb the steep hillside, guiding hikers up a set of stone steps as the path threads between two large stone formations. At the top of this short climb, a small spur on your left takes you above the falls, while a right-hand (north) turn takes you to the parking lot.

Nearby Attractions

Collectively, Hemlock Cliffs, Saalman Hollow, Pott's Creek, and Oil Creek make up Shooting Star Cliffs, protected by The Nature Conservancy. If you're interested in visiting the adjacent 100-acre **Saalman Hollow Nature Preserve,** contact them at 317-951-8818 or visit tinyurl.com/saalman. Access is very limited, and you must obtain permission in advance.

Directions

From Louisville, take I-64 West across the Ohio River into southern Indiana. At Exit 86, turn right (north) on IN 237 toward English. Go 2.6 miles and turn left (west) on Union Chapel Road (County Road 8). Drive another 2.6 miles and bear right (west) on Hatfield Road (CR 8/CR 13). Drive about 1.6 miles until you see the U.S. Forest Service sign for Hemlock Cliffs. Stay straight on National Forest Road, which dead-ends into the parking lot. But be forewarned . . . respect the NO PARKING signs that grace both sides of the road, and don't be surprised if the parking lot is full.

NOT EVEN CINDERELLA COULD SQUEEZE INTO THIS DELICATE LADYSLIPPER.

Mount St. Francis Lake Trail

SCENERY: ★ ★ ★ ★ ★
TRAIL CONDITION: ★ ★ ★ ★ ★
CHILDREN: ★ ★ ★
DIFFICULTY: ★ ★
SOLITUDE: ★ ★ ★

JUST HOW INVITING CAN ONE BENCH GET?

GPS TRAILHEAD COORDINATES: N38° 20.122' W85° 54.102'

DISTANCE & CONFIGURATION: 2.0-mile balloon, with more mileage readily available

HIKING TIME: 1 hour

HIGHLIGHTS: Lakeside trail, wildflowers

ELEVATION: 890' at trailhead, descending to 820' at low point

ACCESS: Daily, sunrise–sunset

MAPS: Available online. A QR code pointing to the trail map is posted at the trailhead.

FACILITIES: Picnic shelter, restrooms

WHEELCHAIR ACCESS: None on trails. However, a 0.3-mile (one-way) paved trail leads from the trailhead to the lakes.

COMMENTS: Well-behaved dogs on leash are welcome.

CONTACTS: Mount St. Francis Sanctuary Center for Spirituality, 812-923-8817; mountsaintfrancis.org

Overview

Mount St. Francis Sanctuary, just 20 minutes northwest of downtown Louisville, is the perfect place for an after-work stroll or a weekend hike with the family. Next to the Mount St. Francis Retreat Center, the sanctuary and its several miles of wooded paths are open to the public. Teeming with wildflowers in spring and rich with fall colors in autumn, the lake trail is an easy 2.0 miles. Longer trails are available for those wanting a deeper spiritual experience and a more rigorous retreat from the trials and tribulations of everyday life.

Route Details

In the late 19th century, 400 acres of woods, fields, and lakes were kindly donated by Mary and Joseph Anderson to the Conventual Franciscan Friars. The Franciscans established a residence here and later a high school seminary for those with the passion to join the order. The seminary was named for St. Francis of Assisi, patron saint of animals and the environment and founder of the Franciscan Order of Catholic friars.

The Mount St. Francis Sanctuary, a religious nonprofit entity, was established more than 100 years after the Andersons' bequest, with the goal of preserving 375 acres of the property and, according to the sanctuary's literature, "to provide a welcoming space for a variety of people to walk, pray, play and enjoy creation." The rest of the property remains under the auspices of the Franciscan brothers, including a chapel, retreat center, friary, youth center, and the Mary Anderson Center for the Arts. In general, the trails are very well marked with such good signage, hikers don't need divine providence to find their way around.

To hike the Mount St. Francis Lake Trail, begin at the small parking lot on your left shortly after you enter the sanctuary. The trail to the lake leaves just west of the small lot and initially follows a paved walk (Trail 1 or Peggy's Path on the sanctuary map) down through the woods. In a little more than 0.1 mile, the path arrives at a small woodland garden where an inviting wooden bench offers hikers a spot of peace and tranquility. The garden is chock-full of native species found throughout Mount St. Francis, including Virginia bluebells, wild blue phloxes, cinnamon and maidenhair ferns, celandine poppies, and large merrybells.

Continue hiking another 0.2 mile on the paved walkway to reach the lakeshore and a small wooden bridge. To walk the trail clockwise, turn left (east)

Mount St. Francis Lake Trail

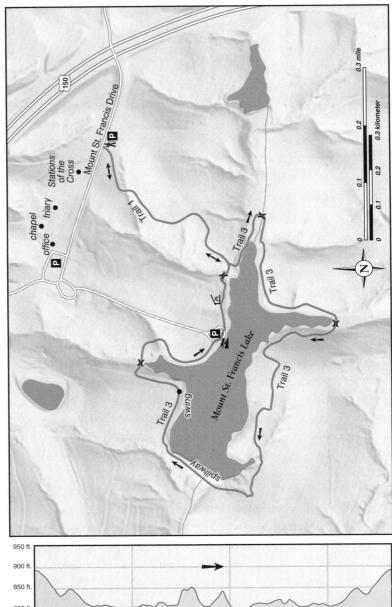

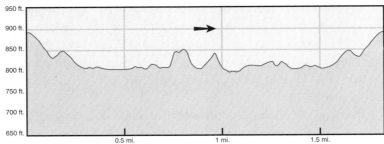

here and follow the edge of the lake (you're now following Trail 3 on your sanctuary map). Bluets love the sun exposure here, their dainty pale-blue flowers can be found clustered along the path. Also be on the lookout for recent beaver activity, as evidenced by gnawed stumps and branches on either side of the trail. Bluegills and striped bass are easily seen in the shallows, among the cattails and other grasses bordering the lake. Throughout the summer, jewelweed, or touch-me-not, grows thickly in the marshy headwaters.

After a few minutes (about 0.1 mile) of walking you'll cross a second bridge. Don't be too intrigued by the path (marked TRAIL 2) that leads uphill to your left, as it just circles back around. Stay on the trail to your right (west) as it hugs the shoreline. Here, spring hikers will be greeted with yellow trout lilies, cheerful white star chickweed, crested irises, Solomon's seal, and more bluets. There's something about hiking Mount St. Francis in the spring, particularly around Easter, that ensnares even the most diehard agnostic.

A third wooden bridge lies just around the corner, about 0.65 mile from the trailhead. Red-eared sliders, the ubiquitous tortoise found in local ponds and streams, frequently sun themselves here, while bullfrogs scramble for the murky bottom. Plop-plop. Take a seat on the bench and contemplate.

At 0.9 miles, a small trail on your right (north of the trail) leads to the slightly hidden St. Kateri's Shrine, quietly overlooking the lake. St. Kateri, also known as Lily of the Mohawks, was an Alonquin laywoman who lived along the New York–Canadian border in the late 17th century. She was canonized by Pope Benedict XVI in 2012 and is known as the patron saint of environment and ecology.

Continue right (north, then west) on the trail, hugging the lake's southern shoreline. Keep an eye out for the yellowish-brown stubs of squawroot, a parasite that attaches to the roots of oak trees. Across the opposite shore you'll see a colorful variety of small fishing boats and canoes, reserved for members of the Mount St. Francis Fishing Club and resident friars. The roof of the small picnic shelter is also visible.

At the far western edge of the lake, the trail crosses a grass-covered spillway before heading north and east to complete the lake loop. The field to your left (north) is often dotted with bright-yellow wild mustard, a beautiful, albeit invasive weed found across Indiana and Kentucky. And how can you pass up that swinging bench?

The trail encircles one last finger of the lake. At 1.3 miles the route ducks back into the woods and passes the hermitage cabin. Silence is golden here, so please respect the signs and tread softly as you pass the prayer retreat at the water's edge. The path then follows the periphery of one more mustard-studded field, home to a multitude of redwing blackbirds. Two small docks extend into the lake. Be mindful of the sign proclaiming NO SWIMMING EXCEPT WITH A FRANCISCAN FRIAR. No kidding. That's what it says.

Walk beyond the picnic shelter and the sculpture climbing the tree at the water's edge. Cross one last bridge before turning left (north) and walking back up the paved trail to the parking lot. Stop by the woodland garden and see how many native wildflowers you can recognize. And try to remember how many others you saw on the trail that aren't growing here.

At the top of the hill, you should see your vehicle. If you have time, look for the small sign across the road from the parking lot, leading walkers to two short loops that encircle the Stations of the Cross and a small sculpture garden. Nod to St. Francis, enshrined in his stone grotto; pause at the sight of the reclining figure at the edge of the gurgling spring; and thank an industrious Eagle Scout for his contribution to the world of the sacred.

Nearby Attractions

If you're up for a longer hike, Mount St. Francis has seven other trails to choose from. Most of them can be accessed from the lake area, but a more efficient way is to park on the opposite side of the retreat center. To reach this alternate trailhead, continue on the entrance road you came in on, driving past the chapel and the youth center to the far northwestern edge of the sanctuary, by the team-building course. Park in the large lot under the water tower that overlooks the open field. A small gravel road leads to Trails 8 and 9, marked with a sign and a box that holds more brochures and maps. Weaving together portions of various trails, hikers can create a scenic 2.4-mile woodland loop.

Hiking west on Trail 8 will take you through open woods and across two small creek drainages. A hard left at the next intersection will take you onto Trail 10 and St. Anne's Shrine, as you travel southeast along a larger creek drainage, a tributary of Little Indian Creek. This portion of the trail will reward spring hikers with prairie trillium, crested iris, bicolored dwarf larkspur, and wild blue phlox. The ever-watchful eye might even spot the elusive jack-in-the-pulpit camouflaged among last year's maple and oak leaves. The woods are equally beautiful in the autumn, with the golden poplar leaves mingling with the reds and oranges of the maples and the yellow beech trees.

At the next intersection, stay east on Trail 6 until it dances along the edge of yet another mustard-punctuated open field. There is a small maze of trails here, but it's difficult to get lost and the best wildflowers can be found along the creek. Finally, bear east again on Trail 9 and hike the last few hundred yards before returning to your vehicle.

Directions

From Louisville, take I-64 West across the Ohio River into southern Indiana. After 4.0 miles, take Exit 119 (Greenville/Paoli) and turn right (north) on US 150 West. At the third stoplight (about 2.5 miles from the interstate), turn left (west) onto St. Anthony Drive and Mount St. Francis (Paoli Pike runs east.). At the top of the hill, park in the small lot on your right. However, if this lot is full, there is more parking past the chapel, near the water tower.

ON YOUR MARK, GET SET, *SLIDE!*

32 O'Bannon Woods State Park:
Cliff Dweller Trail

SCENERY: ★ ★ ★ ★
TRAIL CONDITION: ★ ★ ★ ★ ★
CHILDREN: ★ ★ ★
DIFFICULTY: ★ ★
SOLITUDE: ★ ★ ★

LLOYD'S CABIN IS AVAILABLE AS A RESPITE FOR DAY HIKERS OR FOR THOSE BACKPACKING THROUGH ON THE ADVENTURE HIKING TRAIL.

GPS TRAILHEAD COORDINATES: N38° 10.614' W86° 18.028'

DISTANCE & CONFIGURATION: 3.0-mile balloon, with more mileage readily available

HIKING TIME: 1.5 hours

HIGHLIGHTS: Beautiful creek drainages, wildflowers, Lloyd's Cabin

ELEVATION: 500' at trailhead, ascending to 820' at high point

ACCESS: Daily, sunrise–sunset. Entrance fee: $7/vehicle for Indiana residents, $9/vehicle out-of-state. Annual permits also available.

MAPS: O'Bannon Woods State Park, USGS *Leavenworth*

FACILITIES: Campgrounds, nature center, picnic tables, grills, shelters, equestrian trails, and swimming pool

WHEELCHAIR ACCESS: Not on this trail, but there is a universal access trail on the park property.

COMMENTS: O'Bannon is popular on weekends during late spring and early fall, and all week long during the summer. Timing is everything if you're looking for a secluded outdoor experience. Dogs are permitted on leash.

CONTACTS: O'Bannon Woods State Park, 812-738-8232; tinyurl.com/obannonsp

Overview

O'Bannon Woods State Park is a rustic version of an all-inclusive resort, without the tiki huts dotting the shoreline or the umbrellas in your drinks. Hiking, camping, swimming, fishing, historical sites, nature center—all are securely nestled in the crook of the Blue River where it empties into the Ohio. What more could you want? Bring the kids. Bring the tent. Bring some adventure to your life—O'Bannon Woods is only 45 minutes away from downtown Louisville. The route described below uses the Cliff Dweller Trail and a portion of the Adventure Hiking Trail to create a 3.0-mile hike.

Route Details

Formerly known as the Wyandotte Woods State Recreation Area, the 2,000-acre O'Bannon Woods State Park is surrounded by the 26,000-acre Harrison-Crawford State Forest. The park was developed in the early 1930s by the Civilian Conservation Corps (CCC), which built many of its roads, stone shelters, and picnic areas. Bordered by the Blue River on the west, Potato Run on the east, and the Ohio River on the south, O'Bannon is characterized by a rugged terrain crisscrossed with hiking and equestrian trails.

In addition to hiking, O'Bannon Woods State Park offers four different campgrounds (two catering specifically to the horse crowd); a swimming pool (with a set of crazy spiral slides); and terrific views of the lazy, rolling Ohio. A fire tower stands guard at the park entrance, and those willing to brave the stairs will be rewarded with commanding views of the countryside.

The **Hickory Hollow Interpretive Center** at O'Bannon Woods is filled with the totally cool exhibits that kids love. Several large display boxes hold beautiful feather, moth, and butterfly collections. Numerous small mammals and large animal heads are mounted and hung on the walls. Live displays include a large snapping turtle, looking menacing in his aquarium, and a rough green snake whose fluorescent hue beats Kermit the Frog's hands down. On rainy days, the one-way bird window and the table with activities and crafts will easily entertain your crew.

Just out the back door of the nature center is a re-created mid-19th-century farmstead, complete with a restored 1850s hay press and barn. On holiday weekends during the summer, the park offers living-history events, with participants in era-appropriate clothing, wooden toys for the kids to play with,

O'Bannon Woods State Park: Cliff Dweller Trail

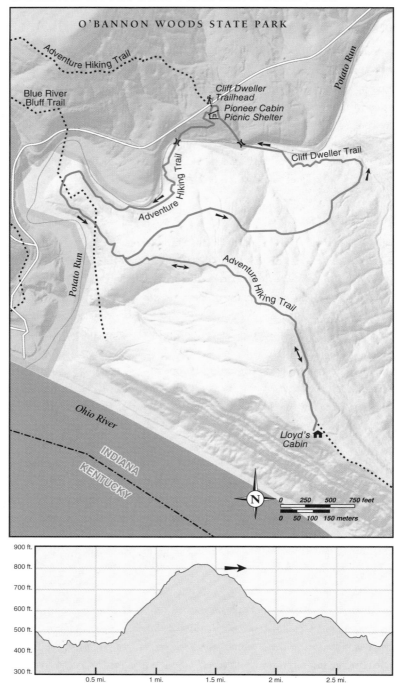

weaving demonstrations, and the like. A 1-mile gravel section of a universal-access trail runs past the homestead.

Cliff Dweller is one of ten hiking trails in the park. At less than 2 miles, it's also the longest trail in O'Bannon Woods that does not permit horses, leaving several other hiking opportunities for the younger ones and for those with less stamina. Conversely, there are several other hiking opportunities nearby for those wanting more mileage.

The Cliff Dweller trail leaves from the scenic Pioneer Cabin picnic shelter and the remains of a homestead built by Louisa and Lewis Langdon in the 1830s. From the small roadside parking lot, the trailhead begins just to the right (south) side of the grassy area, next to the large brown trail sign for the Adventure Hiking Trail, Lloyd's Cabin, and the Cliff Dweller Trail. At the start of the hike, you will see blazes of various colors for multiple trails, which some of you might recognize as the flag of Ireland, the vertical tricolor of green, white, and orange.

The orange-blazed Cliff Dweller Trail gently descends into the Potato Run creek drainage, which is chock-full of wildflowers in the spring, including cutleaf toothwort, yellow trout lilies, rue anemones, and several kinds of violets. The trail soon crosses Potato Run, which may require some rock-hopping after heavy rains but turns fairly dry by midsummer. Here, Indians collected bluish-gray chert, or flint, which they used to make tools and weapons such as spear points, arrowheads, and knives.

The trail continues along the creek for the first 0.5 mile or so, and then Ts 0.75 mile from the trailhead. Bear right (southeast) at the T to diverge from the Cliff Dweller Trail in order to follow the Adventure Hiking Trail (AHT), which is blazed in green and white.

The AHT begins a strong ascent through hardwood forest and then runs through a nice thicket of spicebush before topping out at Lloyd's Cabin, a total of 1.4 miles from the trailhead. The park system is in the process of building some new horse trails on top of this ridge, so be sure to stay on the green-and-white blazed AHT.

Lloyd's Cabin, complete with outdoor fire pit, picnic tables, and hiker's log makes for the perfect lunch spot. The cabin was rebuilt by Lloyd's grandsons in remembrance of him after his death in 2010. The shelter can also be used by thru-hikers as they pass along on the 26-mile AHT. Chances are the place will be vacant, allowing you to slip off that pack, roast a few hot dogs or nestle foil-wrapped sweet potatoes in newly created coals. A spring-fed pool near the cabin will provide enough water to be sure the fire is safely extinguished. If the day is too warm for a fire, just linger as long as you can.

Once you leave the cabin, retrace your steps on the AHT and hike northwest back to where the AHT joins back up with the Cliff Dweller Trail. Bear right (east) at this intersection to continue following the loop counterclockwise. The trail descends back into the Potato Run drainage, and, if the creek is running, to a small cascading waterfall. In another 0.2 mile, the trail takes a sharp right (north) turn to cross the creek once again. Head back up the hill to the Pioneer Picnic Shelter.

Nearby Attractions

O'Bannon Woods offers plenty of hiking trails, including the **Rocky Ridge Trail** (2.0 miles), the **Sharp Spring Trail** (1.0 mile), and the **Tulip Valley Trail** (2.0 miles). A more rugged option is the **Ohio River Bluff Trail,** a 1.5-mile hike along the river at the far southern end of the park. This loop can be accessed at several points, including Shelter House 2, which sits atop a rocky bluff overlooking the Ohio, or the Sassafras Shelter, which sits just above the river in a beautiful grove of trees.

The most demanding hike in the park is the rugged 25.5-mile **Adventure Hiking Trail**, which runs through both O'Bannon and the Harrison-Crawford State Forest. However, this is a linear trail and must be hiked as an out-and-back or with a shuttle set up. Overnight backpackers must register with either the Harrison-Crawford or O'Bannon Woods park office. Five overnight shelters sit along the trail, and primitive camping is permitted.

If all that hiking has left you famished, head for the **Overlook Restaurant** in Leavenworth, just 10 miles from O'Bannon Woods. (1153 West State Road 62, 812-739-4264; theoverlook.com). Perched on a spectacular bluff overlooking the Ohio River, the restaurant serves up fine Southern fare. Both the scenery and the deep fryer go nonstop. There's no need to ask for a window seat—the artful arrangement of the three indoor dining rooms, along with an outdoor deck, guarantees that every diner has a gorgeous 180-degree view of the mighty Ohio.

Save room for dessert—the homemade treats range from coconut cream pie to Death by Chocolate and hummingbird cake. (Supposedly, it takes 150 male hummingbirds to equal a pound; fortunately, no avifauna are harmed in the making of this delectable confection.) The local brews and signature cocktails might make those two bed-and-breakfasts you passed look even more inviting.

Directions

From Louisville, take I-64 West across the Ohio River into southern Indiana. At Exit 105 (Corydon), turn left (south) on IN 135 and drive 1.8 miles. Turn right (west) on Ohio River Scenic Byway (IN 62) and drive 7.0 miles. Turn left (east) on IN 462, which becomes Old Forest Road. The park office is another 2.9 miles ahead, at the park boundary.

O'BANNON WOODS STATE PARK OFFERS GORGEOUS VIEWS OF THE OHIO RIVER.

Pioneer Mothers Memorial Forest

SCENERY: ★ ★ ★ ★
TRAIL CONDITION: ★ ★ ★ ★ ★
CHILDREN: ★ ★ ★
DIFFICULTY: ★ ★
SOLITUDE: ★ ★ ★

THIS STONE SIGN IS BUT A MERE TODDLER COMPARED WITH MANY OF THE TREES FOUND HERE.

GPS TRAILHEAD COORDINATES: N38° 32.064' W86° 27.484'

DISTANCE & CONFIGURATION: 2.6-mile out-and-back

HIKING TIME: 1 hour

HIGHLIGHTS: Old-growth forest

ELEVATION: 827' at trailhead, descending to 587' at low point

ACCESS: Anytime year-round; free admission

MAPS: Available for download (free) at tinyurl.com/PioneerMothers

FACILITIES: None

WHEELCHAIR ACCESS: None, although from the northern trailhead off state route 150, the trail is a 0.5-mile abandoned paved road.

COMMENTS: The trail can be reached from US 150 as well as IN 37. Dogs are permitted on leash.

CONTACTS: Hoosier National Forest, 812-547-7051; fs.usda.gov/hoosier

Overview

What a great place to make you feel young again! Pioneer Mothers Memorial Forest is 88 acres of old-growth woods just outside Paoli, Indiana. The ancient trees stand in silent testimony to the centuries they have survived on this earth. Their stubby arms and towering canopies prove that old lives have a grace all their own. In 1974, the area was made a National Registered Landmark, and recent excavations discovered a 14th-century Native American village site.

Route Details

What gift of nature should we leave our children? Many would argue that we must leave nature just as we found it. But others maintain that a growing population—and its attendant demand for goods and services—calls for the consumption of at least some natural resources.

One compromise is to set aside parcels of land to protect an entire eco-system. And that's exactly what the Cox family did. The land here is pretty much the way Joseph Cox found it when he first purchased the property in 1816. He set aside 88 acres (of a larger 258-acre tract) to preserve as old-growth forest. What an amazing vision he had!

The land eventually passed to his grandson, also named Joseph Cox, and upon his death in 1940 the property was sold for $23,000 to the Wood-Mosaic Company of Louisville. After the sale was advertised in the local paper, the community launched a massive fundraising effort and, together with the U.S. Forest Service, bought the land back from the lumber company at the same purchase price. Donations from the community mandated that no trees ever be cut from the parcel and, in acknowledgment of a $5,900 donation from the Indiana Pioneer Mothers Club, that a rock-wall memorial be built.

So what's the difference between old-growth and virgin forest? Theoretically, a virgin forest has never been exploited by humankind: no mining, no timbering, no agrarian use. Obviously, the number of forests on Earth today that would qualify as virgin are few and far between.

Alternatively, an old-growth forest is just that—old. The trees and accompanying ecosystem have been left undisturbed for sufficient time that the forest has returned to its native, or virginal state, leading to a high level of biodiversity and a full range of growth and decline. That's exactly what you'll find at Pioneer Mothers. Young trees. Old trees. New growth. And decay.

Pioneer Mothers Memorial Forest

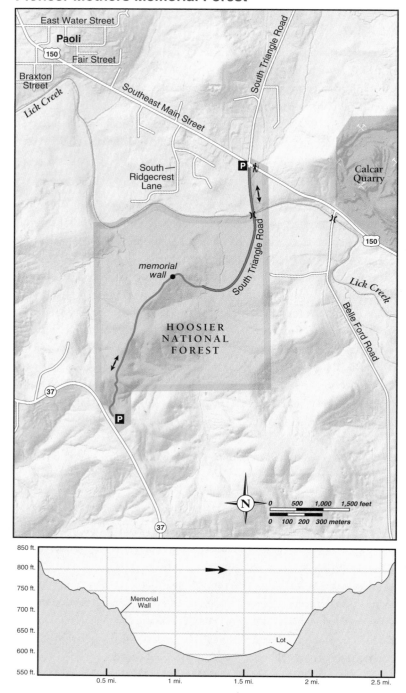

So how do you tell the age of a tree? Of course, cutting it down and counting its rings is one approach, albeit deadly for the patient at hand. We could also drill into the base of the trunk, remove a core sample, and use sophisticated DNA sampling to provide a best estimate. But that also creates a pathway for insects and disease.

Then again, we could sit quietly and observe the differences between big trees and little trees. An old tree that has stood the test of time truly does stand as evidence of endurance. These trees have withstood heavy winds, scathing fires, ice storms, and other natural maladies. Their trunks reach for the light as their arms have been lost to survival. Branches become stubs, and knots form where wounds are suffered. Root flare, where the trunk emerges from the earth, is another indicator of age in the woodland.

When entering Pioneer Mothers Memorial Forest, don't expect to see the aged giants of the redwood forest or the twisted trunks of 400-year-old bonsai. The differences between the young and old trees are much more subtle here, as girth is not the only litmus test for determining age.

The trail begins at the northern trailhead parking lot, not far from a busy state highway. Of course, when some of these trees first sprouted, the road was but a set of wagon-wheel tracks or an animal trail at most. Hike south on the abandoned paved road that goes over scenic Lick Creek. The paved road is slowly succumbing to mother nature and makes for a wonderful walking surface. Hike 0.5 mile until you reach an unused parking lot, then head straight across the lot to pick up the hiking trail on the other side. A short 0.2 mile up this dirt path leads you to the well-built rock wall engraved with INDIANA PIONEER MOTHERS' MEMORIAL. Does that refer to the women who first settled these lands? Or to the early trees whose seeds and young sprouts have populated these forests?

Beyond the wall, the dirt trail continues another 0.5 mile. The path ascends a gentle hillside, blocking out much of the vehicle noise as it follows a narrow ridge. Black walnut, yellow poplar, white oak, hickory, and ash thrive amid the blooms of dwarf larkspur, bloodroot, and wood poppy. Though spring is beautiful here, winter hiking is perhaps more impressive, as the trees' stark silhouettes transform these behemoths into modern-art sculptures.

Continue hiking until you reach the southern trailhead off IN 37. You'll probably want to turn around here and slowly stroll the 1.3 miles back to your vehicle.

Nearby Attractions

If you're looking for a longer hike in the region, try a section of the 12.7-mile **Youngs Creek Trail.** Also part of Hoosier National Forest, it's just a few miles south of Pioneer Mothers. Although the trail is open to horseback riders and mountain bikers, it's in very good condition thanks to ongoing maintenance. The area is beautiful and only occasionally used. Much of the surface is graveled, adding a delicate crunch to your hiking step.

Several parking areas and trailheads are available, and maps can be downloaded from the website in "Contacts" (page 190). Perhaps the prettiest section of Youngs Creek lies off IN 37 and County Road 550 South. From Pioneer Mothers, turn left (south) on IN 37 and drive 5.0 miles. Turn right (west) on CR 550 South and drive 1.3 miles to the intersection with Burma Road (CR 450/CR 525 South). Limited parking is available on the left (south) side of CR 550.

The 3.6-mile balloon trail starts at the end of the parking lane and travels along a seasonal creekbed flush with color in the fall and wildflowers in the spring. Hike 0.5 mile until you come to a T, where the balloon starts. Turn right (south) to walk the loop counterclockwise. In 0.3 mile, the trail Ts again. Bear left (southeast) and hike 2.4 miles. This section of the trail will take you up a small drainage and back down again.

At the next trail intersection, bear left (south) again; another 0.4 mile of hiking brings you back to the start of the loop. Turn right (north) here to backtrack the final 0.5 mile to your vehicle.

Directions

From Louisville, take I-64 West across the Ohio River into southern Indiana. At Exit 119 (Greenville/Paoli), turn right (north) on US 150 West and drive 36.0 miles. Just southeast of Paoli, South Triangle Road (50 E) and Christ the King Catholic Church will be on your right. At this junction, turn left (south) into the small parking area or the northern trailhead. The brown sign with white lettering, mysteriously marked with 2 3 2 4 0 0 0, signifies you're in the right place. The southern trailhead parking lot is 2.0 miles south of downtown Paoli, just off IN 37. The parking area for Pioneer Mothers Memorial Forest will be on your left (east of the highway).

34 Spring Mill State Park Loop

THESE STEPS LEAD TO TWIN CAVES, WHICH SHOWCASES THE WONDERFUL KARST TOPOGRAPHY OF THE REGION.

SCENERY: ★ ★ ★ ★
TRAIL CONDITION: ★ ★ ★ ★ ★
CHILDREN: ★ ★ ★
DIFFICULTY: ★ ★
SOLITUDE: ★ ★ ★

GPS TRAILHEAD COORDINATES: N38° 44.044' W86° 24.849'

DISTANCE & CONFIGURATION: A 2.5-mile balloon on a very short string (5.5 miles with optional side trip)

HIKING TIME: 1.5 hours

HIGHLIGHTS: Several creeks appear from and disappear into caves as the trail traverses an old-growth forest. Side trip includes nature center and pioneer village.

ELEVATION: 652' at trailhead, ascending to 735' at high point

ACCESS: Trails open daily, sunrise–sunset. Entrance fee: $7/vehicle for Indiana residents, $9/vehicle out-of-state. Annual permits also available.

MAPS: Available at the website below and the park entrance gate; USGS *Mitchell*

FACILITIES: Campground, historic inn, swimming pool, and picnic shelters

WHEELCHAIR ACCESS: None on the trail

COMMENTS: Timing is everything! This place can be packed on holiday weekends and anytime during the summer. But during the off-season, you may have the trail to yourself. Dogs are permitted on leash.

CONTACTS: Spring Mill State Park, 812-849-3534; tinyurl.com/Spring-MillSP

Overview

This park hits on all cylinders. Hiking without getting your boots muddy. Creeks disappearing underground and popping out of caves. Wildflowers. Hot showers. Kids having a blast. With the possible exception of gastronomic delights,

Spring Mill State Park Loop

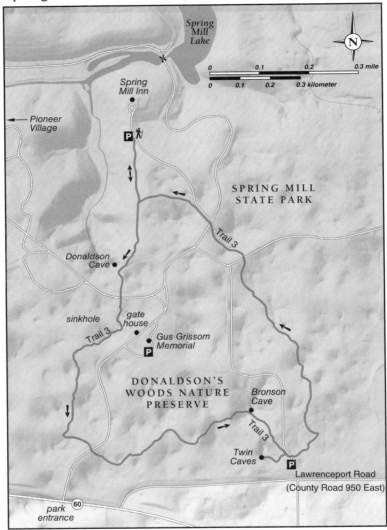

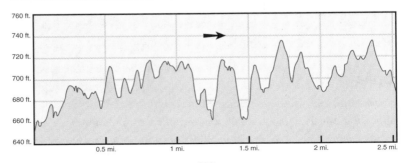

if Spring Mill State Park doesn't have it, you may not need it. But best of all, Spring Mill State Park has a beautiful 2.5-mile loop trail that traverses Donaldson's Woods Nature Preserve and passes through a stand of old-growth forest. The heavily wooded path winds its way past both Bronson and Twin Caves before returning to the beautiful Spring Mill Inn.

Route Details

If you've never been to Spring Mill State Park, it's worth spending a little time getting to know your surroundings. The park sits upon the Mitchell Plateau, and parts of Spring Mill have more than 100 sinkholes per square mile as a result of the karst geography of the region. The constant flow of groundwater was essential in creating an early-1800s industrial village that at one time housed more than 300 people. These pioneer-age titans of local industry used the power of the water to operate several gristmills, a wool mill, a sawmill, and even a distillery.

By the early 1920s, however, the pioneer village was in a state of considerable disrepair. In the early 1930s, the Civilian Conservation Corps jumped in and began renovating the historical log structures, building exquisite stone walls and erecting quaint picnic shelters throughout the park. The restored Pioneer Village consists of 20 log buildings, most of which are original to the park. The village (admission is free with your park-admittance fee) is open daily, March–mid-October, 9 a.m.–5 p.m. The three-story limestone gristmill still grinds corn on occasion; park employees, dressed in period clothing, work at the apothecary, loom house, and other shops in the village.

Spring Mill State Park is home to three nature preserves: Donaldson's Woods, Donaldson Cave, and Mitchell Sinkhole Plain. Although the forest is listed on park brochures as virgin timber, the Indiana Department of Natural Resources notes that the 145-acre Donaldson's Woods is one of only a few "undisturbed" old-growth forests remaining in Indiana, including centuries-old white oaks and massive tulip poplars. Virgin versus undisturbed . . . either way, it's older than you and me put together, and undeniably more stunning to look at.

The main route through Donaldson's Woods Nature Preserve is listed as Trail 3 on state park maps. The trail both begins and ends at the eastern edge of the parking garage adjacent to the Spring Mill Inn. Hikers can access Trail 3 at other points, but parking is easy here and the old inn is fun to explore.

The trail itself is a path of finely crushed gravel 4–5 feet wide, covered with leaves in the fall and winter. With the exception of a few short sets of stairs and a couple of brief climbs, the trail is relatively flat, following a gently rolling terrain. With all the points of interest along the trail, it's perfect for young kids or anyone with a short attention span.

From the trailhead, the trail splits almost immediately. Be sure to read the trail signs carefully. Continue straight (south) to walk the loop counterclockwise and to follow the signage in the most logical order.

The trail quickly rewards spring hikers with a nice display of shooting stars, bloodroot, wild ginger, and trillium before reaching the Donaldson Cave overlook. Although you can't see the cave from here, you can't miss the sound of falling water. Unfortunately, the cave is closed indefinitely because of white-nose syndrome, a fungal disease that has endangered the local bat population.

Go left at the next intersection, toward Bronson and Twin Caves. About 0.3 mile into the hike, the trail crosses the park road close to the entrance gate. A large sinkhole will be on your right. If any little ones are joining you on this trip, it's an excellent time to start that conversation on karst geology, explaining that persistent (typically acidic) water flows begin to eat away at the carbonate (typically limestone) rock below, leaving a depression or sinkhole in the ground. Once you see one sinkhole, it's easy to recognize the hundreds of other sink-holes that pockmark the face of Spring Mill.

In another 0.5 mile, the trail crosses the main park road. Traffic is usually sparse here, but proceed with caution. You don't want to look like the squirrels that were unsuccessful in crossing busy streets.

Bronson Cave is the next point of interest, about 1.2 miles from the trailhead. Here, one of the many creeks in the park mysteriously appears from nowhere, only to disappear into the adjacent cave. Have a seat on one of the benches or read more about the Mitchell Plateau. You really needn't be in a hurry.

From early spring until midsummer, the woods here are generously stud-ded with mayapple, also known as Adam's apple, mandrake, raccoon berry, wild lemon, Indian apple, duck's foot, and umbrella plant. (Who thinks up all these names?) While the fruit of the mayapple is edible in small amounts, the leaves and roots are poisonous. Native American lore sadly tells of Cherokee consum-ing the plant as they marched along the Trail of Tears—unable to face a forced relocation, they chose another fate.

Just past Bronson Cave, the trail makes a sharp but brief ascent to the small parking lot where the Twin Caves boat tours operate. Immediately to your right is a beautiful circa-1920s stone arch and a set of stairs leading to the caves. During the off-season or off-hours, feel free to descend the steps to explore the area. In the summer, the park service offers tours from this location. Customers are loaded into small flat-bottom boats at the mouth of Twin Caves. Park employees then guide the boats upstream into the cave using their gloved hands to press on the roof of the rock. It's about a 20-minute ride into the cave and out again.

The trail picks up again on the opposite side of the parking lot between the handicap parking signs. Be sure to stop and read the informative marker for George Donaldson, the Scotsman who bought this land and then prohibited logging on 181 acres of it in 1865. The next 0.5 mile showcases some of the oldest and most impressive trees in the park. In the fall this section of the trail is magnificent, with the pale golden poplars towering over the smaller red- and orange-leafed sugar maples and yellow pawpaw trees. Two more road crossings and you're back to the start of the loop. Turn right (north) at the Y, and you're back to the parking garage and the Spring Mill Inn.

Nearby Attractions

A longer 5.5-mile hike combines **Trails 3, 4, and 5** on the Spring Mill State Park map. Each of these trails is a loop that begins and ends very close to the Spring Mill Inn. Start at the parking garage, just south of the inn, as described at the beginning of the hike profile. Walk south on Trail 3, bearing right (west) at the first Y in the trail. Just past the Donaldson Cave Overlook, bear right (west) on a short spur of Trail 3 that will connect you with Trail 4.

The Trail 4 loop can be hiked in either direction to take you past several points of interest. The trail circles past the Hamer Pioneer Cemetery and Hamer Cave and skirts the southern edge of the Pioneer Village before bringing you back to Trail 3 once again.

Bear right (south) on Trail 3 and complete the loop as described above, taking you past Bronson Cave and Twin Caves, and through Donaldson's Woods. Once you've completed the Trail 3 loop, walk to the north side of the inn and pick up Trail 1, a short spur that will link you with Trail 5, which loops around the lake and nature center before bringing you back to the inn and parking structure.

Directions

From Louisville, take I-65 North across the Ohio River into southern Indiana. At Exit 19 (Henryville), turn left (west) on IN 160 W toward Salem and drive 39 miles. Turn right (north) into Spring Mill State Park.

35 Spurgeon Hollow North Loop

SPURGEON HOLLOW LAKE AS SEEN FROM THE KNOBSTONE TRAIL.

SCENERY: ★★★★★
TRAIL CONDITION: ★★★★★
CHILDREN: ★
DIFFICULTY: ★★★★
SOLITUDE: ★★★★★

GPS TRAILHEAD COORDINATES: N38° 42.785' W86° 2.631'

DISTANCE & CONFIGURATION: 8.2-mile loop, with more mileage readily available

HIKING TIME: 4 hours

HIGHLIGHTS: Deep woodland and ridgetop trail, scenic creek crossings, lake views

ELEVATION: 562' at trailhead, ascending to 877' at high point

ACCESS: No official hours, but day hikers should be off the trail by sunset.

MAPS: Available online at knobstonehikingtrail.org and tinyurl.com/KnobNorth

FACILITIES: None

WHEELCHAIR ACCESS: None

COMMENTS: Check in.gov/dnr/fish-and-wildlife for current hunting-season dates. Dogs are permitted on leash or under control.

CONTACTS: Knobstone Hiking Trail Association; knobstonehikingtrail.org

Overview

If you've ever wanted to hike part of the 58-mile backcountry Knobstone Trail, Spurgeon Hollow is an excellent choice. Two conjoined loops form the northern terminus of the Knobstone—the Delaney Parkland Spurgeon Hollow trails. Leaving from the Spurgeon Hollow Trailhead, hikers have three basic choices: the northern loop (8.2 miles), the southern loop (8.6 miles), or the outer parts of both loops (12.0 miles).

The described route combines portions of both Spurgeon Hollow and Delaney Park Trails to follow the aforementioned northern loop. The route offers relatively flat ridgetop and creekside hiking, with intermittent steep climbs and descents. While the trails are well marked and easy to follow, this hike may not be a good choice for the faint-of-heart.

Route Details

The Knobstone Trail follows much of the Knobstone Escarpment northwest from Deam Lake to Delaney Park. Considered a linear trail, the Knobstone is frequently used for multiday backpacking trips and as a training ground for those wanting to do longer jaunts, such as the Appalachian Trail. For day-hikers, most of the Knobstone Trail consists of out-and-backs leaving from one of eight different trailheads. But at the northern terminus, two adjacent loops—the Delaney Park and Spurgeon Hollow Trails—provide more interesting options.

The Delaney Park Trailhead can be quite busy, particularly from late spring to early fall, as the park is popular with campers and anglers. A $5 admission fee is charged as well. On the other hand, the Spurgeon Hollow Trailhead receives considerably less use, the trail covers the same hiking area, and parking is free.

The Spurgeon Hollow Trail leaves from the far corner of the parking lot, near the lake and the trailhead sign. Before heading out, be sure to carry plenty of water—the creeks tend to run dry as the year progresses.

Follow the trail 0.2 mile as it hugs the northeastern shoreline of Spurgeon Hollow Lake. The path is mostly flat and offers spring hikers a wildflower display of wood poppy, jack-in-the-pulpit, wild ginger, dwarf larkspur, trillium, and phlox. The ferns along the trail grow thigh high by the Fourth of July. But be forewarned: this short section of trail can also get quite buggy in the summer, when gnats, mosquitoes, and chiggers come out in full force.

To begin the loop, turn left (north) at the trail sign to Delaney Park to hike the trail clockwise. The ground is very acidic, as evidenced by the ground cedar,

Spurgeon Hollow North Loop

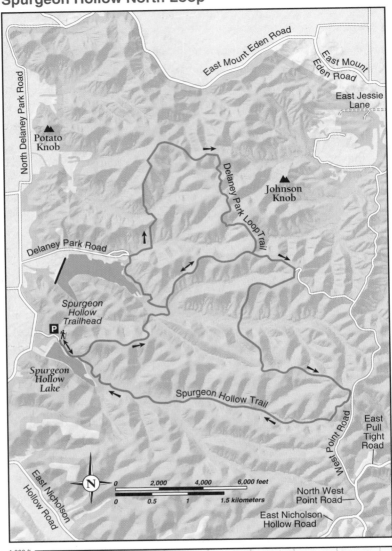

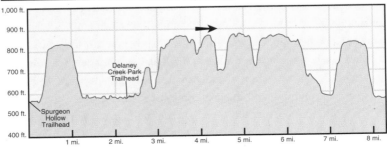

ferns, and pines that thrive here. The trail immediately begins a sharp ascent to a narrow ridgetop. Here the trees belie their age. The thin soils and exposure to the elements have kept the trunks of the oaks and hickories relatively small in circumference. But the lack of lower limbs and the gnarled stubs along their trunks indicate that the trees here are older than they might appear. Viburnum, wood sorrel, alumroot, and wild roses become increasingly prolific as the earth underfoot becomes dry and rocky. A 0.25-mile upward slog will bring you to the top of the ridge and, during the warmer months, a much-needed breeze.

The trail runs ridgetop for a few hundred yards, past a small kettle pond nestled among the hardwoods. As part of the Knobstone Trail, Spurgeon Hollow is blazed with blue-and-white paint and has mile markers placed at appropriate intervals. Just past mile marker 44, be on the lookout for these blazes, as the trail bears left (northeast) and descends the other side of the ridge to Clay Hill Hollow and the upper drainage of the lake at Delaney Creek Park. About 1.3 miles from the Spurgeon Hollow Trailhead you'll cross a shallow stream, and the creekside is blanketed with jack-in-the-pulpits and wood poppies in late spring.

Shortly after mile marker 46, the Spurgeon Hollow and Delaney Park Trails converge and share a section of trail. Stay straight (west) at this intersection to head toward the Delaney Park Trailhead. Going right (north) is both the northern side of the Spurgeon Hollow Trail and the southern side of the Delaney Park Trail. Take a look at the accompanying map and it will make more sense.

So now you're on the Delaney Park loop trail, traveling along the eastern side of the lake. The trail remains wide and level, evidence of the day-hikers that use this trail. You may hit a few muddy spots, but it's nothing to worry about, as you'll be enjoying the periodic views of the lake through the trees.

About 2.3 miles from the Spurgeon Hollow Trailhead you'll reach the Delaney Creek Trailhead and the northern terminus of the Knobstone Trail. Our route will take a sharp right turn to continue hiking the Delaney Creek loop clockwise. The trail follows along the creek for about 0.2 miles and then makes a thigh-burning climb up to a ridgetop covered with some of the largest sassafras trees you may have seen. With left- and right-handed mitten-shaped leaves that, when crushed, some claim smell just like Froot Loops, sassafras trees are easily identifiable. In case you were wondering, the Indiana champion sassafras tree is located in Harrison County and stands 60 feet tall, with a spread of 52 feet. Now that would make a lot of sassafras tea.

The trail begins to narrow as you take the path less traveled, and you'll see several trees blazed in blue, which is confusing but irrelevant to our hike. For the next 3.0 miles the trail traverses steep hillsides, rides high over ridgetops, and crosses the occasional country lane, before plunging back to creek drainages scattered upon the valley floor. Another steep climb followed by a long descent takes you through wild-turkey haunts and pileated-woodpecker territory. But almost immediately the trail climbs once again, reminding you why people find the Knobstone a good proving ground for the Appalachian Trail.

After reaching a large clearing about mile 5.6, the Spurgeon and Delaney Creek loops join once again. Stay right (west) for an enjoyable 1.2-mile gentle descent into Clay Hill Hollow. The trail brings you back to the T junction below Delaney Creek Park; turn left (south) to retrace your steps back on the Spurgeon Hollow Trail. You now have 1.2 more miles of hiking, one creek crossing, and one long ascent followed by one steep descent, to take you back to your vehicle.

Nearby Attractions

The Knobstone Trail, first mapped and built in the 1970s, has grown to become the **Knobstone Hiking Trail (KHT)** that runs 160 miles in length, from 10 miles north of Louisville to 30 miles south of Indianapolis. The KHT is composed of four distinct sections: Knobstone Trail, Pioneer Trail, Hoosier National Forest Knobstone Trail, and Tecumseh Trail. The continuous trail is open to both day-hikers and backpackers and requires no permits, fees, or reservations.

In 2013, the Knobstone Hiking Trail Association was formed and is dedicated to the "completion, preservation, and promotion" of the KHT. As a nonprofit, the association relies on donations from people like us. KHT offers guided hikes, organized workdays, and planned thru-hikes. From their website you can also purchase a wide variety of maps and request free hiking trail brochures. See knobstonehikingtrail.org for more information.

For a much shorter thru-hike, consider walking through the scenic **Medora covered bridge**, located just east of Medora, Indiana, and less than 20 minutes from the Spurgeon Hollow Trailhead. The covered bridge, which spans the East Fork of the White River, was built in 1875 at the cost of $18,142 and took 6 months to build. For driving directions and more information, see medoracoveredbridge.com.

DELANEY CREEK PARK ALSO OFFERS CAMPING, CABINS, AND A SWIMMING AREA, INCLUDING A SANDY BEACH.

Directions

From Louisville, take I-65/US 31 North across the Ohio River into southern Indiana. At Exit 7, turn left (west) on IN 60 and drive 22.0 miles to Salem. Once in Salem, turn right (north) on IN 135, bear right around the lively town square, and continue north on IN 135. After 4.0 miles, turn right (east) on North Delaney Park Road. Drive another 4.5 miles and, immediately after you cross an old iron bridge, turn left (north) to stay on North Delaney Park Road. Drive another 5.8 miles and turn right (east) at the sign to Spurgeon Hollow. The gravel road dead-ends in 0.3 mile, at the lake and at the trailhead.

36 Yellow Birch Ravine Nature Preserve

SCENERY: ★ ★ ★ ★ ★
TRAIL CONDITION: ★ ★
CHILDREN: ★ ★ ★
DIFFICULTY: ★ ★ ★
SOLITUDE: ★ ★ ★ ★

THE HIDDEN ENTRANCE TO DOUBLE FALLS

GPS TRAILHEAD COORDINATES: N38° 19.570' W86° 32.975'

DISTANCE & CONFIGURATION: 3.6-mile out-and-back

HIKING TIME: 3 hours

HIGHLIGHTS: Creekside hiking, waterfalls, natural arch, sandstone outcrops

ELEVATION: 575' at trailhead, ascending to 671' at high point

ACCESS: Daily, sunrise–sunset

MAPS: Limited availability online

FACILITIES: None

WHEELCHAIR ACCESS: None

COMMENTS: Parking is extremely scarce. Dogs are permitted on leash.

CONTACTS: Indiana Department of Natural Resources, 317-232-4200; in.gov/dnr/nature-preserves

Overview

The 441-acre Yellow Birch Ravine is not for everyone: parking is limited, trails are difficult to follow, boots get muddy, and feet get wet. Yet adventurous hikers have the opportunity to glimpse multiple waterfalls, hidden caves, and a natural arch, all tucked deeply beneath sandstone outcrops and lush mountain laurel. But as we traverse this fragile landscape, our environmental footprints will be long lasting and weigh heavily on the survival of the rare plant species this preserve was designed to protect.

Route Details

For those of you who have hiked Hemlock Cliffs or the Red River Gorge, you are well aware of the damage inflicted by too many hikers trying to see too many things in too small a space. Add to that a fragile ecosystem of highly erodible sandstone, thin soils clinging to steep hillsides, and rare and endangered plants, and we have a recipe for destruction. So, if you decide to explore Yellow Birch Ravine, be kind and be respectful. Do not walk in the creeks unless absolutely necessary (flora and fauna live here, too, you know). Do not clamber off-trail to reach where you think no one else has been. And do not post your pictures on social media. Let's keep this place as pristine as others have found it before us.

The small parking lot off Trestle Road only holds three or four cars at best. As always, try and visit during the week, early mornings, or late afternoons, including crisp winter days. From the same trailhead, three different trails go in three different directions and can be hiked in any order. Let's take the three short trails in the following order: Double Falls, Ravine Arch, and Yellow Birch Ravine.

From the parking lot, carefully cross Trestle Road to the east side of the road. From here a single trail leads into the woods, before coming to a Y in 0.1 mile. Bear right and cross a very small stream and head northeast. The trail will cross the stream multiple times and may be hard to find in places. But step lightly and continue up this delicate drainage for about 0.4 mile. As you get deeper up the drainage, several nice limestone and sandstone outcrops will be on both sides of the stream. The stream and the trail will end at Double Falls. Enjoy your view from where you are—there's no need to climb any closer. After viewing, carefully backtrack to the aforementioned Y.

Back at the Y, bear right (north) to hike along another stream 0.5 mile to Ravine Arch (as some have begun to call this natural stone bridge). The woods in

Yellow Birch Ravine Nature Preserve

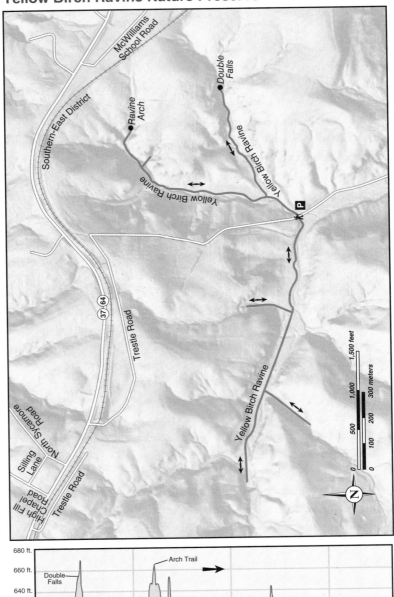

the low-lying areas tend to be beech-maple forest, while oak-hickory dominates the drier ridgetops. Once again, the stream and the trail will intersect several times before ending at Ravine Arch. With a 25-foot span, Ravine Arch can be difficult to discover until you are almost underneath it. Again, don't be tempted to climb any closer on the backs of this fragile ecosystem.

But what is it . . . an arch or a bridge? In general, natural arches are composed of sandstone and/or limestone, in which some of the softer rock has eroded away under the caprock, primarily due to water or weather. If an arch traverses a body of water, such as a creek, it becomes a bridge. When water levels are low, Ravine Arch is dry underneath. But when the creek is running high, water can actually flow under the arch and tumble down the rock face of the falls.

After you return to the now-familiar Y once again, head straight back to the road and cross to the west side of the parking lot. The Yellow Birch Ravine Trail begins here and travels west for approximately 0.8 mile. Again, the trail follows the creek, but the path is much easier to follow than the trails on the east side of the preserve.

Yellow Birch Ravine has been well known to botanists for many years. Floristic surveys have documented multiple endangered, threatened, and rare plant species, including both filmy and hay-scented fern, two different species of ladies' tresses orchids, Lloyd's clubmoss, and ground pine. We can never be too careful when we walk these trails.

The last hike leads to several other waterfalls and rock houses. Once more you will be following a stream, an upper tributary of Otter Creek. If you get turned around, just remember: water always flows downhill and the parking lot is downhill from here.

Nearby Attractions

If you don't mind a little more bushwhacking, consider **Cave Valley River State Natural Area**, about an hour north of Yellow Birch Ravine. Park near the gated road and the sign for the natural area. Walk around the gate and hike down the gravel road, which at one time led to a tourist attraction that offered boat rides into Endless Cave for 10¢. Where the road splits, veer left, although you are free to wander. Trails are not well marked, but following the creek is always a good bet. There are multiple waterfalls and other smaller caves in the vicinity, and the wildflowers are spectacular in the spring.

To enter the cave, you must apply for a permit from the Indiana Department for Natural Resources at tinyurl.com/EndlessCave. Directions from Campbellsburg, Indiana: Drive north on North Sycamore Street, which becomes North White River Road, 1.7 miles. Veer left onto North Cave River Valley Road and drive another mile. Cave River Valley Natural Area will be on your right.

From Yellow Birch Ravine you are only 13 minutes north of **Hemlock Cliffs,** making this a twofer opportunity. In addition, you are only 15 minutes south of **Patoka Lake State Park.** The park claims 26,000 acres of land and water, including freshwater jellyfish and bald eagle nesting sites.

Driving home you might want to stop at the yummy **1816 Restaurant** in Corydon. With options ranging from poutine topped with smoked pimento cheese and fried pork belly to a venison meatball sub smothered in mozzarella cheese and pomodoro sauce, you won't leave hungry: 100 East Chestnut Street, Corydon, 812-225-5342; 1816kitchen.com.

Directions

From downtown Louisville, take I-64 West to Indiana. At Exit 86, turn right (north) onto IN 237 toward English. Drive 3.8 miles, then take a left (west) onto Governors Trace, which turns into Otter Creek Road. Drive another 3.8 miles. Turn right (north) onto Trestle Road. In 1.5 miles you will see the tiny gravel parking lot on your left (west of the road), sporting what could be the world's smallest nature preserve sign.

YELLOW BIRCH RAVINE IS POPULAR IN THE SPRING FOR ITS WILDFLOWER DISPLAYS.

Indiana: North of Louisville and East of I-65

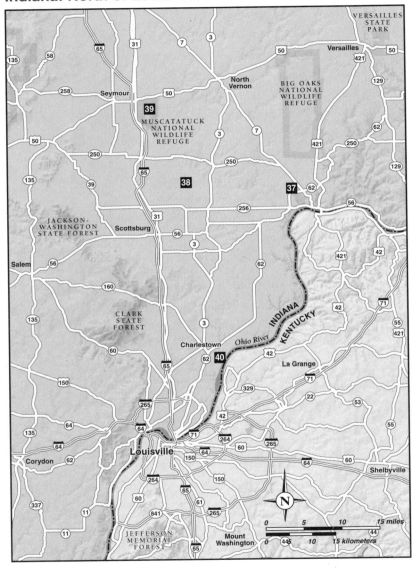

VIEWS OF HARDY LAKE IN EARLY FALL *(See Hike 38, page 219.)*

37 Clifty Falls State Park:
Clifty Falls Canyon

SCENERY: ★★★★★
TRAIL CONDITION: ★★★★
CHILDREN: ★★★
DIFFICULTY: ★★★★
SOLITUDE: ★★

THE STONEWORK AT THE PARK IS POETRY IN MOTION BY WAY OF ITS FORM AND FUNCTION.

GPS TRAILHEAD COORDINATES: N38° 46.209' W85° 26.232'

DISTANCE & CONFIGURATION: 3.8-mile loop; 4.3- and 6.0-mile loops also described below

HIKING TIME: 2.5 hours

HIGHLIGHTS: Multiple waterfalls, intimate canyon setting, spring wildflowers

ELEVATION: 834' at trailhead, descending to 538' at low point

ACCESS: Park is open daily, 7 a.m.–11 p.m.; trails close at sunset. Entrance fee: $7/vehicle for Indiana residents, $9/vehicle out-of-state.

MAPS: Available at park entrance and the website below

FACILITIES: Restrooms, picnic tables and shelters, nature center, playground, campground, swimming pool

WHEELCHAIR ACCESS: Clifty Falls Overlook is ADA compliant; however, the stone wall precludes views for those in wheelchairs.

COMMENTS: Dogs are permitted on leash.

CONTACTS: Clifty Falls State Park, 812-273-8885; tinyurl.com/CliftyFalls

Overview

Within Clifty Falls State Park, the 178-acre Clifty Canyon Nature Preserve presents southern Indiana at its finest. This loop trail, which takes in views of three of the preserve's waterfalls, follows the western edge of a small, intimate canyon formed by Clifty Creek, before crossing the stream and climbing to the eastern rim. Autumn hikers are rewarded with the gorgeous colors of mature hardwoods, while spring hikers are treated to a profusion of wildflowers such as hepatica, blue-eyed Mary, Dutchman's-breeches, and trillium (including the large, showy white variety). Multiple options exist for those wanting either shorter or longer hikes.

Route Details

The Clifty Creek Canyon loop combines five trails—8, 2, 5, 6, and 7, in that order—for a traverse of the northern half of Clifty Canyon Nature Preserve. The park is dissected by Clifty Creek as it flows toward the Ohio River, forming a long, narrow gorge. Only one trail in the park, Trail 2, crosses the creek, allowing you to travel from one side of the gorge to the other. Because most of Trail 2 lies in the actual creekbed, spring hikers will want to come prepared with waterproof boots.

The loop begins at the small picnic area immediately to the west of the North Gate park entrance, off IN 62. Leave your vehicle in the picnic area near the Trail 8 trailhead parking lot and start at the kiosk. But before you begin hiking, you may want to grab a view of Big Clifty Falls from the overlook at the main parking lot.

After leaving the picnic area, Trail 8 descends a short set of wooden stairs before crossing a small tributary of Little Clifty Creek. The noise of vehicular traffic soon subsides as the sound of falling water rises from the small canyon below. The trail follows the western edge of the creek along an old roadbed and past Big Clifty Falls, although no views are apparent from this side of the gorge.

About 1 mile from the trailhead, the trail descends once again. At the bottom of the hill, bear left (east) on the switchbacks and continue down toward the creek. At the creek crossing, looking upstream, you'll see a NO EXIT sign as Trail 2 eventually dead-ends at the base of Big Clifty Falls. If you want to take a side trip on Trail 2, you can hike north up the creekbed to the falls, adding a little more than a mile (round-trip) to your day. Although the view of Big Clifty

Clifty Falls State Park: Clifty Falls Canyon

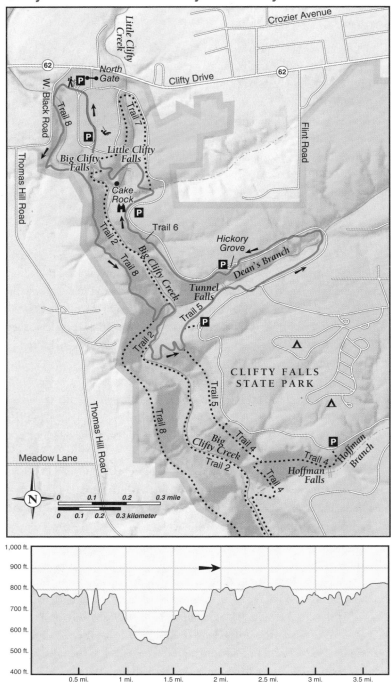

Falls is quite beautiful, walking in the creekbed can be difficult, especially when water levels are high.

To continue on our loop trail, turn right (south) on Trail 2 and follow the creek downstream for a scant 0.15 mile. Again, you'll be hiking in the creek itself. It's very rare for a trail to actually run in a creek due to the possibility of damaging such a fragile ecosystem, but enjoy the glimpses of fossils and aquatic life as you jump from one interesting rock to another. Soon you'll see a sign on the east side of the creek pointing left toward Trail 5. Take the trail up a challenging set of switchbacks as you climb out of the gorge on the opposite side of the creek.

After ascending a small set of wooden stairs, the trail Ts with a wooden walkway running north and south. Turn left (north) on Trail 5 toward Tunnel Falls. You're very close to an old railroad tunnel that is seasonally closed to protect the resident bat population. The Madison and Indianapolis Railroad Company built the 600-foot-long tunnel in 1852. The project was abandoned in bankruptcy, but its legacy includes parts of the trail system you're now walking on. Another 0.2 mile of hiking brings you to the Tunnel Falls Overlook.

At 83 feet high, Tunnel Falls is the highest waterfall in the park. Summer foliage may partially obstruct views from the overlook, so this may be a good time to remind yourself that the journey is the reward. In general, the waterfalls in the park are best viewed in late winter and early spring, when water flows are at their highest and the trees haven't yet leafed out.

To continue the loop, stay on Trail 5 until it crosses a small tributary (Dean's Branch) and merges with Trail 6 at Hickory Grove. Hike north on Trail 6, past Lookout Point, until you reach Trail 7. The bridge across Little Clifty Falls is scenic, but you must take the lower trail, marked RUGGED, for the best waterfall views. Despite their names, both Big and Little Clifty Falls stand 60 feet high.

Trail 7 follows the ridgetop past Cake Rock before climbing a final set of stairs for an overlook view of Big Clifty Falls and the canyon below. Just north of Big Clifty Falls are a picnic pavilion, bathrooms, and play field. Cut north across the parking lot until you see the Trail 8 picnic area and your vehicle. For other trail loop options, read below.

Nearby Attractions

Several other nice loop options exist at the park. To make the hike detailed above into a longer 6.0-mile loop, stay on Trail 8 (do not cross the creek at the midpoint) and continue hiking south until Trail 8 crosses Clifty Creek at the far southern end of the park. Cross the creek (on Trail 2) to pick up Trail 3, then hike north on the eastern side of the canyon. Trail 3 will take you up Hoffman Branch and above Hoffman Falls, before connecting with Trail 4. Hike north on Trail 4 (toward Lilly Memorial). Finally, use Trails 6, 7, and 8 (as described above) to complete the loop.

A third hike option is a 4.3-mile loop, starting at the small parking lot just south of Tunnel Falls. Follow Trail 5 south, just past the old railroad tunnel. Then pick up the switchbacks that lead west, down into the canyon. Once you reach Clifty Creek, walk upstream (north) a scant 0.15 miles until you see another set of switchbacks on your left heading west up the hillside. This side trail will T into Trail 8. Turn left (south) until you reach the creek again, at the southern end of the park. Cross the creek using Trail 2, then follow Trails 3, 4, and 5 back to your car.

Upon leaving the South Gate of the park, turn left (east) on IN 56 East and drive a short distance to historic downtown **Madison,** on the Ohio River. This scenic riverfront town is filled with small shops, cafés, and beautiful old homes. The Madison Chautauqua Festival of Art, held every fall, is well worth the drive.

If you enjoy state parks, try **Versailles State Park,** a 30-minute drive north of Clifty Falls. In addition to almost 7 miles of hiking trails, the park has added more than 20 miles of mountain biking trails; tinyurl.com/VerStP.

Directions

From I-265 north of downtown Louisville, and east of I-65, take Exit 10. Using the third exit off the roundabout, drive north on IN 62 E. Drive about 29.5 miles, where IN 62 and IN 56 merge. Turn right (east) on IN 56. Drive 5.1 miles. Then bear left onto IN 62 E. In 3.0 miles the North Gate entrance to Clifty Falls State Park will be on your right.

38

Hardy Lake State Park

THE LEVEL TRAILS AT HARDY LAKE ARE PERFECT FOR SAUNTERING AT YOUR OWN LEISURELY PACE.

GPS TRAILHEAD COORDINATES: N38° 46.800' W85° 42.172'

DISTANCE & CONFIGURATION: 1.9- to 3.4-mile loop

HIKING TIME: 1–2 hours

HIGHLIGHTS: Easy hiking with lake views

ELEVATION: 644' at trailhead, with no appreciable change in elevation

ACCESS: Trails open daily, sunrise–sunset. Entrance fee: $7/vehicle for Indiana residents, $9/vehicle out-of-state. Annual permits are also available.

MAPS: Available at the gatehouse and online at tinyurl.com/HardyLakeTrails

FACILITIES: Full campground facilities and marina

WHEELCHAIR ACCESS: None on trail

COMMENTS: Dogs are permitted on leash.

CONTACTS: Hardy Lake State Park, 812-794-3800; tinyurl.com/HardyLakeSP

Hardy Lake State Park

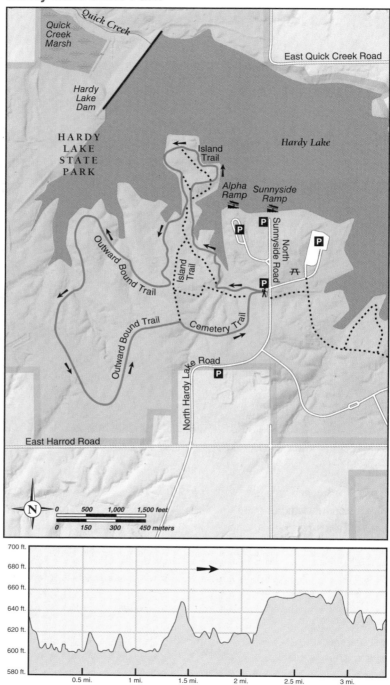

Overview

Even the kids can survive a 50-minute drive from downtown Louisville, in exchange for a day in the woods. If it's the dog days of summer, add a few hours at the sandy beach and enjoy the warm waters of Hardy Lake. Then as the sun begins to set, sit around the campfire before snuggling deep inside your sleeping bag. Sunrise might bring coffee at camp or some crappie fishing on the 741-acre lake. But be sure to save an hour or two to hike the trails at Hardy Lake State Park.

Route Details

Whether you plan a simple day trip or a full week of camping at Hardy Lake State Park, there's plenty to keep you entertained while leaving plenty of time for that much-needed rest and relaxation. The state park is very family oriented and kid friendly, with everything from wagon rides through the campground to free crafts classes and breakfast with the raptors. Situated within the Hardy Lake State Recreation Area, the surrounding forest is also popular during hunting season.

Hardy Lake State Park offers a full-service campground with 149 electric sites, flush toilets, and hot showers, as well as a smaller primitive campground with only 12 sites. Four boat launches are scattered around the lake, and campers can leave their boats moored overnight at the small marina. Two short and easy hiking trails are located close to the campgrounds, providing access to the beach and bathhouse, as well as the hiking trails discussed below.

If you are visiting the park as a day user, trailhead parking is located just past the main gate, on the left (west) side of the road. The parking lot holds 15 cars or so, but a much larger lot is located just across the road at the beach house. This trailhead provides access to the three primary trails in the park.

If you're looking for an easy but scenic hike, the 1.9-mile Island Trail is perfect. The path is wide and relatively flat with good lake views. Most kiddos can hike this trail and still have energy to swim at the beach and visit the raptor display next to the park office.

But if you're looking for a little more mileage, you can weave together all three trails into one big loop. The route will follow both Trail 4 (Island) and Trail 2 (Outward Bound) but will use Trail 3 (Cemetery) to access both from the trailhead parking lot. Looking at the trail map will help you make sense of this.

Starting at the trailhead, take Trail 3 (the Cemetery Trail) to reach the two other trails. To walk the loop counterclockwise, follow Trail 3 on your right (north) of the kiosk. In 0.2 mile Trail 4 begins, so turn right (north) and start walking toward the lake. The trail is wide, allowing you to walk comfortably side by side with your fellow hikers. Be on the alert for beaver activity, great blue herons, and the local deer population.

But timing is everything! If you're hiking this trail on July 4th weekend, both quiet and solitude will elude you. You may want to choose a more peaceful time, such as the off-season or early morning or evening.

As you reach the far north end of the loop, Trail 4 heads south, following another arm of Hardy Lake. Watch for the large five-way poplar tree trunk on your right, just west of the trail. Poplars are renowned for their ability to grow straight and tall. But this trunk has a wild hair and decided that at 15 feet off the ground it would grow in five different directions. Shagbark hickory trees are also prolific in the surrounding woods.

Trail 4 soon joins Trail 2 and Trail 3. You'll want to turn right (west) on Trail 2 (Outward Bound) to complete a 2.0-mile loop that gives you a good look at the backwaters of the lake. The hardwoods here are what is referred to as a climax forest, in which the tree species will remain essentially unchanged as long as the ecosystem is not disturbed. Both beech-maple and oak-hickory forest examples are found here.

Trail 2 dead-ends into Trail 3 (Cemetery), which also takes hikers through an oak-hickory climax forest. Bear right (south) on Trail 3. This trail is named for the McClain Cemetery, with headstones dating back to the 1700s. Hikers are asked politely not to enter the cemetery and to respect the wall that has been erected around the graves. To complete your 3.4-mile loop, stay on Trail 3 until you return to the parking lot.

Nearby Attractions

Hardy Lake was built as a water reservoir and not for flood control. As a result, the water line fluctuates very little and makes for some great freshwater fishing. Spinning, fly-fishing, and bait casting are all popular here but are typically done from a watercraft. However, there are two fishing piers at Hardy Lake, one near the marina and the other near the beach. A variety of species are caught here, including bass, crappie, bream or bluegill, and redear sunfish, although walleye and muskie are occasionally brought to net. A small pond, known as the "Family Fishing Hole," is located just west of the park office.

From Lake Hardy State Park you are a 35-minute drive from **Muscatatuck National Wildlife Refuge Visitor Center.** The refuge has several short trails that can also be combined for longer hiking. See the entry for Muscatatuck on the following pages for more information.

Directions

From downtown Louisville, take I-65 north into Indiana. At Exit 29, turn right (east) onto IN 56 E; drive 4.2 miles. Then take a left (north) on IN 203 N (which later becomes County Road 350 E) 6.5 miles. Last, turn right onto County Road 400 E (also known as North Sunnyside Road.) into the park.

FALL HIKING BRINGS FEWER INSECTS AND MORE SOLITUDE.

39

Muscatatuck National Wildlife Refuge

SCENERY: ★ ★ ★ ★
TRAIL CONDITION: ★ ★ ★ ★ ★
CHILDREN: ★ ★ ★
DIFFICULTY: ★ ★
SOLITUDE: ★ ★ ★ ★

THE WATERS OF MUSCATATUCK SHIMMER WITH A THIN LAYER OF ICE.

GPS TRAILHEAD COORDINATES: See individual hike snapshots.

DISTANCE & CONFIGURATION: Five short loops, 3.9 miles total

HIKING TIME: 3 hours

HIGHLIGHTS: Migrating waterfowl, including sandhill cranes and trumpeter swans

ELEVATION: No significant elevation change on any of the featured trails

ACCESS: Daily, 1 hour before sunrise–1 hour after sunset; free admission

MAPS: Available at the nature center

FACILITIES: Nature center, restrooms

WHEELCHAIR ACCESS: Yes, at the nature center and on the paved 0.4-mile Chestnut Trail. An interpretive auto tour is also available.

COMMENTS: Time your visit carefully. In the quiet of winter, the refuge can provide solace for some and boredom for others. Similarly, the heat and humidity of summer can discourage hikers. Muscatatuck is open for a limited hunting season; call the refuge for current hunting schedules. A good pair of binoculars might be a wise addition to your day pack. Dogs are permitted on leash.

CONTACTS: Muscatatuck National Wildlife Refuge, 812-522-4352; fws.gov/refuge/muscatatuck

Overview

Established in 1966, Muscatatuck National Wildlife Refuge protects 7,800 acres of restored wetlands as a landing ground for waterfowl and other birds as they migrate through south-central Indiana. The U.S. Fish and Wildlife Service has worked diligently at Muscatatuck to convert farmland to a mixed ecosystem of forest, aquatic, and grassland habitat. The proposed 3.9-mile hike encompasses five trails at Muscatatuck, a Native American word meaning "land of winding water." Spring and fall may be the best times to see the migratory waterfowl as they travel between South America and northern Canada, although sandhill cranes are frequently seen throughout the winter.

Route Details

After entering Muscatatuck National Wildlife Refuge, drive 0.4 mile to the Charles E. Scheffe Visitor Center. Start your visit by picking up some maps and learning more about the refuge. Big kids and small ones will enjoy the birding room, which has lots of hands-on displays, a bird window with one-way glass overlooking several feeders, a video describing Muscatatuck, and a small gift shop with an excellent selection of books.

Before the 19th century, this region was primarily swamp forest that frequently flooded. By the 20th century, however, most of the land had been clear-cut and drained for agricultural purposes. The U.S. Fish and Wildlife Service now uses a sophisticated system of pipes and pumps to keep water flowing in and out of the refuge, creating a natural wetlands for the roughly 15,000 migrants who pass this way. Muscatatuck can be a civil engineer's dream or nightmare, depending on the weather.

The migratory waterfowl residing at the refuge include wood ducks, mallards, northern shovelers, and hooded mergansers. Along the fencerows and open meadows, indigo buntings, American redstarts, and Baltimore orioles are frequently seen. In 1998, trumpeter swans were introduced to the refuge; more-recent visitors include sandhill cranes. These cranes, with their flamboyant courtship rituals, are among the largest birds on Earth and usually arrive at the refuge in late October and again in March. Call 812-522-4352 to find out if the cranes are present.

A careful examination of the trail map indicates five short hikes in the refuge. The following description covers each of these trails, presented in the order in which visitors would normally drive through the refuge.

Muscatatuck National Wildlife Refuge

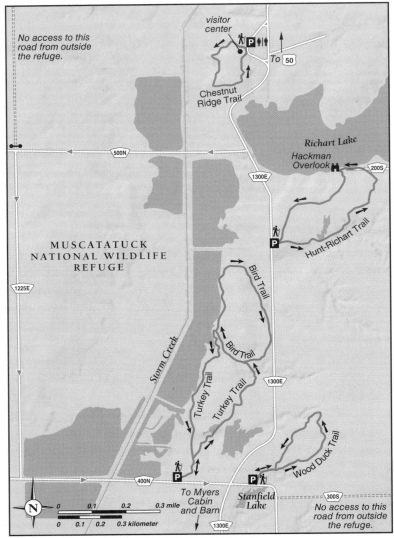

Chestnut Ridge Trail   *(0.4-mile loop; 15 minutes' hiking time; N38° 57.578' W85° 47.922')*

This paved trail starts directly behind the visitor center and has a small interpretive pamphlet available. Benches provide a nice respite if the insects aren't too aggressive.

After your walk, drive 0.4 miles south on the main road (County Road 1000W) and turn right (west) on the one-way gravel road (CR 500N) just across from Richart Lake. Refuge signs then direct you left (south) on CR 1225E and left again (east) on CR 400N. Multiple turnouts are available for parking and viewing the waterfowl. (*Note:* The county roads listed here aren't marked on the refuge map, nor are they marked on the roads themselves, but I've marked them on our trail map for navigational purposes.) The parking lot for your next hike is on your left, just north of CR 400N.

Turkey Trail and Bird Trail *(1.9-mile figure-eight; 40 minutes' hiking time; N38° 56.438' W85° 48.123')*

These two trails, just east of Storm Creek, are accessed from the southern parking area, as indicated on our trail map. If you want to hike Bird Trail, you have to hike Turkey Trail first.

Start at the Turkey Trailhead and walk counterclockwise (heading right, or northeast). You'll immediately notice huge sassafras trees on both sides of the trail. Shortly you'll come to a shallow pond, edged with large bald cypress, their skinned knees protruding from the ground and water. In recent years, the beaver population at Muscatatuck has exploded and you will see some of their handi- or toothwork here. Just past the pond, Turkey Trail joins Bird Trail. Continue straight (west) until Bird Trail departs north. Follow the Bird Trail loop clockwise until it rejoins Turkey Trail. You can then follow the western half of Turkey Trail through sycamores, sweetgums, poplars, and oaks.

After your hike, continue driving 0.2 mile on the gravel road until it intersects the main road. Turn right (south) on CR 1300E, and drive 2.0 miles toward the turnoff for the Myers homestead and Lake Linda.

Side Trip: Myers Cabin and Barn *(Just a short stroll to travel more than a century back in time)*

The Myers cabin was built between 1880 and 1885 by Louis Myers and his family of seven, using beech logs harvested off the land. The first floor includes a living area and the parents' bedroom. A summer kitchen was set up on the back porch. The five kids slept upstairs unless it was too hot, in which case they slept outside. Louis's wife, Nancy, lived here until she died in 1948.

The barn is built of poplar logs held together with wooden pegs. One of the Myerses' sons became a nurseryman and planted the seedless hybrid persimmon trees growing across the road from the cabin. Fall visitors will enjoy the juicy fruit and a taste of yesteryear.

After exploring, drive the main road (CR 1300E, which becomes CR 1000W) back north to the Wood Duck Trail, just north of Stanfield Lake. Turn right (west) toward the lake, and the trailhead parking lot will be immediately on your left.

Wood Duck Trail   *(0.75-mile balloon; 15 minutes' hiking time; N38° 56.416' W85° 47.874')*

Perhaps the prettiest wooded path in the refuge, this small loop can be walked clockwise or counterclockwise. Pawpaw, swamp chestnut oak, and many other native species reside here. Some of the larger beech trees are used as nesting spots by wood ducks and barred owls.

To reach the final hike, drive north on the main refuge road until you see the trailhead, just south of Richart Lake.

Hunt-Richart Lake Trail   *(0.9-mile loop; 20 minutes' hiking time; N38° 57.054' W85° 47.794')*

Yet another loop, this trail can be hiked in either direction. Once lakeside, be sure to stop at the Hackman Overlook. The views of Richart Lake are lovely; many shorebirds can be seen wading in the shallows, and otters frequently pop their heads up for air.

Nearby Attractions

If you are unfamiliar with the sounds and calls of sandhill cranes, as well as their elaborate mating dances, be sure to watch a few online videos before you visit Muscatatuck. The cranes can frequently be heard at the refuge, even though you might not be able to see them.

Most of the lakes at Muscatatuck are open for fishing, subject to Indiana state regulations. The use of gasoline and electric motors is prohibited; canoes and kayaks are only permitted on Richart Lake. There are generous daily catch limits for bluegill, sunfish, crappie, bass, catfish, and other species that swim these waters. Due to the shallow waters, the use of an indicator (or bobber) is much preferred. See the Muscatatuck website for more information.

If you consider yourself a bit of a birder, the 50,000-acre **Big Oaks National Wildlife Refuge (NWR)** is only about a 40-minute drive east of Muscatatuck on US 50. A limited amount of hiking is available on the trails just south of Old Timber Lake. Big Oaks NWR has been identified as a "globally important bird area" due to the Henslow's sparrows that breed here, as well as 200 other species of birds found in the refuge. For more information, see fws.gov/refuge/big_oaks.

Directions

From downtown Louisville, take I-65 North across the Ohio River into southern Indiana and drive 50.0 miles. At Exit 50A, turn right (east) on US 50 toward North Vernon. The main entrance to Muscatatuck Wildlife Refuge will be 2.6 miles ahead on your right, just south of US 50. During the winter months, large flocks of sandhill cranes can frequently be seen in the corn fields prior to the refuge entrance, on your left, north of the highway.

COULD YOU IMAGINE A FAMILY OF SEVEN LIVING HERE TODAY?

STEP BACK IN TIME AND EXPLORE THE HISTORY OF THE ROSE ISLAND AMUSEMENT PARK.

GPS TRAILHEAD COORDINATES: N38° 25.638' W85° 37.777'

DISTANCE & CONFIGURATION: 1.2-mile–5.5-mile loop options

HIKING TIME: 2 hours

HIGHLIGHTS: Multiple creek views, historic park and bridge, spring wildflowers

ELEVATION: 661' at trailhead, descending to 427' at low point

ACCESS: Daily (including holidays), 7 a.m.–sunset. Entrance fee: $7/vehicle for Indiana residents, $9/vehicle out-of-state. Annual permits are also available.

MAPS: Charlestown State Park, tinyurl.com/CharlMap; USGS *Charlestown*

FACILITIES: Restrooms, picnic tables, water, and campsites in the park; no facilities at the trailhead

WHEELCHAIR ACCESS: Short paved section at the trailhead

COMMENTS: Pets must be leashed. Guided wildflower walks are advertised locally.

CONTACTS: Charlestown State Park, 812-256-5600; tinyurl.com/CharlPark

Overview

The Rose Island Loops nestle along Fourteenmile Creek in Charlestown State Park, an easy 20-mile drive north of downtown Louisville. Sharing the same trailhead, each loop descends to the creek and back up again. In the spring, Fourteenmile Creek and adjacent tributaries yield spectacular wildflower displays that include wild geranium, trillium, bluebells, bloodroot, and many rare species found only here. The hike also provides close-up views of Devonian fossil outcrops and several examples of karst topography. A short hike across a restored bridge leads to the remains of the historic Rose Island Amusement Park, where Fourteenmile Creek flows into the Ohio River.

Route Details

Established in 1996, Charlestown State Park originally was part of the Indiana Armory Ammunition Plant (INAAP). Subsequent land donations from the INAAP have allowed the park to grow to more than 5,100 acres, making it the third-largest state park in Indiana. The Rose Island Loops comprise three loop trails, all of which share the same trailhead and parking area. At the far end of the lot, a kiosk displays a trail map (none for the taking) and several old photos of Rose Island Amusement Park.

Hikers have a variety of choices: If you just want to hike down to the site of the old amusement park, you're looking at 1.2 miles round-trip. If you add loop Trail 3 to this hike, your total will be 2.9 miles. Finally, hiking to the old amusement park site, plus loop trails 3 and 4, results in a total of 5.5 miles. To hike the route counterclockwise, follow the paved road, which begins behind the kiosk, about 0.3 mile toward Fourteenmile Creek. The road quickly descends among towering yellow poplars, sycamores, and maples. Soon the beautifully restored 1912 Portersville Bridge spanning the creek comes into view. Here you will notice Trail 3 on your left leaving the road and heading north into a forest of deciduous hardwoods. But we'll continue straight across the bridge for a short jaunt to the remains of the historic Rose Island Amusement Park.

Technically not an island but a spit of land formed by the junction of Fourteenmile Creek and the Ohio River, the 0.9-mile gravel trail begins just across the restored bridge. Interestingly, the 1912 bridge was not original to the site, but was moved from Vincennes, Indiana, to where a 400-foot suspension bridge once carried visitors to reach the amusement park.

Rose Island Loops

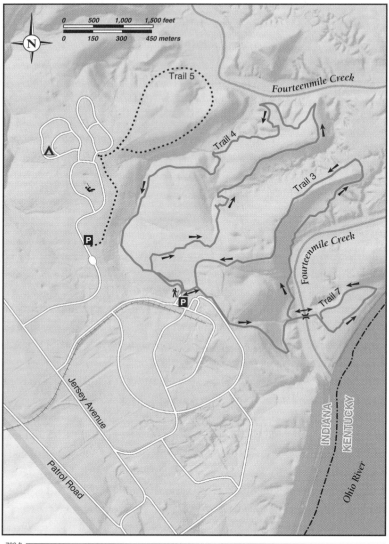

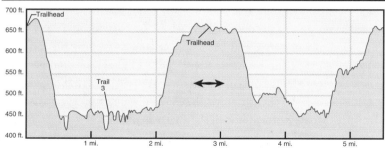

In 1923, local businessman David B. G. Rose purchased the park, which was built around 1880 and originally called Fern Grove. He immediately launched a series of improvements, including a swimming pool, roller coaster, merry-go-round, ice plant, and alligator pit. For 25¢ (15¢ for children) visitors could travel aboard the steamboat *Idlewild* (now the *Belle of Louisville*) from the Kentucky side of the river, while Hoosiers arrived via the suspension bridge (which also charged a 25¢ toll). The gravel path takes you past the old swimming pool and the former sites of where the dance hall, cottages, dining hall, and hotel once stood. The trail reaches the river at the original steamboat landing, where three stone pillars remain, before circling back toward the bridge.

After Mr. Rose sank his heart and $250,000 of his cash into Rose Island, he managed to keep it afloat throughout the Great Depression. But it was the Great Flood of 1937 that did in the amusement park, inundating the property with 10 feet of water. This same flood covered 60%–70% of Louisville, and it took three weeks for the waters to recede. The damage was so devastating that Rose Island never reopened.

After you finish exploring the historic park, cross back over the steel bridge to find Trail 3. Turn right (north) just after the bridge to follow the trail along Fourteenmile Creek. After crossing two small footbridges, the trail continues along the bottomland as the main creek disappears from view. Up along the small ridge to your left (west), a string of low, rocky outcrops will appear. Known as Devils Backbone, this ridge was most likely formed by the combined effects of glaciation and erosion as Fourteenmile Creek flowed into the Ohio River. With perhaps less scientific rigor yet more colorful appeal, local legend has it that the ridge was once part of a stone fortress built by Prince Madoc and early Welsh explorers in the 12th century.

As the trail makes a U-turn from northeast to southwest, the moss-covered rocks of Devils Backbone will stay on your left as you steadily ascend out of the creek drainage. The trail tops out with a distant view of the southern banks of the Ohio River. A short (0.2-mile) walk through a transition meadow of grasses and red cedars brings you back to the blacktop road. If you want to add Trail 4 to your hike, the path begins a few yards north of the trailhead parking lot. To hike the loop counterclockwise, turn right (northeast) at the beginning of the Trail 4 loop for the best creek views. The trail is flat the first half mile, before descending into a deciduous hardwood forest of hickories, maples, and beeches draped with ancient grapevines. If you've brought kids along, try to keep a straight face and tell them this is where the original *Tarzan* movies were filmed.

A little more than a mile from the trailhead, a small spur appears on your right (just north of the trail), providing an overlook of Fourteenmile Creek. The trail then meanders along several smaller tributaries. Spring hikers will love the sound of rushing water and the spectacle of blooming wildflowers. From here the trail ascends once again, back through the same transitional meadow. Turn right (south) on the blacktop road to get back to the parking lot.

Nearby Attractions

Next to the boat launch, **Trail 6** takes hikers on a 2.3-mile loop atop a bluff overlooking the Ohio River and Twelvemile Island. The trailhead is across the road from the Riverside Overlook, at the far southern edge of the park. The trail crosses a small footbridge over a waterfall before descending to the bluff bottom. The wildflowers here rival those along the Rose Island Loop trails.

Just a stone's throw from Charlestown State Park is the 121-acre **Nine Penny Branch Nature Preserve.** A 2.4-mile trail takes you to a small overlook, then crosses Nine Penny Branch creek just below a small waterfall, before forming a nice loop through old-growth forest. Remnants of an aging stone wall are all that remain of the stagecoach route that once passed this way. One story has it that it cost 9¢ to ride the stagecoach, though none of the passengers are talking.

To get to the nature preserve after leaving Charlestown State Park, turn left on IN 62 W. Drive 0.6 mile, then take a right onto Monroe Street. In 0.3 mile, take another right onto Tunnel Mill Road. After 2.5 miles and a few dogleg twists in the road, the nature preserve will be on your left. See tinyurl.com/NinePenny for more information. *Note:* At the time of this writing, both the web page description and the map at the preserve parking lot do not indicate the loop trail that begins atop the hillside, after you cross Nine Penny Branch Creek.

Directions

From downtown Louisville, take I-65 North across the Ohio River into southern Indiana. After 6.7 miles, take Exit 6A to merge onto I-265 East, toward Clark Maritime Center. Shortly before I-265 ends (after about 3 miles), exit on IN 62 East (Ohio River Scenic Byway), heading right (northeast). Charlestown State Park will be 8.5 miles ahead, on your right. To reach the trailhead, go through the main entrance to the park, then immediately bear right. Drive 1.9 miles until you see the sign for Trails 3 and 4, and Rose Island. Turn left and drive 0.5 mile to the parking lot.

A 25¢ TOLL IS NO LONGER REQUIRED TO CROSS THE BRIDGE AT FOURTEENMILE CREEK.

Appendix A:
Outdoor Retailers

ACADEMY SPORTS + OUTDOORS
academy.com

JEFFERSON MALL
4901 Outer Loop #144
Louisville, KY 40219
502-966-1650

BASS PRO SHOPS
basspro.com

RIVER FALLS MALL
951 E. Lewis and Clark Pkwy.
Clarksville, IN 47129
812-218-5500

CABELA'S
cabelas.com
5100 Norton Healthcare Blvd.
Louisville, KY 40241
502-365-9020

DICK'S SPORTING GOODS
dickssportinggoods.com

OXMOOR CENTER
7900 Shelbyville Road
Louisville, KY 40222
502-420-6400

RIVER FALLS MALL
951 E. Lewis and Clark Pkwy.
Clarksville, IN 47129
812-288-2194

SPRINGHURST TOWN CENTER
3555 Springhurst Blvd.
Louisville, KY 40241
502-429-0776

STONEYBROOK SHOPPING CENTER
3500 S. Hurstbourne Pkwy.
Louisville, KY 40299
502-499-9029

ORVIS
orvis.com
4288 Summit Plaza Dr.
Louisville, KY 40241
502-425-0198

QUEST OUTDOORS
questoutdoors.com

ST. MATTHEWS
4600 Shelbyville Road
Louisville, KY 40207
502-290-4589

Appendix B:
Hiking Clubs

**KENTUCKY AND INDIANA HIKERS
AND WALKERS**
tinyurl.com/kishaw

LOUISVILLE HIKING MEETUP
meetup.com/louisvillehiking

LOUISVILLE HIKING CLUB
meetup.com/louisvillehikingclub
facebook.com/louisvillehiking

ORIENTEERING LOUISVILLE
orienteeringlouisville.org

**LOUISVILLE RUNNING AND
WALKING CLUBS**
louisvillerunningcompany.com
/groups

**SIERRA CLUB, GREATER
LOUISVILLE GROUP**
louisville.sierraclub.org
P.O. Box 20606
Louisville, KY 40250
502-649-0139

Appendix C:
Public and Private Agencies

**INDIANA DIVISION OF
NATURE PRESERVES**
in.gov/dnr/nature-preserves
800-457-8283

**INDIANA DIVISION OF STATE PARKS
AND RESERVOIRS**
in.gov/dnr/state-parks
800-457-8283

**JEFFERSON MEMORIAL FOREST
(WILDERNESS LOUISVILLE)**
louisvilleky.gov/government
/jefferson-memorial-forest
502-368-5404

**KENTUCKY STATE NATURE
PRESERVES COMMISSION**
eec.ky.gov/Nature-Preserves
502-573-2886

KENTUCKY STATE PARKS
parks.ky.gov
502-564-2172

LOUISVILLE PARKS
louisvilleky.gov/government/parks
502-574-7275

THE NATURE CONSERVANCY
nature.org
859-259-9655

OLMSTED PARKS CONSERVANCY
olmstedparks.org
502-456-8125

THE PARKLANDS OF FLOYDS FORK
theparklands.org
502-584-0350

Index

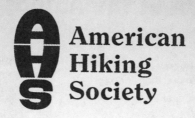

American Hiking Society

PROTECT THE PLACES YOU LOVE TO HIKE.

Become a member today and
take $5 off using the code **Hike5**.

AmericanHiking.org/join

American Hiking Society is the only
national nonprofit organization dedicated
to empowering all to enjoy, share, and
preserve the hiking experience.

About the Author

After having spent more than 20 years as a university researcher and professor, **Valerie Askren** traded the ivory towers of academia for the hardwood forests and sandstone arches of Kentucky. The proverbial outdoorswoman, she has swum in Africa's Lake Malawi, climbed China's Mount Tai, sailed the coast of southern France, biked Nova Scotia, backpacked across Canada, and survived the biting cold of farm life in Ukraine. She spent her honeymoon kayaking the Grand Canyon with her husband, Ben.

Photo: Emma Askren

Valerie's background in natural-resource economics and her love of the wilderness translated into a second career writing guides to the outdoors, including *Hike the Bluegrass and Beyond, Fly Fishing Kentucky, Backpacking Kentucky,* and *Backcountry Cuisine.*

Valerie lives in Lexington, Kentucky, where a peaceful wooded path, beautiful public garden, or historical walking trail is always close at hand.